SEARCHING FOR FEMINIST SUPERHEROES

WORLD COMICS AND GRAPHIC NONFICTION SERIES

Frederick Luis Aldama, Christopher González, and Deborah Elizabeth Whaley, editors

Other Books in the Series

James Scorer, *Latin American Comics in the Twenty-First Century: Transgressing the Frame*

J. Andrew Deman, *The Claremont Run: Subverting Gender in the X-Men*

Jeffrey A. Brown, *Super Bodies: Comic Book Illustration, Artistic Styles, and Narrative Impact*

Peyton Brunet and Blair Davis, *Comic Book Women: Characters, Creators, and Culture in the Golden Age*

Mark Cotta Vaz, *Empire of the Superheroes: America's Comic Book Creators and the Making of a Billion-Dollar Industry*

Anna Peppard, ed., *Supersex: Sexuality, Fantasy, and the Superhero*

Allan W. Austin and Patrick L. Hamilton, *All New, All Different? A History of Race and the American Superhero*

Jorge J. Santos Jr., *Graphic Memories of the Civil Rights Movement: Reframing History in Comics*

Benjamin Fraser, *The Art of Pere Joan: Space, Landscape, and Comics Form*

Jan Baetens, *The Film Photonovel: A Cultural History of Forgotten Adaptations*

Marc Singer, *Breaking the Frames: Populism and Prestige in Comics Studies*

Matt Yockey, ed., *Make Ours Marvel: Media Convergence and a Comics Universe*

Mark Heimermann and Brittany Tullis, eds., *Picturing Childhood: Youth in Transnational Comics*

David William Foster, El Eternauta, Daytripper, *and Beyond: Graphic Narrative in Argentina and Brazil*

Christopher Pizzino, *Arresting Development: Comics at the Boundaries of Literature*

Frederick Luis Aldama and Christopher González, eds., *Graphic Borders: Latino Comic Books Past, Present, and Future*

SEARCHING FOR FEMINIST SUPERHEROES

Gender, Sexuality, and Race in Marvel Comics

Sam Langsdale

University of Texas Press
Austin

The Louann Atkins Temple Women & Culture Endowment is supported by Allison, Doug, Taylor, and Andy Bacon; Margaret, Lawrence, Will, John, and Annie Temple; Larry Temple; the Temple-Inland Foundation; and the National Endowment for the Humanities.

Portions of chapters 3 and 4 were previously published in "Moon Girls and Mythical Beasts: Analyzing Race, Gender, and Monstrosity," *Signs: Journal of Women in Culture and Society* vol. 45, no. 2: pp. 395–420. © 2019 by The University of Chicago.

Printed in the United States of America
First edition, 2024

♾ The paper used in this book meets the minimum requirements of ANSI/NISO Z39.48-1992 (R1997) (Permanence of Paper).

Library of Congress Cataloging-in-Publication Data

Names: Langsdale, Samantha, author.
Title: Searching for feminist superheroes : gender, sexuality, and
race in Marvel Comics / Sam Langsdale.
Other titles: World comics and graphic nonfiction series.
Description: First edition. | Austin : University of Texas Press, 2024. |
Series: World comics and graphic nonfiction series |
Includes bibliographical references and index.
Identifiers: LCCN 2023054058
ISBN 978-1-4773-2978-8 (hardcover)
ISBN 978-1-4773-2979-5 (pdf)
ISBN 978-1-4773-2980-1 (epub)
Subjects: LCSH: Feminism in comics. | Women superheroes. |
Transgender superheroes. | Lesbian superheroes. |
Queer comic books, strips, etc. | Social justice in comics.
Classification: LCC PN6714 .L355 2024 |
DDC 741.5/3522—dc23/eng/20240314
LC record available at https://lccn.loc.gov/2023054058

doi:10.7560/329788

For all the feminist heroes who fill my bookshelves and grace my everyday: you save me.

CONTENTS

INTRODUCTION | "A WILLFUL METHOD"

Searching for Feminist Superheroes

Throughout the last fifteen years, superheroes have again become an integral part of mainstream popular culture in the United States. A proliferation of films, TV series, videogames, comics, fan conventions, and merchandise has ushered superheroes into almost every corner of American media. For scholars of superhero comics and comics-related media, the genre has the potential to be analyzed from any number of angles, including its history and evolution into a multi-billion-dollar industry; its relationship to US nationalism and its reflection of underlying social issues; and its ability to inform cultural hopes and ideals and to influence the politics surrounding representation. Despite this polyvalence, recent popular discourse has turned towards the genre's capacity to glorify violence and to uphold white supremacy, heteropatriarchy, imperialism, and even fascism. Recent TV shows such as HBO's *Watchmen* (Lindelof 2019), Amazon's *The Boys* (Kripke 2019), or *Invincible* (Kirkman and Racioppa 2021); films such as Todd Phillips's *Joker* (2019); and myriad op-eds about, or interviews with, creators like Alan Moore and Eric Kripke all suggest a reemerging cynicism towards the genre. Relatedly, recent scholarship on superhero comics has also cultivated a focus on the genre's problems. Texts like Sean Guynes and Martin Lund's edited volume *Unstable Masks: Whiteness and American Superhero Comics* (2020), Esther De Dauw's *Hot Pants and Spandex Suits: Gender Representation in American Superhero Comic Books* (2021), and Allan Austin and Patrick Hamilton's *All New, All Different? A History of Race and the American Superhero* (2019) overwhelmingly point towards the genre's historic and ongoing tendency to generate media informed by white supremacy, racism, heteronormativity, and sexism.

Given this context, I suppose I should not have been surprised when, after a panel presentation during which I and two of my colleagues had given (what I thought were) nuanced, persuasive papers about feminist friendship in superhero comics, I was approached by an audience member who asked me why I was reading superhero comics if I was interested in feminism. Admittedly, I *was* a bit gobsmacked. Had we not just spent sixty minutes explaining exactly why? But I also understood. My interlocutor's question, and the popular and scholarly discourses of which it is a part, was absolutely warranted. Even cursory histories of the representation of women and girls in superhero comics point to overwhelming trends of underrepresentation and marginalization, oversexualization and objectification, and the near ubiquity of whiteness, cisnormativity, heterosexuality, and able-bodiedness (Cocca 2016, 6–16; Peppard 2017; De Dauw 2021, 1–15). Statistics reflecting the current state of affairs are hardly better. According to scholar Carolyn Cocca, "Female characters starred in about 15% of superhero comics in 2020, with about the same percentage being written or drawn by a female creator. In 2015 it was about 12%, in 2010 about 6%, and in 2000 about 5%. Women star in about 16% of superhero TV shows on air or in development, and in about 18% of films scheduled for release or in development." As Cocca notes, "Given that women are 50% of the population, these proportions are quite low" (2021, 7). There is no denying that superhero comics and comics-related media that do not center straight, white, heterosexual, nondisabled men and that do not employ white supremacist, heteropatriarchal, nationalist ideological frameworks are numerically marginal. But they do exist, and to continue to focus only on the problems at the center of the genre amounts to further marginalizing (even if inadvertently) more inclusive, progressive texts and the various ways they make meaning.

Searching for Feminist Superheroes: Gender, Sexuality, and Race in Marvel Comics begins with the recognition that female-led superhero comics, with diverse casts of characters that cultivate inclusive feminist storytelling and art, exist on the margins of the US mainstream superhero genre. However, the purpose of this book is not to focus primarily on why these comics are marginalized, but rather to show how the margins as a site of innovation and productivity have enabled the creation of feminist superhero texts. Moreover, by employing feminist philosophies as lenses through which to analyze the comics in question, I suggest that feminist superheroes have the potential to contribute to liberatory social imaginaries that are crucial to working towards a more just world. Such a study is warranted for a number of reasons: First, as superheroes continue to proliferate across media, there is a protracted potential to lose sight of historically excluded creators, characters, and audiences without an express effort to construct more equitable frameworks of scholarship. Second, reducing more inclusive superhero comics to their minority status is to ignore the power of the margins and the multiple and meaningful ways comics may impact audiences. As scholars like andré carrington have argued, the potential of the margins exists even in mainstream media: "Marginality and popularity can coincide as names for multiple facets of the same cultural phenomenon. This is especially true for works of genre fiction, which are both deeply invested in market imperatives that buttress the existing social order and, occasionally, more imaginative or diversionary than texts that present realistic treatments of everyday life" (2016, 14). And third, as US popular culture continues to manifest as a battleground between oppressive and progressive social norms, capitalist modes of cultural production, and people's desires to envision a better elsewhere, focusing on feminist superheroes provides one way to prove that the fight goes on; nothing about the genre is inevitable.

METHOD AND TERMINOLOGY

To determine whether, and to what extent, solo comics featuring Spider-Woman, America Chavez, the Unstoppable Wasp, and Ironheart may be read as feminist, I will pair close textual reading with analyses of contemporary discourses of race, gender, sexuality, and disability using feminist philosophies as interpretive tools. This combined approach speaks to the themes that make this book a work of feminist cultural studies broadly, and of feminist comics studies more specifically. As Morag Shiach argues, cultural studies is concerned with the relationship between culture and power and is "interested in the practices and texts through which individuals and groups come to understand or to imagine themselves as social beings" (1999, 3). Accordingly, *Searching for Feminist Superheroes* is, on the one hand, aimed at analyzing the limitations and possibilities for generating feminist representations of girls and women in comics in our white supremacist, imperialist, capitalist, heteropatriarchal cultural context. On the other hand, because the nature of reading comics is an interpretive process (i.e., meaning-making happens "in the gutters"), this book also aims to demonstrate how feminist philosophies can enrich readings (scholarly or otherwise) of female-led superhero comics.

More specifically, comics scholar and artist Scott McCloud suggests that the gutter, the space between comics panels, "plays host to much of the *magic* and *mystery* that are at the very *heart of comics*! Here in the limbo of the gutter, *human imagination* takes two separate images and *transforms* them into a single idea" (1994, 66).[1] In other words, comics readers are never passive recipients of messages delivered by creators; instead, readers actively make meaning by incorporating their past experiences in their imaginative attempts to bridge the gaps between images so that a continuous narrative comes into view. This interpretive process, which McCloud calls "closure," is not actually limited to the gutters of comics. However, I have chosen to use "gutters" in this discussion as shorthand for comics as a space in which worlds are constructed by creators *and* readers, and both bring their real experiences to bear on telling and consuming stories. In fact, Frederick Luis Aldama argues that the creation and consumption of comics is a co-creative process:

> When we open a comic and begin to read and view its pages, we *co-create*. The authors and artists select in *and* out details (writing and visuals) that at once hit our perception system *and* guide our imagination to thrill in their filling in of gaps; our emotions and thoughts fill in and complete drawn figures, gestures, dialogue, and character interaction, for instance. When we fill in the gaps, we co-create and we make the story our own. We don't change the story; we follow the carefully selected visual and verbal cues that make up the blueprint to *co-create* the story. We become chiasmic transformers, all while not changing the DNA of the story itself. (2017, 91)

This conception of comics and how they are read is constructive for my examination of feminist superheroes for several reasons. Comics should not be seen as mirror images of our reality, but Aldama's analysis nevertheless points to techniques creators use to reconstruct reality by selecting and omitting "building blocks" of our reality to compose their storyworlds. Comics readers similarly integrate their real identities, experiences, and ideologies into their interpretations of the gaps, signposts, and cues creators use to "make up the blueprint" of the comic. Importantly, according to Aldama, "The wonderfully generative capacity of this co-creating potential in comic book readers . . . not only allows readers and audiences to imagine movement and three dimensions in the static, two-dimensional in-print comic book story-world spaces, but also allows them to feel and think about identities and experiences distant from their own" (2017, 90).

For example, creators may choose to focus on a character with marginalized identities to incite co-creative readers to understand and relate to that character's experiences of marginalization, whether the reader shares that identity in reality or not. Creators' abilities to reconstruct realities that draw from, but are not limited to, our reality also enable them to compose visual and verbal cues that guide readers to imagine a world free from such marginalization. Therefore, my method of pairing close reading with discourse analysis aims to demonstrate how US norms of gender, sexuality, and race (among other aspects of identity) may inform which building blocks creators choose to include or exclude in reconstructing reality and how these same norms may impact readers' abilities and desires to co-create that reality via their interpretations of visual and verbal cues.

Moreover, by recognizing the potential for comics to open readers' eyes to the experiences of marginalized subjects, and to help them imagine a world free from such marginalization, this book focuses on comics that are attentive to but not entirely determined by the overlapping systems of social oppression that affect US women. Because this kind of analysis is based on my abilities and desires as a comics reader, each chapter is, on one level, an account of how I, as a feminist scholar, comics fan, woman, and social being, have filled in gaps, completed gestures, and followed the map composed by the relevant creative team. That is, these interpretations are, in many ways, my own co-creations. However, throughout each chapter I endeavor to demonstrate the specific ways I use feminist philosophies as tools for interpreting the figures, gestures, and dialogue of each comic such that any co-creative reader with the same tools might identify a similar set of blueprints.

My reason for employing feminist philosophies as comics studies tools becomes clear when one considers Mary Midgley's definition of philosophy. She argues that it is not some grand abstract hobby but rather a very necessary skill set that has much in common with plumbing.

> Plumbing and philosophy are both activities that arise because elaborate cultures like ours have, beneath their surface, a fairly complex system which is usually unnoticed, but which sometimes

> goes wrong. In both cases, this can have serious consequences. Each system supplies vital needs for those who live above it. Each is hard to repair when it does go wrong, because neither of them was ever consciously planned as a whole. There have been many ambitious attempts to reshape both of them, but existing complications are usually too widespread to allow a completely new start. (1992, 139)

The value of being able to look at the inner workings of a system is, as Midgley suggests, most obvious when problems arise. While the breakdowns of our ideological and ethical systems are not always as immediately obvious as a dripping faucet or a flooded drain, we are eventually faced with discomfort and social malfunction. It takes skill—and practice—to turn inwards and ask what "in the structure of our thought" is wrong, and it is even harder to readjust, shift, and change (1992, 140). Like Midgley, I see the value in philosophies as tools for examining how our cultural norms around identity have amalgamated through generations, how they are complex in their imbrications, how they are taken for granted as inevitable, and, as a result, have become a source of great social discomfort. Feminist philosophies in particular can help us to see the underlying systems of gender as they intersect with other structures of identity, to diagnose the failings of taken-for-granted norms, and to devise strategies for change.

Of course, feminism itself might be conceived of as a vast, complex philosophical and political system with many crisscrossing pipes intended to meet diverse and sometimes competing demands. Because of the plurality of feminisms over time and across geographies, it would be neither possible nor desirable for me to attempt to "plumb" the histories, movements, practices, or structures of thought that fall under the term "feminism" in the space of this book.[2] Instead, my aim in the chapters that follow is to pick up and use the various feminist philosophical tools that seem most suited to the job.

Having said that, the one tool that is required consistently throughout the book is a working definition of feminism. Historian Estelle Freedman defines feminism as "a belief that women and men are inherently of equal worth. Because most societies privilege men as a group, social movements are necessary to achieve equality between women and men, with the understanding that gender always intersects with other social hierarchies" (2003, 22). Recognizing how gender intersects with other social hierarchies is the basis for intersectionality. This term—coined by Kimberlé Williams Crenshaw to address the ways Black women's experiences are affected by compounding inequalities—has been a mainstay of much social justice–oriented scholarship (Collins and Bilge 2016, 1).

In its proliferation, though, its meaning and usage have expanded such that no single definition conveys its significance. However, Patrick Grzanka's summation is helpful: intersectionality reflects how "race, class, gender, sexuality, and other dimensions of identity and inequality shape the contours of social life and structures in the United States and around the world. Intersectionality, [is] the study of how these dimensions of inequality co-construct one another" (2014, xiii).

Because the aim of this book is to conduct intersectional feminist analyses of superhero comics, each chapter critically examines how white supremacy, capitalism, patriarchy, and heteronormativity (among other social hierarchies) co-construct each other, until representations of white, affluent, heterosexual men are disproportionately privileged and presumed to be the genre norm. The particular comics I have selected for discussion all either explicitly critique those norms, actively subvert them, or do both. True to the co-creative process, these texts can also be read as presenting visual and verbal cues that illuminate the diversity of women's lived experiences as they are shaped by race, class, sexuality, and embodiment while also imagining alternative realities that exceed the limits of our own overlapping systems of oppression. Calling attention to these feminist imaginaries of liberation in superhero comics is an important part of philosophical plumbing. As Midgley suggests, the changes needed to shift blockages often come from the arts: "They can show us a new vision" (1992, 140).

To achieve true intersectional justice, we need to do far more than simply reimagine superhero comics, of course: "Any powerful new idea calls for a great deal of change, and the more useful that idea is going to be, the more need there will be to work out these changes fully" (Midgley 1992, 140). According to historians like Freedman, women have been politically agitating for unmitigated access to their rights as human beings for more than two centuries, and even a brief look at contemporary US issues like women's healthcare, equal pay, political access, representation, and domestic violence makes it clear that a feminist future is far from being realized. Nonetheless, it is my hope that in searching the margins for feminist superheroes, this book demonstrates the creative ways some comics producers and readers are pushing our structures of thought in more egalitarian directions.

What quickly becomes apparent when one focuses on comics that are critical of the status quo—and that invite readers to imagine feminist futures—is that they do *not* align with accepted definitions of the superhero genre. For example, if a superhero is "a heroic character with a universal, selfless, prosocial mission," as Peter Coogan suggests (2013, 3), a feminist character who is Black or a person of color, who is poor or working class, who is disabled, or who is queer could apparently never be a superhero in a white supremacist, capitalist, ableist, heteronormative, patriarchal society since true justice would include personal (as well as collective) liberation, and, arguably, could not be said to be selfless.

One might also struggle to characterize feminism as a universal mission since, as Freedman argues above, feminist praxis requires that specific measures be taken to address women's inequality, in particular. Similarly, if Coogan is correct in suggesting that a superhero "is generically distinct, i.e., can be distinguished from characters of related genres (fantasy, science fiction, detective, etc.) by a preponderance of generic conventions" (2013, 3), then comics like *America* or *Ironheart* are off the table because their creators purposefully align their texts with other literary traditions like Latin American feminist literature or Afrofuturism.

Jeffrey Brown has argued that "at its core, the superhero genre is about boundaries" (2015, 137). This creates problems for understanding *Spider-Woman* as a superhero comic since Jessica Drew's journey from pregnant superhero to working mom transgresses boundaries on bodily, professional, and representational levels. What is important to note here is that these definitions can be read as *descriptive* of the majority of the genre rather than *prescriptive* of what superhero comics must do or be. As descriptions of most superhero comics, Coogan's and Brown's analyses (among several others) are accurate in many ways. However, as I've suggested, identifying superhero comics based only on these criteria excludes many promising texts.

So, following feminist scholar Sara Ahmed, this book adopts a willful method to seek out what has been excluded. Ahmed writes: "Willfulness might be what we do when we are judged as being *not,* as not meeting the criteria for being human, for instance. Not to meet the criteria for human is often to be attached to other nots, not human as not being: not white, not being male, not being straight, not being able-bodied" (2014, 15). As I show throughout the four chapters of this book, characters like Jessica Drew/Spider-Woman, America Chavez,

Nadia van Dyne/The Wasp, and Riri Williams/Ironheart fail to meet the criteria for "superhero" in terms similar to those Ahmed outlines. Thus, to insist on their designation *as* superheroes is to be willful. This decision to "read sideways or across" the de facto boundaries of the superhero genre also makes this book a work of "*not philosophy*" (Ahmed 2014, 15). That is, part of the discussion for each fictional woman or girl analyzed in the following chapters focuses on what they are not—not monstrously embodied, not stereotypically hypersexual, not hyperindividualistic, not derivative.

The search for feminist superheroes constitutes, in some ways, what Ahmed describes as "a *philosophy of the not*." Methodologically, *Searching for Feminist Superheroes* is also a "not philosophy" insofar as it is interdisciplinary. Certainly, I cite many philosophers in this book and have argued above for their utility in reading comics; however, like Ahmed, I reference philosophers alongside many thinkers who are not philosophers, and in no way am I aiming to suggest that feminist philosophies are the *most* or the *only* effective tools for co-creative comics studies. As I suggest in the conclusion, the process of searching for feminist superheroes is one I hope others from across comics studies will join. The four chapters that follow are not intended to be representative of the culmination of this search; rather, they are entries into what will ideally become a living archive of feminist superheroes.

By way of invitation to others who may also wish to seek out feminist superheroes, it seems useful to discuss further the criteria that led me to the four comics discussed in the chapters that follow. First, all the titles selected for analysis are female-led, insofar as they are titular comics focusing primarily on one girl or woman (although there is a tendency for the protagonists to work closely with friends, sidekicks, and teams). This does not necessarily mean that the creative teams of each book are led by women. Women and nonbinary creators have been far outnumbered by men in mainstream superhero comics publishing throughout its history. The disparity between the number of female characters discussed and the number of female or nonbinary creators behind them is indicative of this industry-wide problem. In fact, only one of the books, *The Unstoppable Wasp*, maintained gender parity in its creative team throughout production. It is also important to note that the gender identities of comics creators do not necessarily tell us anything about their politics. We typically assume that creators who share the same identities as their characters can speak more authentically to the kinds of experiences that character might have. But even when women comics creators write or draw female characters, there is no guarantee that the comic will have a feminist ethos.

Relatedly, while cis men may not be able to write or draw female characters based on lived experience, it is still possible for them to include and omit building blocks of our reality in their reconstructions of comics storyworlds in feminist ways. Indeed, that is precisely what I suggest writers like Dennis Hopeless and Jeremy Whitley and artists like Javier Rodriguez, Joe Quinones, and Luciano Vecchio do. Male superheroes may also be capable of feminist praxis and may also be portrayed in feminist ways.[3] However, given the marginal status of women and girls in superhero comics, and, by extension, in scholarship focused on superheroes, my decision to focus on women and girls (as well as some nonbinary characters) is rooted in my own feminist politics.

Aside from each comic being female-led and eponymous, each text represents a specific run that is examined in its entirety. This approach allows for a more in-depth examination of how each text "[comes] to understand or to imagine" girls and women "as social beings"; it lends to more detailed discussion of the choices of specific comics creators; and it helps to cultivate a sharper focus on the particular feminist concerns being explored.

I have also chosen comics that, thus far, have not received much scholarly attention.[4] While particular comics focused on characters like Kamala Khan/Ms. Marvel, Carol Danvers/Captain Marvel, X-Men's Storm, or DC's Wonder Woman all have the potential to be read as feminist texts, these characters have also been discussed across numerous academic publications. My aim with this book is to add to an already rich conversation on feminism and representation in comics by bringing different characters to the table.

Second, all of the comics discussed are Marvel comics: as one of the "big two" publishers, Marvel produces texts that are unquestionably part of the superhero genre. Moreover, as Brown observes, "Marvel superheroes have interacted with issues of cultural diversity ever since Stan Lee and Jack Kirby redefined comic book relevance in the 1960s" (2021, 5). Although not always done well or with any reliable degree of authenticity, Marvel's superheroes have been depicted dealing with issues of race, gender, sexuality, and nationality for decades. Similarly, while initiatives such as "Marvel NOW" and "All-New All-Different Marvel" have been rightfully scrutinized for failing to deliver the kinds of "diversity" promised, these moves did at least begin to expand casts of creators and characters in the 2010s. As Brown notes, these initiatives indicated that "the world of Marvel superheroes was changing and diversifying in a way that reflected real-world changes and an increased awareness of identity politics. The editorial directive was that Marvel's fictional universe should resemble the 'world outside our windows'" (2021, 3).

Marvel has also become a flashpoint amid ongoing debates about identity politics and conservative versus progressive values in the United States. This is evident not only in the launch and then seemingly inevitable cancellation of titles intended to appeal to a more diverse audience but also in real-world events. "The Milkshake Crew" incident, for example, unfolded in 2017 when a group of female creators and staffers took an afternoon break from their jobs at Marvel to grab milkshakes. Because they had the "audacity" to take a selfie with their milkshake treats and post it to Twitter, they were met with a barrage of misogynist responses decrying the inclusion of women in the industry (Rosza 2017).

Similar sexist behavior erupted leading up to and following the release of Marvel's first solo female superhero film, *Captain Marvel* (Boden and Fleck 2019). In response to movie posters, for instance, sexist fans demanded that Brie Larson should be pictured smiling to look more appealing (Clark 2018; Cavanaugh 2019). Antidiversity fans also attempted to "review bomb" the film prior to its release (Francisco 2019), and Larson was met with hostility when she suggested that her film should not be reviewed by white men only (Lang 2018). Marvel's history of creating comics focused on "othered" identities and their recent attempts to hire more marginalized creators to tell authentic stories about marginalized characters have proven promising for identifying feminist superheroes. The controversies around women working for or featured in Marvel media further point to the ways these stories matter in contemporary US culture.

It is not to say that one could not conduct this kind of research amid other superhero comics publishers. DC comics is, of course, the home of the first and perhaps most famous feminist superhero, Wonder Woman. And as Anna Peppard shows in her discussion of the controversy over the naming of Wonder Woman as an honorary UN ambassador, her stories also matter deeply to real people (2020, 7–8). Nonetheless, because during the last ten years Marvel seems to have asked themselves a question akin to "Can we make comics that will speak to a feminist audience?," focusing on their superheroes has been most productive for this particular study.

Third, all of the comics discussed in this book are what Adrienne Resha has characterized as "Blue Age comics." Reflecting on the responses developed by publishers like Marvel to address changing identity politics and on the rise of digital reading and comics sales platforms, Resha argues that the 2010s marked the beginning of the latest wave in the periodization framework of superhero comics. She writes: "This Age is, thus far, defined not by diversity but by diversification. New heroes (like Kamala Khan and Miles Morales) have appeared, and old heroes (like Carol Danvers and Clint Barton) have been made different. The Blue Age is further distinguished in name from the Golden, Silver, and Bronze Ages because blue, unlike gold, silver, and bronze, is intangible. The color blue is as immaterial as (some of) the digital comics and culture that define the Blue Age" (2020, 70).

Comics from this age are important from the perspective of feminist cultural studies because their availability via online retailers means they are arguably more accessible to readers who may have felt unwelcome in comics bookstores or who may have been precluded from buying from brick-and-mortar stores because of disability (Resha 2020, 72–73). Resha also coined the term "Blue Age" to signify the blue used in the icons of social media platforms like Twitter (branded X as of 2023) or Facebook, highlighting how readers of many current comics can demonstrate their preferences online in ways typically obscured by sales figures that are not readily available to scholars (2020, 77). For my purposes, the social interaction between readers and creators is important because it provides another way to determine whether and how a particular comic is meaningful to feminist audiences. In chapter 4, for instance, I discuss how a fan-led Change.org petition to hire Eve Ewing preceded her being offered the job to write *Ironheart*.

Blue Age comics are also relevant for this study because of their focus on "legacy heroes"—that is, characters who have been reimagined in supposedly more progressive ways or new characters who take up the mantle of established heroes but who are also intended to diversify Marvel's roster of characters. The girls and women in chapters 1 through 4 are all legacy heroes in one way or another. These comics, Resha writes, are "new and different" insofar as they feature more women, people of color, and characters of other marginalized identities, while simultaneously being "not all-new or all-different." In other words, they are still recognizable as superhero comics (2020, 69–70). Although I did not use this aspect of Blue Age comics as a criterion for selection, all four of the comics analyzed in this book also adhere to

Resha's description because they were all canceled after only five or six issues (e.g., *The Unstoppable Wasp*) or were ended earlier than expected (e.g., *Ironheart*). Marvel's official response to fans who are unhappy with these decisions is always to point out that the books in question simply did not perform in terms of monthly sales. However, Resha argues that this is also indicative of Blue Age readers who "do not understand the preorder system of the direct market[;] they trade-wait, or they simply prefer to purchase and read comics digitally. Blue Age readers are not content to let publishers exploit them in exchange for representation" (2020, 79).

In any case, the somewhat ephemeral nature of Blue Age feminist superhero comics is an important reminder that, as Resha argues, "'diversity' in comics and their transmedia derivatives is at least as much about commodification as it is about representation, if not more" (2020, 78). As impactful as I think the four comics discussed in this book are, they are also the product of a media conglomerate's attempts to sell as much as they can to as many readers as they can. Both are true and are a reminder that, as Midgley suggests, we cannot free ourselves on new visions alone.

The fourth requirement that led me to the specific comics analyzed in the chapters that follow is direct engagement with intersectional feminist issues that are either of ongoing or newly pressing concern for US feminists in the Blue Age. In chapter 1, *Spider-Woman* highlights ongoing feminist concerns with reproductive justice and with harmful discursive norms of motherhood. *America* in chapter 2 combats the erasure of queer female sexuality, critiques the violence of binary thinking, and challenges xenophobic, nationalist anxieties around borders and migration. *The Unstoppable Wasp* in chapter 3 enables analysis of androcentrism, combats women's marginalization in STEM fields, and emphasizes the importance of feminist friendships. Finally, in chapter 4 *Ironheart* speaks to the need to center and value Black lives, evaluates what it means to be good and evil under authoritarian rule, and imagines a liberatory future that has the power to challenge oppressive social structures.

Of course, these are not the sum total of contemporary feminist concerns. Nor is this a complete list of superhero comics that explore intersectional feminist issues. For example, although I discuss the need for greater representation of trans and nonbinary characters in chapters 1 and 2, all four of the comics featured in this book are centered on fictional cis women. This is not because I do not see trans rights as an integral part of concurrent intersectional feminism. Rather, it reflects a lack of source material. Marvel has only recently begun introducing more trans women characters like Shela Sexton/Escapade, and at present, she (like her predecessors) remains a minor character. The paucity of trans creators, characters, and opportunities to celebrate trans lives through superhero stories is deeply concerning since trans people are one of the most vulnerable populations in the US today. To continue to exclude trans people is to signal that their stories don't matter and that their voices aren't an important part of our visions for the future. This is unacceptable.

Thus far, Marvel has also failed to produce a superhero comic that takes as its primary concern the increasing threat posed by the climate crisis. As environmental justice scholars and advocates have shown, social systems of oppression are exacerbated by environmental degradation to the point that those who are impacted most by the intersections of racism, sexism, capitalism, and nationalism also suffer most from climate change. While I consider this to be a primary feminist concern, there is, as yet, no Marvel comic that has included that aspect of our reality in a superhero storyworld in a meaningful way.

On one hand, these omissions point to a limitation resultant from my decision to focus on Marvel comics. DC comics has historically included more trans characters than Marvel (Billard and MacAuley 2017), and Gail Simone's DC trans woman character Alysia Yeoh is not only appearing in more comics, in more central roles, but was also slated to be played by trans actress Ivory Aquino in the film adaptation of *Batgirl* (Vary 2022).[5] Similarly, G. Willow Wilson and Marcio Takara's current DC comic, *Poison Ivy* (2022–present), frames the climate crisis as Ivy's primary motivation for action and makes use of real ecological research to show how harmful things like industrialization or factory farming have been. On the other hand, like all discrete projects, this book cannot cover everything, and my hope is that others interested in joining the search for feminist superheroes can address the omissions created by the parameters of my research.

Finally, the comics discussed in this book were chosen because every titular character analyzed in chapters 1 through 4 has or will appear in other comics, comics-related texts, films, video games, animated series, or all of the above. While it has traditionally been the case that comics scholars have denied any direct correlation between comics sales and the appearance of other kinds of comic book media, recent films and TV series suggest this may be changing. The MCU (Marvel Cinematic

Universe) film *Avengers: Infinity War* (Russo and Russo 2018) resulted in the sale of half a million Infinity Gauntlet trade collections, and the Disney+ series *WandaVision* (Shakman 2021) elicited WandaVision-related comics to sell out to the point of being on backorder for months (Johnston 2018; Enlow 2021). Similarly, when newly appointed co-chair and CEO of DC Studios James Gunn announced that there would be a film adaptation of the DC comic *The Authority*, trade paperbacks once again sold out (Johnston 2023). Therefore, the potential for these female characters' appearance across media to inspire audiences to seek them out in the comics in question seems increasingly possible.

Moreover, while each girl or woman analyzed in this book, as a female superhero, may still be numerically marginal, their impact cannot be so easily reduced when they appear in multiple transmedia texts. As Enrique García argues, when underrepresented characters are launched "into other media venues such as animation, video games, and live-action filmmaking," the shift can lead "to the diversification of other narrative mediums and to a more solid presence of underrepresented groups in the global narratives produced in the United States" (2018, 169). While the brief discussions I provide at the end of each chapter cannot do justice to what it means for the girls and women studied in this book to be transmedia characters, my aim is to aid scholars and fans in making demands for better, more inclusive representations of girls and women in superhero texts wherever they appear.

THE DARK PHOENIX PROBLEM

One final clarification I can offer regarding the texts I have included in this book is to discuss some that I have not. My first crack at feminist comics scholarship was an essay written on *The Dark Phoenix Saga*. I had grown to love the character Jean Grey/Phoenix through the X-Men films, which led me to go back and read the comics. After a deep drink of "killjoy feminism" while earning my PhD, I knew Chris Claremont and John Byrne's book had its problems, but I also wondered if using creative methods of analysis would reveal resistant readings. By comparing Jean Grey/Phoenix to Donna Haraway's paradigm of the "promising monster," I was able to establish the kind of scholarship I wanted to do: constructively critical *and* creative, rigorous *and* reparative.

In my chapter for the edited volume *Comics and Sacred Texts: Reimagining Religion and Graphic Narratives*, I note that there are few comic book characters that have undergone reincarnation (literally) as many times as Jean Grey (Langsdale 2018). Jean begins as the demure Marvel Girl and transforms throughout the comics into various manifestations of the Phoenix, each one more powerful and volatile than the last. For feminist fans and scholars like me, the Phoenix is both delightful and disappointing owing to representations of her sexuality, agency, and identity. For example, in Claremont and Byrne's *X-Men: The Dark Phoenix Saga* (2006), Jean is a confident sexual subject unafraid to exhibit desire and initiate intimate moments with her lover.

However, the *Saga* also links female desire and sexuality with psychoses, chaos, monstrosity, and destruction. These sexist links are developed both verbally and visually. When Jean appears as the Dark Phoenix, her behavior is often characterized as "out of control," and readers are encouraged to see Jean as being "at the mercy" of the Phoenix Force. Jean's fate is sealed when her supposedly unwieldy power leads her to commit an act of mass destruction, a cosmic crime for which she pays with her life. Despite my efforts to read against the grain, I nevertheless concluded that *The Dark Phoenix Saga* was not exactly feminist.

When I learned of a new Dark Phoenix comic, I became hopeful that I would be able to revisit Jean's story in the first chapter of this book. *Phoenix Resurrection: The Return of Jean Grey* (Rosenberg et al. 2017–2018) attempts to reimagine the violence wrought in *The Dark Phoenix Saga* and to create a version of Jean that allows for the full complexity of her character. While this text mitigates some of the problematic gender politics in *The Dark Phoenix Saga*—namely, Jean gets to live—further scrutiny reveals lingering issues with respect to female sexuality and empowerment. As part of Marvel's Legacy line, an initiative designed to take things back to Marvel's "iconic history," *Phoenix Resurrection* is steeped in nostalgia that demonstrates a longing for innocence, most particularly in Jean. The result is a postfeminist, postracial comic that relies on its ability to replicate Jean's trauma and thus punish her yet again "for the original sin of Dark Phoenix" (Linton 2019), all under the aegis of bringing Jean back in a way that sets the stage for "who she can be again." Far from being an innovative reimagining of the character, the Jean who appears at the conclusion of the book is depowered, infantilized, and desexualized. Thus, despite the potential for a more feminist story, I found myself once again wondering why it was so hard for comics creators to imagine a storyworld in which a woman with access to power is not murderous, rapacious, and monstrous. How was I going to include Jean's story in my book on feminist superheroes when she continued to be co-opted to uphold patriarchal norms?

According to Carolyn Cocca, the ending of *The Dark Phoenix Saga* displeased much of the creative team but was nevertheless ordered by editor-in-chief Jim Shooter, "who felt Jean's genocide required consequences" (2016, 127). Many fans were also distraught about the conclusion, including future *Phoenix Resurrection* writer Matthew Rosenberg. In a letter in the back matter of issue #1, Rosenberg explains that Jean's initial death, and subsequent reincarnations, led to a feeling that she was the heart of the X-Men and that her sustained absence needed to be corrected (Rosenberg et al. 2017). *Phoenix Resurrection,* he argues, is, on the one hand, a eulogy. Because eulogies are backward-looking literary devices focused on good or happy memories, many are inherently nostalgic, expressing a longing for what was. This kind of approach to *Phoenix Resurrection* is apparent even before one gets to Rosenberg's letter reminiscing about reading X-Men comics in his childhood. Although the first several sequences of issue #1 concentrate on a contemporary amalgamation of X-Men, Jean's first appearance on the page is drenched in nostalgia. She appears in a bright pink waitress uniform, standing next to a woman named Gladys, outside a 1950s-style diner. Her hair is drawn up into a girlish ponytail, her face framed and accentuated by a soft, long fringe. She wears pink nail polish, cosmetics, has a slim waist and a large bust. She is relatively unsure of herself and tries to maintain a pleasing demeanor despite a growing sense of confusion.

This hyperfeminine performance dominates how Jean is represented throughout the five issues of *Phoenix Resurrection*. We eventually learn that this is a fabricated reality created by the Phoenix Force in an attempt to comfort the newly resurrected Jean and ease her back into becoming the Dark Phoenix. The implication of this scenario is that Jean initially feels most at ease in an environment that evokes white, upper-middle-class fantasies of suburban 1950s America. This kind of postfeminist depiction suggests that when women choose normative beauty standards as they have been dictated by patriarchal culture, there is no need to scrutinize how those same standards may also contribute to women's marginalization (Tasker and Negra 2007).

As a sexual subject, she is virtually a nonentity before issue #5 (Rosenberg et al. 2018). In fact, various visual design decisions reinforce Jean as an object of the male gaze. For example, in issue #3, even after she has just been sexually harassed by a character reminiscent of young Wolverine, Jean reacts in a panel composed with a low angle that draws the viewer's gaze up her almost entirely bare leg towards her rear, which is exposed as she raises her arms towards her head, a gesture that also accentuates her chest (Rosenberg et al. 2018). That her face is almost entirely obscured further emphasizes the to-be-looked-at-ness of her body.

As Jeffrey Brown writes: "Where male characters usually strike heroic action poses, superheroines are far more likely to be illustrated as pin-ups or centerfolds" (Brown 2013b, 134). Once we arrive at issue #5, Jean's agency as a sexual subject is still largely absent; however, there is arguably a strong return to depicting female sexuality and empowerment as deadly. Once the X-Men locate the alternate reality the Phoenix Force has created for Jean, they begin to postulate on how it works. Beast suggests that the dome under which they stand is like an egg from which Jean, as the Dark Phoenix, will hatch if all goes according to the Phoenix Force's plan. If such an event occurs, death becomes imminent (Rosenberg et al. 2018). As Cocca, Linton, and others have observed, X-Men often come into power at puberty; their power, therefore, aligns with a sexual awakening. For Jean, her transition from the demure Marvel Girl to the Phoenix signals an awakening not just of her sexuality but also of her lethalness.

Phoenix Resurrection doubles down on this kind of alignment: by the time Jean appears in a black-and-red Phoenix uniform, there can be little doubt about the connection between a sexually awakened woman and danger. Further, whereas *The Dark Phoenix Saga* distorted Storm's image in service of Jean's fantasies, *Phoenix Resurrection* largely eradicates the connection between the two women.[6] This erasure, which appears alongside the diverse cast of X-Men who appear throughout the book, gives it a postracial sensibility that implies racism does not exist and therefore cannot be a part of white women's subjectivity (Kamaloni 2019). When the Phoenix Force does finally conjure what Jean truly desires in an attempt to win her over, a resurrected Scott Summers appears briefly to tell his wife he loves her, to kiss her, and then to say goodbye again once both he and Jean realize the unnaturalness of being reunited. This is the first step in containing Jean's desire: it is expressed heteronormatively and then relinquished.

To further contain, or rather diminish, her power, Rosenberg adopts a narrative resonant of the alternate ending Claremont and Byrne originally had planned (Cocca 2016, 127). Over a number of pages Jean converses with the Phoenix Force, refusing its request to once again merge with her. She recognizes that her life was saved because of its intervention, but she is certain that she will never truly live if it does not leave her. Jean exhibits agency in knowingly rejecting the Phoenix Force, but in so doing, she also suffers the fate of so many previous female superheroes in becoming significantly depowered. While this scenario is not quite as gruesome as the "psychic lobotomy" Claremont and Byrne proposed, it nevertheless evokes a similar excising of the parts of Jean that made her goddess-like, a creative choice that, as Matthew Linton writes, "says much about the cultural treatment of feminine identities and power" (2019). Jean is then transformed so that she is back in her Marvel Girl uniform of the 60s, which seems only to confirm the ways her "welcome back" is contingent upon the containment of her womanhood, her sexual agency, and her power.

Svetlana Boym writes that "nostalgia inevitably reappears as a defense mechanism in a time of accelerated rhythms of life and historical upheavals" (2001, xiv). Susan Faludi argues that following the civil rights and feminist movements in the 1960s and 1970s, in the late 70s and into the 80s there was a cultural backlash against the great strides that had been made for oppressed groups (1991). To diminish and contain the fought-for changes, mass media, advertising, and popular culture began to espouse the "costs" of such radical social shifts. Similarly, after Americans elected the first Black president and nominated the first woman to lead the Democratic presidential ticket in 2016 (the same year Faludi published a new edition of *Backlash* and wrote a new, contemporary introduction), Americans elected an aspiring autocrat promising to "make America great again" to the presidency. Interestingly, following Marvel's "diversity initiatives," the Marvel Legacy initiative began in 2017, with the aim of reinvigorating the company's iconic characters, and to "remind readers of Marvel's rich history" (Rothman 2017).

In principle, Jean's resurrection story within the Marvel Legacy storyworld is not necessarily a problem. As a heteronormative white woman, she doesn't really speak to the goals of the initiatives aimed at diversifying comics. Nevertheless, the creative team's choice to use *Phoenix Resurrection* to essentially send her back to "factory settings" undermines any claims about improving Jean's circumstances as a character. Letting her live seems like a low bar, and, as suggested above, simply allowing her to make a choice—particularly one that reifies a patriarchal vision of who can and should have access to power—is hardly liberatory from a feminist perspective.

I do not want to be dismissive of the various meanings fans have found in Jean's stories. As discussed above, Jean was my gateway to superhero comics and to comics studies, and many queer comics fans and critics have found Jean's transformations relatable (Century 2019). But to try to read *The Dark Phoenix Saga, Phoenix Resurrection,* or any other rendition of this narrative as feminist is, I argue, to try to "change the DNA of the story" (Aldama 2017, 91). Further, the proliferation of adaptations that faithfully recreate the seeming inevitability that Jean as the Phoenix poses an immense threat and must be eradicated suggests that media producers have no interest in radical retellings. The 2019 film *Dark Phoenix* (Kinberg), for example, goes some way to change the setting in which Jean slowly loses control, but ultimately, her inability to handle the weight of the Phoenix Force drives her mad and again results in her death.

In the opening pages of the retcon[7] comic *Jean Grey,* writer Dennis Hopeless (an author whose other comic, *Spider-Woman,* appears in this volume) uses caption boxes over a panel depicting a flashback to Jean's original death to describe Jean as "a genocidal madwoman corpse, all decked out in her burgundy bad-guy clothes" (Hopeless et al. 2017). As Linton asserts, these iterations all seem to betray a deep distrust of "feminine identities and power" (2019, 14).

I see no indication in these texts that the creators are choosing to reconstruct reality to ameliorate patriarchal gender norms. Even while I cannot rule out more subversive readings, I also have no reason to believe that the creative teams of recent Dark Phoenix stories willfully chose building blocks of reality for their storyworlds that would speak to women's lived experiences and render their characters as complex, desirous, yet fully human subjects. So until Marvel hands the reins over to creators who use their "will to style" to reconstruct reality in a way that frees Jean from the yoke of patriarchal fears of feminine power and to imagine her in ways that exceed gender norms requiring her purity and submissiveness, I do not believe she belongs in this book.

Instead, the characters analyzed herein reflect the plurality of women's experiences. Their storyworlds demonstrate what Aldama calls a purposeful "will to style": that is, the responsibility creative teams feel to fully understand "the building blocks of reality that they are reconstructing as well as the degree of presence of a willful use of skills and technical devices to give shape to the making of new pop-cultural phenomena" (2017, 4). Whether or not the creative teams of the comics analyzed in the pages that follow identify themselves as feminists, I argue that they all demonstrate the will to understand well the building blocks of reality that shape women's lives and willfully use their skills to create comics that can be read as feminist superhero texts. The women and girls discussed are not simply ciphers of their creators' desires and fears; instead, they are compelling characters that demonstrate the responsibility their creative teams feel to represent the dynamism and complexity of women's identities and experiences.

AUDIENCE FOR AND STRUCTURE OF THE BOOK

While this book is informed by and in conversation with many scholarly texts on the superhero genre generally, they are too numerous to list here. In addition to the texts mentioned previously, this book coincides most closely with scholarship on superhero comics and superheroes and identity.[8] Even more acutely, this book is aligned with works concerned with representation of girls and women in the superhero genre.[9] In its cultivation of a specifically feminist reading of female superheroes, *Searching for Feminist Superheroes* relates most closely to Lillian Robinson's *Wonder Women: Feminisms and Superheroes* (2004) and Cocca's *Superwomen: Gender, Power, and Representation* (2016). This book differs from Cocca's insofar as her work traces the history of specific characters across media to analyze their evolution (or lack thereof) relative to cultural shifts, whereas my focus is on close textual readings of specific comics in dialogue with dominant discourses of identity to determine whether, and in what ways, they can be read as feminist. In that way, I see this book as a kind of follow-up to Robinson's *Wonder Women*; although she found most contemporary female-led superhero comics to be postfeminist at best, her argument that comics that are informed by a feminist ethos produce feminist superheroes resonates with my own aims.

My insistence on centering my analysis on comics that *can* (at least to some extent) be read as feminist—as opposed to focusing on how and why various comics actively marginalize girls and women—is also resonant of the kind of work done in Ramzi Fawaz's *The New Mutants: Superheroes and the Radical Imagination of American Comics* (2016), Adilifu Nama's *Super Black: American Pop Culture and Black Superheroes* (2011), and andré carrington's *Speculative Blackness: The Future of Race in Science*

Fiction (2016). That is, this book, in parallel to the work of Fawaz, Nama, and carrington, does not deny the effects of overlapping systems of oppression that marginalize certain groups but rather focuses on a "reparative" reading that illuminates the creativity, innovation, and "world-making possibilities" of the comics produced in the margins.

Because this book also uses feminist philosophies as interpretive tools for analysis, it does arguably align with several "philosophy and . . ." books: for example, *Superheroes and Philosophy: Truth, Justice, and the Socratic Way* (Morris and Morris 2005). In relation to these texts, *Searching for Feminist Superheroes* makes an important contribution, since feminist philosophical analyses are absent from the vast majority of "philosophy and . . ." books, including *Superheroes and Philosophy*. Further, as the majority of authors who contribute to these books are men, I also bring much-needed gender diversity to the subfield. One recent exception to these trends is Jason Held's edited volume *Wonder Woman and Philosophy: The Amazonian Mystique* (2017), which, while it centers specifically on the character of Wonder Woman, similarly makes use of feminist philosophy as a lens through which to read superhero comics.

As asserted above, because *Searching for Feminist Superheroes* is also a work of "not philosophy," it is accessibly written, and popular media journalism informs each chapter. My aim is to appeal to an interdisciplinary audience of scholars and students, including those interested in comics studies; in superhero studies; in the intersection of race, gender, sexuality, and media; in cultural studies; and in women's and gender studies. *Searching for Feminist Superheroes* is also for superhero fans who are concerned with the politics surrounding representations of race, gender, and sexuality.

The organization of the book is chronological, beginning with a chapter on *Spider-Woman* (published 2015–2017) and concluding with a chapter on *Ironheart* (published in 2018). Having said that, the book may be read in any order since each chapter presents a unique case study of the comic in question. Reading the book in its entirety is, of course, the best way to understand how feminist philosophies may be employed as tools for reading the visual and verbal clues generated by Blue Age creators. Their willful reconstruction of the building blocks of reality results in comics that both acknowledge how US norms of gender, race, sexuality, nationality, and disability shape women and girls' lives *and* imagine feminist storyworlds that exceed the limitations of our own world.

Chapter 1 presents an analysis of *Spider-Woman,* which was written by Dennis Hopeless with art by Javier Rodriguez. In 2015 Hopeless and Rodriguez revealed that the star of their story would be a very pregnant Jessica Drew. Far from being a gimmick, Jessica's storyline as a hero and a mother demonstrates what I argue is a feminist reading of maternity. The chapter begins by engaging with established scholarship on pregnant superheroes to demonstrate how Jessica's pregnancy departs from prior sexist representations. Rather than being framed as punishment, an accident, or a mistake (as were the pregnancies of other female superheroes), Jessica's decision to become a mother is characterized as informed and purposeful. While the book does not fully address all the choices (or barriers) people have when it comes to their reproductive rights, the comic does show clearly the patriarchal context within which Jess makes her decision.

Because she decides to pursue motherhood as a single woman, Jess is confronted with sexist attitudes that the creative team critiques via visual and narrative devices that transgress genre norms that prioritize paternity over maternity. By examining how the degradation of pregnancy and maternity is rooted in broader cultural systems of dichotomous thought, I show how *Spider-Woman* not only frees Jess of genre norms but also channels a Kristevan model of motherhood in its content and composition. In other words, Jessica's transition from pregnant hero to working mom recalls Julia Kristeva's theories of the maternal "subject in process": the model is both reflective of women's unique experiences of maternity and accessible to anyone who can open themselves up to the "other." Kristeva's maternal subject in process is reflected in *Spider-Woman* in its honest depictions of the simultaneous toil and joy women experience as mothers, its promotion of collaborative childcare, its compositional fluidity, and its inclusion of a gender-swap story arc.

Although I am unconvinced that Hopeless and Rodriguez intend for Jess's gender-swap narrative to be representative of trans experience, this aspect of the book nevertheless provides a much-needed opportunity to explore the interconnectedness of trans rights and reproductive justice, as well as to demand more and better trans representation. Ultimately, then, *Spider-Woman* can be read as feminist in its defiance of the trend in mainstream superhero comics that characterizes motherhood as untenable for superheroines and in its representation of (m)othering as dynamic, communal, and (gender) fluid.

Chapter 2 centers on *America*, written by Gabby Rivera with art by Joe Quinones. From the moment Marvel announced an America solo title, both the character and her writer made headlines. Rivera—the first queer Latina hired at Marvel, writing Marvel's first lesbian Latina character—marked a real departure from the company's status quo both behind the scenes and on the page. Despite complaints from anti-diversity comics fans who accused Marvel of virtue signaling with the new title, Rivera, Quinones, and the rest of the creative team defy genre norms through constructing an explicitly queer feminist storyworld, subverting racist stereotypes, embracing borderlands subjectivity, and aligning *America* with other rich Latinx literary traditions.

Unlike many previous Latina superhero characters, Quinones's character design of America avoids hypersexualization and instead depicts America as muscular yet beautiful, wearing costume elements that tie her to real Black and brown communities. The remaining cast of main characters in the comic is made up of queer Black people and people of color who are integral to the storyworld and to America's growth as a superhero. Together, America and her queer found family not only fight the kinds of intergalactic monsters characteristic of the genre, they also combat rising fascism and white supremacy.

America's ability to punch star-shaped portals through space and time, her queer identity, and her frequent use of dialogue in both Spanish and English evoke what feminist philosopher Gloria Anzaldúa called a "new *mestiza* consciousness." Similar to Anzaldúa's work more broadly, *America*'s dialogue and composition disrupt patriarchal binaries, deconstruct essentialist categories, and draw attention to the real acts of violence inflicted on Latinx people whose lives are impacted by the formation and enforcement of the US-Mexico geopolitical border. In true Anzaldúan fashion, America works towards justice by forming coalitions, honoring the hybridity and plurality of her heritage, modeling transcultural feminist praxis, and fighting against politics of exclusion.

The creative team of *America* further challenges genre conventions by aligning their comic with other Latinx literary traditions. By showing how *America* incorporates aspects of other Latinx superhero and independent comics like *Love and Rockets*, I argue that despite its early cancellation, *America* cannot be dismissed as only a marginal Marvel comic. Instead, like some of the comics it emulates in story and form, *America* can be read as a part of a feminist Latinx literary tradition. The creative team's willful use of visual and narrative devices serves to construct a queer, feminist storyworld that is populated by a diverse cast of characters, who combine with America's borderlands powers and identity to connect her to a feminist Latinx literary tradition and reinforce *America* as a feminist superhero text.

Chapters 3 and 4 share two characteristics that are important to comment on before getting into the specifics of each. First, both chapters focus on comics about girls. Hillary Chute writes that "in the graphic novel world, girls are the new superheroes" (2017, 531). Despite historical associations of comics with men and boys, a recent proliferation of media centered on girlhood and starring girls indicates that this is no longer indicative of our current reality. That two of the chapters in this book are focused on comics about girls serves as evidence that even "Marvel and DC are investing more, in every medium, in young women superheroes" (Chute 2017, 540). This shift is important from a feminist perspective because it affirms that there is nothing inherently masculinist or androcentric about the superhero genre.

It is also encouraging because the use of girl characters makes comics more inclusive of girl readers who may have developed the skills to imaginatively relate to stories through point-of-view characters unlike themselves but who have had far fewer opportunities to directly relate to protagonists via their own life experiences. Conversely, offering boys the opportunity to relate to girl protagonists in superhero comics is valuable because such texts can expand boys' imaginations and strengthen their abilities to relate to others (Cocca 2016, 3–4). Girl characters are also important for a feminist analysis of superhero comics because as adolescents still learning about the world, their struggles to understand complex issues and to figure out who they want to be allows creators to explore gender, race, sexuality, power, and social norms in relatable ways (Stanley 2017). For many feminist philosophers, questioning norms and unsettling deterministic logic are key. As such, girls like Nadia and Riri, who, as adolescents, naturally raise questions about the world around them, make for ideal superheroes.

The second characteristic chapters 3 and 4 have in common relates to this proclivity for girls to explore complex issues. In the case of *The Unstoppable Wasp* and *Ironheart,* Nadia and Riri both articulate concerns with the nature and use of violence. The history of violence in superhero comics has largely been detrimental for female characters. Aside from the normative alignment of violence with masculinity—thus casting any violent female characters as somehow unnatural or insufficiently feminine—depictions of violence in superhero comics also tend to cast female characters as victims. As Cocca notes, throughout much of the history of superhero comics "female characters were subject to sexualized violence and/or 'killed, maimed, or depowered' at much higher rates than their more numerous male counterparts, generally as a plot point to further a male character's development" (2016, 12). Because of this history, the use of violence in female superhero comics has been a point of critique for feminist scholars who argue that the uncritical adoption of physical violence in female-led titles contributes to postfeminist, androcentric texts.

Reflecting on the history of representations of female superheroes, Michael Goodrum argues that depictions of two women characters fighting have traditionally offered little more than a masculinist fantasy: "Although fights between superpowered women can be read as an exercise in female empowerment," he writes, "it is also possible to interpret them as being staged for sexual gratification" owing to hypersexualized character designs and skimpy costumes (2014, 107). Cocca similarly notes how the use of violence by female characters may, in some ways, seem subversive of gender norms and may allow viewers to vicariously feel empowered, but she also highlights the fact that the overwhelming majority of female characters who use violence strongly resemble their male counterparts insofar as they are "white, conventionally attractive, and almost always portrayed as heterosexual," thus undermining their subversive potential (2021, 27).

Moreover, the neoliberal, individualist tendency for superhero comics to focus on what Rebecca Wanzo identifies as "muscular power as the ideal fantasy of agency" (2015, 318) does very little to address structural forms of oppression or the need for collective liberation. As Cocca argues, "A punch to one white man's jaw from a glowing female fist doesn't dismantle multiple and overlapping systems of inequalities" (2021, 88). What I appreciate about *The Unstoppable Wasp* and *Ironheart* is the fact that both comics take these kinds of questions and concerns seriously. Both Nadia and Riri spend time asking themselves and the people around them what it means to use violence to address conflict, how their own use of violence reflects on who they are as people, and whether it is possible to do their jobs as superheroes without physical violence. Neither girl comes to a neat, easy conclusion—which, I argue, is the only responsible option.

Because their respective comics offer stylized reconstructions of our own reality (wherein Black girls are subjected to racialized violence, alarming numbers of children are killed by gun violence, and girls and women are still the group most vulnerable to domestic violence), I think it would be unproductive to ignore the ways violence is a reality for girls, whether we want them to throw punches or not. As I demonstrate in the remaining two chapters, the creative teams behind Nadia's and Riri's comics do not take for granted the superhero genre's tendency to frame violence as the answer to problems, but neither do they ignore the need for girls to be able to defend themselves from harm. Their nuanced—and sometimes messy—explorations of violence arguably add to the ways each comic may be read as feminist.

In addition to analyzing the use of violence, chapter 3 centers on the various ways *The Unstoppable Wasp*, written by Jeremy Whitley with art by Elsa Charretier and others, may be read as feminist. While *The Unstoppable Wasp* is an eponymous comic, it is also a comic about a superhero team. Traditionally, Marvel superhero teams have been composed of more men than women, and, when human or human-approximate, more white characters than characters of color. They are also often led by male characters, even when said males fail to exhibit the qualities that make a good leader. Despite this precedent, *The Unstoppable Wasp* focuses on a superhero team that, in its mission and membership, offers a powerful critique of the homogeneity of the status quo.

The comic begins with the main character, Nadia van Dyne, gathering brilliant young minds historically overlooked based on gender, race, class, sexuality, and disability. Nadia's stated motivation for forming G.I.R.L. (Genius In action Research Labs) is, on the one hand, to redress the historical sexism of superhero teams and, on the other, to call out and disprove androcentric assumptions about intellectual prowess, heroism, and leadership. In addition to taking measures to address the homogeneity of superhero teams, the creative team of *The Unstoppable Wasp* also ameliorates sexist representations of girls and women in STEM (science, technology, engineering, mathematics). Each girl or woman in the comic is characterized as having STEM-related acumen. The inclusion of STEM-focused pedagogical features throughout the comic, as well as back matter featuring interviews with real women in STEM, combats girls' and women's marginalization in the sciences and "queers" science in terms of ideal practitioners and methods.

The cast of *The Unstoppable Wasp* is diverse in age, race, sexuality, disability, and class, which enables exploration of intergenerational and cross-racial friendships among girls and women in complex, dynamic, and sometimes difficult ways. I assert that as a result, the book models the varieties of friendship feminist theorists like María Lugones and Elizabeth Spelman have argued are crucial for collective liberation. Therefore, using feminist philosophies of androcentrism, queer feminist science studies, and philosophies of feminist friendship as interpretive tools, chapter 3 argues that *The Unstoppable Wasp* may indeed be read as a feminist text.

Chapter 4 focuses on *Ironheart,* written by Eve Ewing with art by Kevin Libranda, Luciano Vecchio, Geoffo, Matt Milla, and Clayton Cowles. Riri Williams, also known as Ironheart, was created in 2016 by Brian Michael Bendis and Mike Deodato. As a fifteen-year-old engineering genius, Riri was introduced as an aspiring superhero who made use of her MIT scholarship to build her own Iron Man suit. Although Riri began her superhero career performing as Iron Man in Tony Stark's absence, she eventually crafted a super-suit and moniker that better reflected her identity as a teenage Black girl.

Despite seemingly good intentions, early iterations of Riri perpetuated various racial stereotypes while also being critiqued by antidiversity comics fans for being derivative and uninteresting. Using Black feminist philosophies as interpretive tools, this chapter analyzes the various means by which Ewing and the rest of the creative team ameliorate the intersectional failures of previous iterations of Riri—how the team "remixes" the superhero genre in order to center Black women's experiences and ways of knowing and incorporates Afrofuturist attributes that allow *Ironheart* to be read as a part of broader cultural movement towards social change.

Unlike many other artists' renderings of Black female superhero characters, Libranda, Vecchio, and others draw Riri in ways that avoid hypersexualization and that depict her adolescence realistically. And, in defiance of the genre's tendency to erase mothers and female mentors from the lives of female superheroes, the creative team of *Ironheart* makes Riri's mother and her childhood best friend integral parts of her life. Riri's storyworld in *Ironheart* is not overdetermined by racialized violence (as it had been in previous comics); instead, the creative team uses Riri's character history to emphasize the importance of Black women prioritizing their mental health, and they expand Riri's range of experiences to include joy, friendship, and belonging.

Ewing's allusions to the philosophies of Hannah Arendt allow her and the rest of the creative team to combat misogynoirist reactions to previous iterations of Riri and to explore what it means to do the right thing at a time, not so unlike our own, when those in power demand immorality. Finally, by including a story arc that takes Riri to Wakanda (home of the Black Panther), Ewing and the rest of the creative team align *Ironheart* with "a resistance movement that employs the imagination in inverting conventional thinking, destabilizing previous analysis of blackness and creating an African space in the future" (Chikafa-Chipiro 2019, 2).

Chapter 4 demonstrates that *Ironheart* can be read as a feminist text because in their nuanced depiction of Black girlhood, their creative remixing of genre conventions to affirm and celebrate Black lives, and their willingness to tackle ongoing real-world political threats, the creators of *Ironheart* prove that intersectional justice is not mutually exclusive to superheroism.

Finally, in the conclusion I return to the question of why I, as a feminist scholar and fan, continue to turn to superhero comics. In addition to the qualities that made the four comics analyzed in this book viable for this study, a number of other attributes come to light when they are read in conversation. The shared themes that appear further demonstrate how superhero comics can evoke feminist ideals of justice, bravery, community, and care.

The centrality of mothers or female mentors, for example, manifests in each of the four comics. The power of collaboration and the support that comes from found families also extends through each text. The aversion to homogenous identity categories and inflexible social systems is another shared trait. And, perhaps above all else, the extent to which each comic is successful in representing the set of experiences unique to the woman or girl in question points to ways other kinds of women could also be meaningfully depicted as superheroes.

My point in outlining these shared characteristics is not to create a strict taxonomy but rather to sketch the beginnings of an archive of the traits that inform contemporary feminist superhero comics. Following the work of Sara Ahmed, I am proposing an archive not as an official registry of documents or as a building where a collection can be housed. Instead, it is the continuation of a conversation begun by scholars who have revealed both the limitations of and expansive possibilities for superhero comics to capture the complexity and power of women and girls. It is also an invitation to all those who are willing to follow the "nots" of the genre to join me in searching for more feminist superheroes.

1 | WHOA MOMMA!

The Feminist Model of Maternity in Spider-Woman

Among the characters discussed in this book, Jessica Drew, a.k.a. Spider-Woman, has the longest and most problematic history from a feminist point of view. Created in 1977 by Archie Goodwin and Marie Severin, Spider-Woman (like She-Hulk) was inspired by the need for Marvel to maintain rights to female versions of their popular male heroes. While it is the case that she was one of only a few female characters to get a solo series early in her existence, a rotating door of writers and artists often made her storyworld uneven in tone and narratively incoherent, not to mention the fact that the series ended in Jessica's death. Over the course of her forty-five-year comics history, Jessica was conceived of as a villain and a hero, an actual spider and a brainwashed human; she has been killed, resurrected, depowered, repowered, replaced by Skrulls, included in superhero teams, and committed to solving common crime. This diverse history distinguishes Jessica from Spider-Man; despite her rather androcentric beginnings, Jessica has generally been characterized in distinct ways and was rarely afflicted by the same harms as her male counterpart. That said, Jessica's character design and visual manifestation across thirty-five years of comics and animation adhered closely to genre norms for female superheroes to be rendered primarily as sex symbols. Her characteristic red-and-yellow superhero suit often seemed to be designed to draw attention to her breasts, hips, and behind rather than to convey anything about her personality or the nature of her powers.

This all changed in 2015 when writer Dennis Hopeless and artist Javier Rodriguez began work on Jessica's new solo series, *Spider-Woman*. Although Blue Age legacy superheroes are typically new or marginalized characters (and sometimes both) who take up the mantle of an older, more normative character, the visual changes and narrative framing of Hopeless and Rodriguez's *Spider-Woman* give Jessica Drew an identity that has rarely been explored in superhero comics, thus aligning her with other legacy heroes in her capacity to diversify the genre. From the cover of the first issue of the series, the focus of Jessica's new adventures becomes clear: she's pregnant. After years of fighting both intergalactic and neighborhood crime, as well as a lengthy imprisonment by the villainous Skrulls, Jessica takes stock of her life and finds that her priorities have changed. Although she was never interested in children before, Jessica (or Jess, to her friends) finds herself wanting to add "mother" to her already long and varied resume.

Despite the genre's history of upholding and adhering to binary norms of gender, *Spider-Woman* depicts Jessica's pregnancy, superheroism, and maternity via situations and plot elements that defy patriarchal dichotomies. For instance, in the redesign of her costume, Marvel frees Jess of the sexually objectifying aesthetic that dominated her comics appearances for the majority of her history. Further, while pregnancy has rarely been explored in superhero comics, scholars like Jeffrey Brown have argued that when female superheroes have experienced pregnancy and motherhood, their stories heavily implied that women cannot be both superheroes *and* mothers. Hopeless and Rodriguez disrupt these sexist tropes by depicting Jessica's journey using storylines and imagery that avoid patriarchal demands for representations of sanitized "good mothers" and that affirm Jessica's ability to be both heroic and maternal.

The creative team's choice to make Jessica's support network of people (consisting of Carol Danvers, Ben Urich, and Porcupine/Roger Gocking) central to her story demonstrates, for example, how cooperative childcare enables women to flourish as multifaceted human beings. In fact, Hopeless and Rodriguez don't just eschew sexist gender norms in their representation of pregnancy and motherhood; they approach these experiences in decidedly feminist ways. By employing the ideas of feminist philosopher Julia Kristeva, I suggest that *Spider-Woman* develops a feminist model of maternity. More specifically, I argue that comics as a medium is akin to what Kristeva calls "poetic language" in its ability to challenge everyday communications and open readers up to "nonexclusive opposites." Rodriguez's multipage layouts, for instance, often feature Jess in multiples that convey movement in space and time and simultaneously present her as multifaceted.

Jess may also be read as an example of what Kristeva has called the "subject in process." Unlike the binary model of gendered subjectivity developed throughout much of the superhero genre, Kristeva's conception of identity is complex, ever-changing, fluid, and unstable. Seen through this lens, Jessica's transition from single woman to pregnant person to mother may be read as a dynamic evolution of self rather than as a monstrous abdication of her superhero identity. And while Kristeva's ideas about the maternal subject are rooted in women's experiences of pregnancy and motherhood, she suggests that they may also serve as a metaphor for the processual and relational division between the self and other, regardless of gender or biology.

After exploring the resonances between *Spider-Woman* and Kristeva's theories of maternality, as well as certain points in Jessica Drew's character history, the chapter concludes by examining how Hopeless and Rodriguez's book enables a discussion about the interrelatedness of reproductive rights and trans rights. While I do not suggest that this version of Jessica can be read as a trans woman, I am interested in how her gender fluidity (as it is presented via cloning narratives or multiverse plots) may help to uncouple reproductive healthcare, pregnancy, parenthood, and bodily determination from cisheteronormative definitions of subjectivity. Addressing the limitations of these connections in *Spider-Woman* also provides an opportunity to call attention to the dearth of trans creators and characters across the superhero genre and to highlight the crucial need for more complex, empathetic, and humane representations of trans lives.

As a character who has undergone so much revision, resurrection, and retconning, Jessica Drew has proven to be the ultimate "subject in process." Hopeless and Rodriguez highlight Jessica's capacity to evolve in order to create a comic that redresses sexist representations of female superheroes, acknowledges the value of pregnancy and motherhood, and extends the right to self-determination beyond the confines of binary gender. From a feminist point of view, these characteristics are exciting because they make the genre more inclusive but also because they demonstrate how much further the genre needs to expand.

BINARIES OF GENDER AND GENRE

Philosophers like Luce Irigaray, Hélène Cixous, and Julia Kristeva are commonly called French feminists because of their engagement with the work of French intellectuals (like Jacques Lacan and Roland Barthes), their use of French as their primary written language, and their shared interests in the social and linguistic nature of subjectivity.[1] Although varied in their methods and scholarly priorities, these women have all explored how the cultural and psychological processes by which the Western speaking subject is formed create and maintain gender inequality. Cixous, for example, has argued that within systems of language—which she sees as the basic structures of Western thought and culture more broadly—dyads are arranged hierarchically. Pairs like activity/passivity, sun/moon, culture/nature, day/night, father/mother, high/low are structured such that the first term is valued over the second term. She goes on to suggest that each of these oppositions is rooted in "the" couple, man/woman. Cixous calls this binary system "phallogocentrism" and argues that it works first to equate all the terms to the left of the slash, and second, to value them above and against the terms to the right (1997). As Rosemarie Tong and Tina Fernandes Botts observe, "Man is associated with all that is active, cultural, light, high, or generally positive, whereas woman is associated with all that is passive, natural, dark, low, or generally negative. Moreover, the first term in the dyad man-woman is that from which the second departs or deviates. Man is the self; woman is the other" (2018, 252–253).

Cixous suggests that Western culture is saturated with phallogocentrism: "Theory of culture, theory of society, symbolic systems in general—art, religion, family, language—it is all developed while bringing the same schemes to light." This repetition serves to privilege "Man," to emphasize his authority, and to violently repress the "Other" that "he uses to sustain himself" (1997, 102). Even though the self can only establish itself because of the existence of the other, and even though no one person can be identified singularly through time, patriarchal discourses often aggressively erase interconnectedness and plurality to present the illusion of a monolithic, static, knowing subject. Further, because phallogocentrism is embedded in language and ubiquitous in Western cultural systems, French feminists like Cixous explain that one does not need to intentionally invest in male chauvinism; rather, it is a byproduct of becoming a speaking subject in a patriarchal system.[2]

One can think, for instance, of our continued use of the terms "superhero" and "female superhero" in comics scholarship. As Carolyn Cocca notes, many people do not feel the need to say "male superhero" because the word "superhero" has normatively been understood as meaning white, male, able-bodied, and heterosexual. There is no reason "superhero" can't mean any and all kinds of characters, but because phallogocentrism informs our understanding of the genre, we typically only specify when talking about characters who are not white, male, able-bodied, and so forth (Cocca 2016, 6). Indeed, Jeffrey Brown demonstrates the numerous ways this same binary logic has traditionally informed the superhero genre beyond its terminology, a process that has similarly resulted in the marginalization of female characters (2015).

Brown argues that the superhero genre is fundamentally premised on a concern with boundaries. He writes that "what the superheroes repeatedly enact for readers is a symbolic policing of the borders between key cultural concepts—good and evil, right and wrong, us and them. Intertwined with these abstract concepts are corporeal boundaries between male and female, mind and body, self and other" (2015, 137). Further, Chris Gavaler suggests that "by establishing a very particular hyper-muscular, able-bodied masculinity as an ideal, the male superhero body projects all other physical variations as inferior and so potentially antagonistic" (2018, 192). As such, within the United States, the good, right, male superhero has overwhelmingly been white, heterosexual, nondisabled, attractive, impenetrable, hypermuscular, and hypermasculine. Brown believes that this normative masculine ideal is maintained by specifically rejecting or repressing anything that is feminine, soft, or fluid.

This rejection acts doubly against female superheroes, who, according to this kind of dichotomous logic, must necessarily embody these devalued traits yet must also display generic superhero qualities (Brown 2015, 137). The female superhero, then, is necessarily (devalued as) feminine, soft, and inviting because she is in opposition to the male superhero who is (valued as) masculine, armored, and impenetrable—*and* she is devalued as a superhero because her capacity to maintain toughness, impenetrability, and power is compromised by her femininity.

These phallogocentric tendencies have resulted in fewer female superheroes throughout the genre's history, and they underpin many of the sexist tropes that have limited the complexity of the female characters that did make it to print. According to Brown, the root cause of "the genre's depiction [of] and reaction to policing female bodily boundaries reveals a deep-seated fear of female reproductive abilities"; thus, it is unsurprising to note how rare pregnant superheroes have been and how monstrous their treatment (2015, 138). Brown reiterates: "In a genre obsessed with armoring, containing, and defending the integrity of self-sufficient and powerful bodies," pregnant bodies are problematic because they indicate penetrability, challenge ideals of corporeal stasis, trouble the illusion of stable identity, and dissolve boundaries between self and other (2015, 139, 140–141). As such, when pregnant female characters have actually appeared in comics, their pregnancy and subsequent maternity are typically treated as a challenge to overcome. In synthesizing the genre, Brown describes the following patterns:

> A quick survey of maternity in comics reveals four consistent tropes: 1) the superheroine chooses to give up her child in order to continue her career, 2) she has to give up her heroic calling to assume motherhood as a full-time role, 3) she repeatedly puts her child at risk because she continues her adventures, and 4) mothers are cast as purely monstrous because they are inherently evil, neglectful, or absent. (2015, 143)

The examples Brown cites to substantiate these claims range across the genre and include titles from DC, Marvel, and Image that all display these tropes.[3] He goes on to note that in conjunction with derogatory depictions of superhero mothers, there is an abundance of fathers and father figures such that "superheroic male characters almost completely displace mothers as parental figures." In terms evocative of French feminism, Brown writes that the genre's "rejection of the maternal is tantamount to an acceptance of patriarchal authority, of the Law as the word of the Father" (2015, 147). Cumulatively, these patterns frame pregnancy as abject and transgressive and motherhood "as dangerous to both the heroes and to the children or as actively working against the greater good" (2015, 151). Given this context, it is not an exaggeration to say that in its disruption of phallogocentrism and its avoidance of misogynistic tropes, Hopeless and Rodriguez's *Spider-Woman* represents a radical departure from the superhero status quo.

In fact, the myriad differences between the narrative and visual choices made around Jessica Drew's pregnancy and maternity and the trends identified by Brown point towards a more feminist model of superhero motherhood. Marvel's redesign of the character and Rodriguez's presentation of her throughout the comic are case in point. Prior to Hopeless and Rodriguez's run, Marvel asked Italian cartoonist Milo Manara to draw a variant cover for a 2014 Spider-Woman comic.

Manara produced a cover featuring Jessica crawling on all fours with her head at the bottom of the page, her back arched, and her behind perched at the top of the page. The pose was a re-creation of one Manara had previously used in his erotic comics art; because it overtly sexualized Jess, it drew swift criticism (Pantozzi 2014). Although this cover did display a particularly egregious example of a "broke-back pose" (to wit, an anatomically impossible pose designed to sexualize a female character's body by emphasizing her curves),[4] it was also one in a long line of sexually objectifying renditions of Jess. Like most other female superheroes, Jess was more often than not drawn in sexy pin-up styles throughout most of her comics history.

Marvel's redesign was refreshing not only because it corrected the Manara misstep but also because it broke more with traditionally sexist representations of Jess. Rather than a skin-tight bodysuit tantamount to body paint, artist Kris Anka chose a costume composed of black pants, flat boots, a leather jacket, and yellow-lensed glasses. When buttoned, the jacket displays the same angular spider insignia of old, and when necessary, web gliders appear under the arms just as they did in previous suits. This functional yet stylish design speaks more to who Jess is as a character and enhances her ability to do her job. For example, the boots, jacket, and two-toned gloves are akin to motorcycle gear, pointing towards Jessica's preferred mode of transportation. When unbuttoned, the jacket looks like modern streetwear, a shift that is particularly useful for Jess, who works as a private investigator. As Marvel editor Nick Lowe says, "Jess needs to go and figure stuff out and dig things up, and you can't really do that head to toe in spandex very well. . . . To operate on the level she wants to, she needs something that can pass for semi-normal and she can turn it on to crazy if she needs to" (Truitt 2014).

The adaptability of the outfit also comes in handy in accommodating Jessica's baby bump. Brown writes that "the pregnant body is so beyond the norm for comics that creators will often go to great lengths to erase its presence" (2015, 141). In marked contrast, Rodriguez makes Jessica's pregnancy abundantly clear on all of the covers for the first four issues in which she is pregnant and in all of the pages within. While Jess proudly shows her jacket's capacity to zip up over her belly on the cover of issue #1 (fig. 1.1) (Hopeless et al. 2015), she is often drawn wearing her jacket hanging open, which frames and accentuates her pregnant stomach. Whereas some comics artists have previously used synecdoche to represent female characters with close-up views of their

Figure 1.1. Jessica Drew shows off her baby bump on the cover of *Spider-Woman* #1 (2015).

breasts, bums, or both, Rodriguez uses the technique to highlight Jessica's baby bump. In issue #3, for instance, Jess's entrance into a room is visually indicated by her shadow cast on a wall in the background and her white belly as it protrudes into the upper right foreground of the panel (Hopeless et al. 2016). Rodriguez's compositional choices subvert genre norms not only because they make what was previously omitted visible but also because they depict female embodiment in nonsexually objectifying ways.

Returning to issue #3, we should note that Hopeless and Rodriguez even take aim at reductive representations of Jessica as a sex object generally, as well as at the Manara cover specifically. After her attempted OB/GYN appointment in an intergalactic hospital goes awry owing to an enemy ambush, Jess finds herself in the position of having to rescue a young Skrull prince who is a cancer patient in the same facility. Upon meeting Jess, the boy says he recognizes her from Earth TV: "You're that Avenger . . . The one with the butt" (Hopeless et al. 2016). Aside from providing a moment of levity, the prince's dialogue implies that versions of Jess like Manara's align with the tastes of a thirteen-year-old boy. Of course, Jess is still drawn in conventionally attractive ways, and pregnant bodies can be beautiful, but their capacity to expand, change, and leak is disruptive of patriarchal ideals for female superheroes.

As Brown suggests, because the pregnant body "bursts forth with increased mass and with various leaking fluids," it violates genre "principles of discipline and containment" (2015, 140). Rodriguez does not shy away from these qualities in his depiction of Jessica. On a splash page in issue #3, Rodriguez draws Jess in multiples as she leaps onto and then traverses an engine room full of gears on her way to rescue the Skrull boy (fig. 1.2) (Hopeless et al. 2016). Rodriguez draws each version of Jess from a different angle as she leaps, swings, and crawls so that she is visible from above and below, in close-up and at a distance. These compositions serve to illustrate her movement through space, but they also highlight how a pregnant body in action stretches, bulges, and protrudes. As nimble as Jess is, she is also bulbous. Later in the issue, as Jessica and Dirk (Jess's nickname for the young Skrull prince) make their way to a safer place in the hospital, Jess is suddenly crippled with pain. Rodriguez draws Jess in close-up as she cries out: saliva stretches between her tongue and teeth and flies out of her open mouth. Just as the enemy Skrulls enter the room and Dirk pulls Jessica into hiding, she says through clenched teeth that her water has broken. In addition to its proclivity to leak fluids and change rapidly, the pregnant body

Figure 1.2. Jess drops, leaps, and crawls through onomatopoetic gears. *Spider-Woman* #3 (2016).

with its permeable boundaries also threatens masculinist superhero ideals about "the body as a means to declare one's own exceptional identity" (Brown 2015, 140).

Issue #2 opens with Jessica fuming to herself in caption boxes about the enemy Skrulls who have ambushed the hospital. Although they begin as an inner monologue, the words shift to a sort of dialogue between Jess and her unborn baby and then back to Jess's own thoughts. At various points she is ostensibly speaking to her baby, but it becomes clear that she is actually (or perhaps also) talking to herself. As Jess tries to talk herself down from fighting the two Skrulls that are holding everyone hostage, for instance, she surreptitiously texts her best friend, Carol Danvers (a.k.a. Captain Marvel), to come to the rescue. The caption boxes read: "I'd only need five seconds distraction to make green stains. But . . . no. Much as I'd love to crack these numbskrulls . . . with great baby—comes the crushing weight of parental responsibility. So mama will just sit here—choking back pride and keeping you safe. Auntie Carol gets to do the violence this time" (Hopeless et al. 2015). The *fluidity* of Jessica's thoughts, from reflections on her situation to discussion with her baby about what to do, *suggests* that even the most interior parts of herself are relational. These pages further blur boundaries between inside and outside through close-up panels of Jessica's belly. As she becomes more agitated, the baby begins to kick, creating a small bulge in Jessica's stomach accompanied by an onomatopoeic sound effect in thick yellow letters that read "KIK." After Jess texts Carol and resolves to sit it out, the baby kicks one more time, which leads to more seemingly dialogic caption boxes: "Hmm . . . I mean . . . you're right. There's just the *two* of them. And they *are* really, really . . . asking for it. We can probably call Auntie Carol from the nurses' station. That could be the end of it. Okay. *Fine*. But just these two" (Hopeless, Rodriguez, et al. 2015).

According to Brown, this blurring between self and other, inside and outside, is considered monstrous by patriarchal superhero standards. But from a feminist perspective, these scenes do valuable work. For example, they help to normalize the real bodily and psychological changes that pregnant people go through in superhero media. They also subvert phallogocentric demands for the "Other" to be repressed in service of the self. Jessica does not cease to be herself because she is pregnant; on display in these scenes is her characteristic humor, quick thinking, and capacity to kick ass. However, her character does change and expand, both literally, with each "KIK," and figuratively. Jessica's body does make her more vulnerable, but as a result her superheroism becomes more collaborative and readers get to see who she is as a team leader, a friend, a hero, and, most importantly, a *caring* mother.

Even amid the danger presented by the Skrull ambush, Hopeless and Rodriguez take care to avoid the trope of superhero mothers inevitably and constantly putting their babies in danger. After Jess and her kicking baby belly agree that it is necessary for everyone's safety to dispatch the first two enemy Skrulls, the other pregnant characters in the room beg Jess to save them from the remaining invaders. As Jess bends forward to stretch out her back, belly drooping into the middle of the panel, she makes it clear that she will not take on the danger alone: "My one and only priority is the safety of this big weird gut. Just like the rest of you. Look, I know this is scary. I'm not trying to freak anyone out. All we have to do is hold out a few more minutes. I promise I can get us through this. But I'm not risking my kid's life so you lot can keep your seats. I'm gonna need your help" (Hopeless et al. 2015). With Jessica's guidance, the pregnant group does manage to further evade the Skrulls and get to safety.

The balance Hopeless and Rodriguez create between keeping Jess proximate to danger (she is a superhero after all) but also allowing her to prioritize her baby's safety continues throughout the book. Once Gerry (Jessica's baby) is born, Jess relies on her support network of friends to help care for him. So on nights when Jess goes out to fight crime, her baby stays with Roger (a.k.a. the superhero-in-training Porcupine), Ben Urich (reporter and Jess's investigative partner), or sometimes even "Auntie Carol." In issue #12 Jess and Roger take their kids to the beach for a day off. Of course, as is often the case in the world of superheroes, danger finds them, and as per their agreed-upon "work schedule," Jess stays with the two children while Roger dons his Porcupine suit to take on the bad guy. While Jess watches Roger's fight from a distance and helps to subtly move beachgoers out of harm's way, she never leaves the children unsupervised or endangers them in any way. The bad guy gets battled, the day gets saved, and Jess continues to defy narrow tropes (Hopeless et al. 2016).

It's not to say that Jess finds the balancing act between being a mother and being a superhero easy. Early in issue #1, a flashback shows Jess debating with herself as to whether it is necessary to give up riding her motorcycle while pregnant (Hopeless et al. 2015). Although it clearly pains her to do so, she feels like that sacrifice is necessary to keep herself and her baby safe. Jeannie Ludlow suggests that this scene borders on the trope of superhero moms having to give up their careers but points out that in other scenarios, even when Jess is expressing doubts or fears related to motherhood, Hopeless and Rodriguez manage to avoid subverting her competence as a superhero (2020, 124).

In fact, in issue #5 Jessica's confession to Roger that she feels like she is "bad at this" and is "overwhelmed every minute" ends with Roger assuring her that what she is going through is perfectly normal for a new parent (Hopeless et al. 2016). Surrounding Jessica with a support network and allowing her to express doubts while she continues to live her life as both mother and superhero is important not only because it amends sexist genre trends; these scenarios also point towards a more feminist model of motherhood. Numerous studies have shown that without support networks of family members, friends, and social services, the sacrifices women make to raise their children take a heavy toll on their mental and physical health and their careers (Luthar and Ciciolla 2015; Schiller, Dorstyn, and Taylor 2021; Emmott, Myers, and Page 2021). In surrounding Jessica with friends who act as caregivers for Gerry—and who are invested in Jess's own mental health—*Spider-Woman* depicts a version of motherhood that alleviates the pressure for women, particularly single mothers, to do it all alone.

This idea that women must "do it all," and, increasingly, do it perfectly, is indicative of harmful discourses that define "good mothers" as those who "glow" during their pregnancy, who "naturally" take to motherhood, and who sacrifice endlessly for their children (Garbes 2018, 5). As Angela Garbes notes, "The pressure, intentional or not, that we place on new mothers—not just to breast-feed but to enjoy pregnancy, to give birth a certain way, to 'bounce back,' to be happy—is unnecessarily stressful and harmful" (2018, 11). The various scenes in which Jess expresses her fears, anxieties, and doubts help to mitigate representations of motherhood that are untenable for most women. Because Jess is also frequently shown snuggling, playing with, and adoring her baby, the comic also implies that struggling with the complex demands of maternity is not mutually exclusive to being a loving mother.

The fact that Jess is a single mother is another notable departure from genre norms. As discussed by Brown above, fathers and father figures far outnumber mothers in superhero comics, and "while maternity is suspect in superhero comics, paternity is often glorified" (2015, 147). Hopeless and Rodriguez acknowledge and critique these patriarchal tendencies in issue #1 during Jessica's maternity leave party. As Jess talks with Spider-Man on one side of the party, on the other side Carol chats with Tony Stark, a.k.a. Iron Man, who asks Carol if she knows who the father is and suggests that "everybody's curious" (Hopeless et al. 2015). That this question arises at a gathering intended to celebrate Jess and her contributions to the superhero community points towards widely held, persistent assumptions about the centrality of fathers even in their absence.[5] Because Tony Stark is a character famous for his arrogance, Hopeless and Rodriguez signpost to the reader that the question is irrelevant at best. Carol goads Tony into posing the question to Jess herself, and the largely wordless panels that ensue clarify the inappropriate nature of this line of questioning.

As Tony approaches Jess and Spider-Man, small squiggly lines appear above Spider-Man's head; these are typically used to indicate the activation of his Spider-sense (i.e., a superpower that tells him something is wrong). The longer Tony stands there, the more pronounced the Spider-sense waves become and the darker the expression on Jessica's face. The panel that indicates that Tony has been put in his place does not actually focus on him but rather on Carol, who looks on in amused surprise, her face colored in a neon green hue, with the onomatopoeic word "KA-ZAT" filling the air behind her head. Tony appears in the next panel with a steaming plate of food on his head, illustrating that Jess used her biokinetic "venom blasts" to, as Carol says, "cook his weenies." It becomes apparent that Tony did not simply ask Jess who the father is, he asked her if she *knew*, implying that he (and, by extension, everyone who is purportedly curious) perceives Jessica to be promiscuous and that her pregnancy is a mistake. This bundle of assumptions reveals prevailing patriarchal attitudes about women's sexualities and reproductive choices being inextricably linked to ideals of the nuclear family.

In this context, any variation on creating a nuclear family is framed as incomprehensible, deviant, or both. However, Jessica deems the circumstances of her pregnancy as being no one else's business. Despite the tendency for people to treat pregnant bodies as public property—expressed, for instance, through the compulsion to touch pregnant bellies without consent (which Hawkeye does at Jess's party)—Hopeless and Rodriguez make it clear that Jess's boundaries are hers to determine. Jess is entitled to and capable of making decisions for herself, even when those decisions do not align with patriarchal heteronormative expectations. That said, while Jessica's pregnancy and maternity disrupt patriarchal genre trends, the scenes in *Spider-Woman* that explore her earlier reproductive choices unfortunately fall short from an intersectional feminist perspective.

In issue #5, Jess stands in her bathroom getting ready for a "night out" while Carol chats to her from the adjacent bedroom. Although Jess has maintained that her baby's paternity is her business alone, she decides to share the story with Carol. Following a short and ultimately unsatisfying relationship, Jess discovered that she had missed a period. Three pregnancy tests concluded that she was not pregnant, but the experience helped her to reassess her feelings about becoming a mother. After several months of consideration and "a bunch of weird research," Jess "made an appointment" (Hopeless et al. 2016). The dialogue insinuates that Jess became pregnant via an anonymous sperm donor and intrauterine insemination.

Being able to choose parenting and having access to reproductive technology comprise an important part of reproductive justice, particularly for Black and Indigenous women; poor, queer, and disabled women; and nonbinary people who have historically been subjected to forced sterilization or denied access to reproductive healthcare for political and economic reasons (Silliman and Bhattacharjee 2002). It's not to say that Jessica's choice isn't meaningful, but as a white, financially secure woman, her "choice" narrative is not particularly disruptive (or critical) of how the ease of this decision is secured by race and capital.

These scenes are also unsatisfying insofar as they do not actually depict how the decision Jessica makes stands in comparison to the other choices available to her. According to Garbes, reproductive choices are only truly "free" when we understand all the options available, have access to education in order to make informed decisions, and, crucially, have access to the healthcare required to pursue any one of the possible choices (2018). The last several decades in the United States have been devastating for people's reproductive freedoms: debates rage about bodily autonomy, families have been separated (Rhodan 2018), laws have been enacted or revoked to restrict access to vital healthcare (Acevedo 2019) and education (Reynolds 2023), and landmark cases that protected people's reproductive rights have been overturned at a federal level (Totenberg and McCammon 2022). As this book goes to press, twenty-four US states have enacted or plan to enact bans on abortion services (Nash and Guarnieri 2023). Needless to say, reproductive choices are far from "free" for Americans, and the topic of reproductive justice remains of crucial importance for many feminists.[6] There is no indication in *Spider-Woman* that Jess faces any of these pressures or considers other options—like abortion or adoption—at the point when she is concerned about an unplanned pregnancy. Because Jessica Drew's storyworld resembles our own in many ways, the lack of representation of the various choices she might make, and the barriers associated with each, reads as a kind of postfeminist narrative. As Lillian Robinson argues, comics that depict a "present time" in which "all gender problems have been solved" but do not "[show] us how such conditions came to pass" do not contribute to feminist efforts to address persistent gender inequities (2004, 138).

My point here is not to argue that Jess should have made a different choice, or even that she should have been made to psychologically struggle with her choice: her desire to be a mother and her choice to parent are valid. Moreover, in a genre that has traditionally denigrated pregnancy and maternity, this depiction of Jess is valuable. Nonetheless, the comic's total lack of acknowledgment of how women's rights to reproduce are connected to other aspects of reproductive justice (like the right to education, healthcare, and abortion) constitutes a limitation on the extent to which Jessica's "choice" may be read as feminist. Despite this shortcoming, much of Hopeless and Rodriguez's treatment of Jessica's pregnancy and motherhood does ameliorate misogynist genre trends, and, as I show below, other aspects of the book further contribute to *Spider-Woman*'s feminist ethos.

THE MATERNAL SUBJECT

Three key concepts developed by French feminist Julia Kristeva can better help us to see the feminist model of maternity in *Spider-Woman*. The first of these is her theory of "poetic language." According to Dani Cavallaro, this is a "type of language that overtly subverts mainstream conventions." She writes: "Poetic language is not exclusively peculiar to poetry. . . . Indeed, it can be found wherever language challenges and reorders the principles of everyday communication and the structures of grammar and syntax, and whenever an artist chooses to experiment . . . with words and images" (2003, 80–81). For Kristeva, poetic language is "polyvalent and multidetermined," it promotes "the coexistence of nonexclusive opposites," and "comes into being only in the margins of recognized culture" (1980a, 65). This, of course, could describe much sequential art! Comics (long considered a marginal medium) work with both images and text; they are not limited to prescribed structures of syntax; while some may be collaboratively created, the process of reading comics is certainly co-creative (i.e., comics are multidetermined); and their meaning cannot be gleaned on one level alone.

Cavallaro observes that Kristeva finds significance in the fact that dominant Western culture has tended to characterize poetic language as "feminine" because of its tendency to manifest "in fluid structures and musical sequences which bring into play unconscious drives and bodily affects." What makes this kind of language explicitly feminist is its capacity to disrupt "the rigid rules" of Western systems of language "and, by implication, of patriarchy" (2003, 82). Again, this discussion of poetic language strongly resonates with certain definitions of comics. Hillary Chute, for example, writes: "The way that time is shaped spatially on a page of comics—through panel size, panel shape, panel placement, and the concomitant *pace* and *rhythm* the page gestures at" can be compared "with music, with its beats and syncopation, and the orchestrated tension of its various phrases and parts" (2010, 7).

Further, Chute suggests that "the form of comics even at its most basic is apposite to feminist cultural production," not least because the hybrid nature of comics challenges "the structure of binary classification that opposes a set of terms, privileging one" (2010, 9, 10). Relevant to this analysis of *Spider-Woman* is Cavallaro's assertion that for Kristeva, poetic language texts "are not necessarily produced by women"; rather, any text "capable of challenging and fragmenting conventional syntax and logic may be considered revolutionary" (2003, 82). Throughout *Spider-Woman*, Rodriguez's page compositions exhibit the qualities of poetic language. His frequent use of multiples, fluid panel design, and purposeful splash pages portray Jess using complex techniques that disrupt patriarchal superhero norms of pregnancy and maternity.

One particularly representative example comes from Jessica's adventures in the intergalactic hospital in issue #4 (Hopeless et al. 2016). After Jessica's water breaks, Dirk manages to whisk her into an operating room where several alien doctors are on hand to perform an emergency C-section. As Jess undergoes surgery, the enemy band of Skrulls attempts to break through the heavy doors with a laser cannon. With only minutes until the cannon perforates the metal, the doctors deliver Jessica's baby and hand him to her (fig. 1.3). The page depicting Jess's first embrace of her baby is divided into two horizontal panels,

Figure 1.3. Jessica's first embrace with her baby. *Spider-Woman* #4 (2016).

with the top panel dominating the page. Using a close-up perspective, Rodriguez draws four multiples of Jess as she first looks at her baby, kisses his cheek, sighs in contentment, and then snaps into action saying to the surgeon, "Okay, Doc. Close me up." Multiple images of the same character on a comics page or panel are often used to convey movement over a span of time and, according to Scott McCloud, can "involve the reader more deeply in the action" (1994, 112).

As discussed above in reference to depictions of Jessica's pregnant body in issue #1 (fig. 1.2), Rodriguez's use of multiples not only conveys Jessica's movement through time; the technique also allows him to demonstrate her dynamism as a character, both physically and emotionally. Whereas most of Rodriguez's multiples of Jess depict many distinct poses with space in between, the four busts shown in figure 1.3 are collaged. Her facial expressions and posture change from one to the next, but the fact that they literally overlap significantly collapses the gesture of time between them, giving the impression that these are stages of one fluid moment. In some ways, this could perhaps be read as a linear progression—first this, then that, then that, and so on. But given the nature of comics as a static medium, all four aspects of Jessica's first moment with her baby remain simultaneously on the page. As McCloud notes, "In comics, the past is more than just memories for the audience and the future is more than just possibilities! Both past and future are real and visible" (1994, 104).

This kind of composition breaks up dichotomous logic: it is impossible to insist that Jess is either an adoring mother or a feisty superhero when she appears as both simultaneously. Each multiple of Jess bleeds into the next, connecting them all, further reinforcing the idea that these aspects of her character are inextricable.

The bottom panel of the page also complicates notions of linear progression and imbues the moment Jessica shares with her baby with further layers of meaning. The operating table with Jess on it, and the various figures around it, are all drawn from a long view in a white silhouette against an otherwise black panel. According to Randy Duncan and Matthew J. Smith, this technique, chiaroscuro, "a stark contrast of light and dark," works to "funnel attention to a particular point in the panel" (2009, 143). In this case, the eye is drawn to the fiery ring being melted into the doors, reminding readers of the imminent danger on the other side. Because the molten ring appears in previous pages of the sequence, accompanied by sound effect lettering reading "HRRSSSHHH," its reappearance in the chiaroscuro panel implies that the blast has been ongoing. Thus, Rodriguez's page simultaneously depicts a nearly all-encompassing moment of tenderness and quietude *and* the din of persistent danger. As readers, we are made aware that Jessica's experience in this moment is informed by a blend of love, awe, contentment, anger, determination, and peril. As art akin to poetic language, Rodriguez's composition defies binary classifications of Jessica, evokes numerous affective states, and summons multiple temporal registers.

The use of dynamic multilayered depictions of Jess, which Hopeless and Rodriguez develop throughout the book, aligns with another of Kristeva's key theories: that of the subject in process. According to Kristeva, poetic language, avant-garde art, and the carnivalesque are valuable forms of expression because they disrupt patriarchal systems of language and culture and enable explorations of the precarity of subjectivity. Contrary to what patriarchal discourses imply, Kristeva argues that the self is not homogenous, static, or stable. Because we as subjects evolve psychologically and physically in conjunction with language acquisition and enculturation, Kristeva (like other French feminists) sees the subject as processual, as continuously unfolding. No matter how neat and tidy phallogocentric systems of meaning appear to be, Kristeva sees language—and by extension the speaking subject—as fundamentally changeable and complex. In other words:

> All identities are unstable: the identity of linguistic signs, the identity of meaning and, as a result, the identity of the speaker. And in order to take account of this destabilization of meaning and of the subject, I thought the term "subject in process" would be appropriate. Process in the sense of process but also in the sense of a legal proceeding where the subject is committed to trial, because our identities in life are constantly called into question, brought to trial, over-ruled. (Kristeva, qtd. in Cavallaro 2003, 78)

In their depiction of Jess as a character very much akin to Kristeva's subject in process, Hopeless and Rodriguez frame the physical, psychological, and social changes Jess undergoes as inevitable and natural rather than as deviant, weak, or monstrous. As such, the trials Jess endures (whether self-imposed or otherwise) may make her more relatable to readers whose lives are similarly impacted by the competing pressures and demands of family, career, and self-care. Jessica's decision to become a mother, for example, demonstrates one of the kinds of growth people undertake when they allow themselves to reevaluate their lives. In issue #5 Jess tells Carol that after her concerns about an unexpected pregnancy turn out to be unfounded (i.e., all the tests were negative), she realized she was disappointed: "I always said I didn't want kids, but that was a decision I made super young and never reevaluated. Now here I was holding a not pregnant pee stick and thinking—holy hell, I want a ***baby***!" (Hopeless et al. 2016). Just as Kristeva suggests about the subject in process, Jess describes calling the assumptions of her younger self into question and realizing that over time, her desires for who she wanted to be had changed. Of course, not all of the proceedings a subject endures are self-directed or navigated in purely psychological terms. As discussed above, Jessica's maternity party in issue #1 clarifies that the people around her are also scrutinizing who Jess is as a mother and a superhero. This kind of social trial of Jess's identity occurs again at the end of *Spider-Woman* in issue #17.

Over the course of the book, Hopeless and the rest of the creative team develop the working relationship between Jessica and Roger/Porcupine into a romantic one. Despite their different "class" statuses as heroes (it is common in superhero comics and fandom to talk about lesser-known characters as D-listers), Jessica and Roger's shared trust in each other and love for Gerry bring them together. To integrate her new romantic relationship with the rest of her social life, Jess throws another party to introduce Roger, *as* her boyfriend, to the rest of her superhero friends. From the moment they arrive, it is clear that characters like Spider-Man, Black Widow, Hawkeye, and She-Hulk are shocked to see Jessica and Roger together. Although Jess already feels judged, Natasha (a.k.a. Black Widow) explicitly articulates what Jess presumes everyone is thinking: "What does she expect us to say? The man dresses up like a hedgehog." After Jess confronts her, Natasha elaborates on what she perceives the problem to be: "We're already expected to bite our tongues about your career change. You belong in the big leagues and everyone knows it. But instead, no, you're wasting yourself playing P.I. down in the dirt. It was bad enough watching you train this buffoon. Now you want to parade him around as your new—" (Hopeless et al. 2017).

On one level Natasha's attitude reflects normative expectations for superheroes to be superior to, and therefore removed from, "common" people and their problems. If, as Brown notes, a crucial element of the superhero profile is the ability to lay claim to an "exceptional identity," then Jessica's decisions (to work in a career that requires no superpowers and to train a "common criminal" to work as a superhero) seriously undermine what supposedly makes her and her peers exceptional. In this sense, Natasha represents the tendency for the superhero genre to police boundaries between "us" and "them," exceptional and normal, self and other. Natasha's complaints also reveal a phallogocentric demand for stasis. According to this logic, superheroes (like all dominant subjects) should be knowable and unchanging. Because motherhood fundamentally changes a person, these critiques also tacitly reify the supposed incompatibility between superheroism and maternity.

On another level, Natasha's comments may be read as indicative of normative expectations for mothers to be asexual. As Susan Griffin argues, because Western culture positions mothers as "symbols of purity," among all their other sacrifices, mothers are also expected to sacrifice their sexuality (2001, 38). Although Natasha's disdain is undoubtedly rooted in a kind of classism, her objection in this moment nevertheless acts to denounce Jessica as a sexual subject.[7] This scenario is upsetting for Jess, but through the process of being put on trial by her peers, she is able to establish a new kind of clarity for herself. Jess interrupts Natasha by shouting, "That's more than enough out of you! I'm @#$!% *happy!* Okay?! For the first time ever, I *love* my stupid life! And, whether you like it or not, my idiot boyfriend is a *huge* part of that" (Hopeless et al. 2017). Jess's response and the events that follow (baby Gerry's freshly realized Spider-powers help him evade everyone except Roger, who saves the day) clarify that Natasha's criticisms, and the social norms they represent, are unjust. However, it is through the process of judgement that the creative team can demonstrate how Jess's ability to adapt and embrace a different set of priorities has ultimately made her more fulfilled. As a subject in process, Jess confronts the scenario and in doing so reveals the perniciousness of the boundary policing endemic to much of the superhero genre and also speaks meaningfully to the real ways mothers are scrutinized. But it also demonstrates how much more complex characters can be when they are allowed to evolve, adapt, and change. By depicting Jessica's identity as processual, the creative team of *Spider-Woman* points towards the irreducibility of what it means for her to be a woman, a mother, and a superhero.

The combination of Kristeva's theories of poetic language and the subject in process—and her claims regarding their power to disrupt patriarchal systems of meaning—is most persuasively explored in her works on the maternal subject. In her essay "Stabat Mater," for example, Kristeva shows how unconventional writing on mothers and mothering-as-a-process can subvert the power of dominant discursive constructions of "The Mother" (1986).[8] As Cavallaro suggests, Kristeva is "interested in images which do not frame the mother figure as a fixed cultural icon but actually show her as fluid and vibrant" (2003, 128). The impression one gets of Kristeva's alternative model of maternity comes not just from the content of her essay but also from its form. Although it begins in a conventional textual format, a second column of bold text erupts on the left side of the page. What begins as a scholarly historical essay on the figure of the Virgin Mary as an emblem of patriarchal ideals of femininity splits into a duet, and sometimes a dialogue, between Kristeva's traditional analysis and her lyrical account of her own experiences as a mother. There is no clear prescription on how to read the essay; the reader must constantly decide how to navigate back and forth between the analysis of patriarchal norms and Kristeva's personal reflections on her body, her child, their relationship, and her identity. Sometimes both columns appear on the page, and at other times only the conventional essay takes up space. Kristeva makes the point that there must be both, and in formatting her essay in such a way, she stresses that the relationship between exegesis and embodied narrative is not always easy.

The content of the personal account also works to unsettle the "inflexible idealization of Mary" Kristeva describes in the scholarly column (Cavallaro 2003, 128). Whereas the Virgin Mary has been discursively constructed as a submissive, endlessly sacrificing, sinless, sexless feminine ideal, Kristeva's own writing on maternity fluidly recounts her sometimes competing experiences of pain, anguish, love, intense joy, and ambiguity. "Stabat Mater" explores how the mother is a split subject: she is both for herself and for the other; she is an "I" and a "we." In formatting the essay as she does, Kristeva positions the reader to experience some semblance of split subjectivity. Even if one is not nor ever will be a mother, the necessary action of navigating both columns of Kristeva's essay, and engaging with how mothers are influenced by normative gendered discourses while also experiencing the messy dynamism of maternity, opens up the split maternal subject to any reader. As Marilyn Edelstein argues, "Kristeva, like other postmodernists, de-essentializes gender; she treats the *maternal* as metaphorically available to both men and women, but also considers *maternity* as a physiological experience shared by many women" (1993, 201).[9]

Just as Kristeva combines the practice of transgressive writing with her theories on the subject in process in order to disrupt patriarchal ideals of motherhood while simultaneously highlighting the multidimensionality of maternity, so too do the creators of *Spider-Woman* employ visual and narrative conventions that eschew the trope of the "good" mother in favor of a more dynamic, messy model of maternity. Moreover, similar to the ways Kristeva's work invites readers to engage with the split maternal subject irrespective of gender, the creators and editors of *Spider-Woman* develop Jess's experiences in ways that are intended to be representative of women's lives as well as relevant and relatable to all readers.

Issue #5 begins with a panel of Jessica standing in the door of her apartment holding a half-eaten pastry and a coffee cup, wearing a baggy T-shirt covered in baby spit-up, her hair disheveled and dark circles under her eyes. As she tries to tell her interlocutors in a sequence of close-up panels about the changes her baby has brought about, a letter-shaped panel that spells out "WAAAAGGHHH!" breaks apart the page and interrupts Jessica's dialogue. Content and form work together here. Jess says, "This baby . . . has ruined my life. People laugh when I say that. It sounds like a joke. But I mean it. I *mean* it. The life I had before is *over*" (Hopeless et al. 2016). Just as Jess describes how her old life has come to a stop, so too do the panels depicting her dialogue abruptly end with the insertion of the letter-shaped panel indicating her baby's cry.

Like "Stabat Mater," this issue begins with a single narrative voice in a conventional format until another voice forcibly disrupts the homogeneity of the page. Further, like Kristeva's essay, this sequence not only demonstrates split subjectivity through form, it also details the sometimes harrowing, sometimes joyful experiences of real mothers. Jess's declaration that her previous life is over echoes Susan Griffin's assertions, for instance: "I am not the same person I was before I had a child. That young woman would not understand me" (2001, 34). Or Garbes, who notes that becoming a mother didn't just change her body in innumerable ways; instead, she writes that "having a baby changed me in a way that I felt deep down—in my blood, bones, and cells—somewhere inside me that I couldn't quite place. I am not the person I once was" (2018, 216). Hopeless and Rodriguez develop the Kristevan nature of this sequence over the next two pages by blending formal conventions with visual and narrative elements that demonstrate the fluidity of the maternal subject. On the second page, speech balloons in which Jess carries on a frank discussion about the changes in her life, the realities of infant care, and her anxieties are paired with four vertical gutters that lend the appearance of a traditional comics page. However, the use and placement of multiples, bleeds,[10] and onomatopoetic lettering create a reading experience akin to "Stabat Mater." The word balloons cascade down from the top of each of the four panels and are contained by the gutters, giving the impression that the four topics of Jess's dialogue unfold in discrete moments in time (fig. 1.4).

But Jessica's movement subverts this impression. She bleeds onto the page by walking from the gutter between the pages into the first panel, and then four more multiples of her bleed under each gutter as she makes various attempts to placate Gerry, until her last figure bleeds off the right side of the page. Gerry's cry emanates from his mouth in the left-most panel and floats in the air behind, over, and around the multiples of Jess and under each gutter. One may begin by trying to read each set of speech balloons and engaging with the topic in each, but attention to the rest of the page complicates this process. Jess's movements onto, through, and off the page give it a continuous feel, and the way Gerry's cry lingers across the panels even as Jessica tries to address his needs shows how relentless her care for him must be. The following page is composed in the same way, perpetuating the timelessness of the sequence even as Jess progresses from one topic of conversation to the next. These pages, like Kristeva's essay, are both informative and affective, continuous and disjointed, a narrative on motherhood and a depiction of mothering as a practice. Similar to Kristeva's insistence that both scholarly exegesis and embodied accounts are needed, Hopeless and Rodriguez seem to suggest that to understand motherhood one must read and witness.

Again, the content of Jess's dialogue further mirrors the complexity of emotions and embodied experiences Kristeva articulates, which so many other women experience. After listing the various fears, worries, and difficulties she has had in caring for her newborn, Jess says:

> The weirdest thing is that I don't mind any of it. Not really. Nothing has ever felt more important than keeping this little person safe. And I love doing it because it feels right and good and normal. Except when it's 3:00 AM and I don't know why he won't stop screaming and I remember that the doctor said sometimes you

Figure 1.4. Jess speaks frankly about the challenges of raising a baby. *Spider-Woman* #5 (2016).

> need to put baby down and walk away for a minute. Because those *never shake a baby* commercials aren't a joke. And then you feel like a monster and . . . (issue #4, Hopeless et al. 2016)

Jess finally stops when she realizes that the people to whom she's been speaking, Hellcat and She-Hulk, are still standing in her front doorway with baby gifts in hand and their eyes and mouths open wide. The messy reality of Jessica's life shocks and worries her friends, who may harbor what Adrienne Rich described as "the stereotype of the mother whose love is 'unconditional'" and who is "a single-minded identity" (2001, 83). Like Kristeva, Rich spoke of her own experiences of maternity using language that transgressed dichotomous logic and subverted sanitized stereotypes of mothers. In fact, Hopeless's dialogue quoted above echoes Rich's sentiments that "my children cause me the most exquisite suffering of which I have any experience. It is the suffering of ambivalence: the murderous alternation between bitter resentment and raw-edged nerves, and blissful gratification and tenderness. Sometimes I seem to myself, in my feelings toward these tiny guiltless beings, a monster of selfishness and intolerance" (2001, 81). What is important to note here is how Rich, like Kristeva, sees maternity as a process that, in its radical reforming of the maternal subject, may elicit contradictory embodied experiences of "anger and tenderness," but which also ultimately *teaches* mothers certain qualities: "patience, self-sacrifice, the willingness to repeat endlessly the small, routine chores of socializing a human being" (2001, 95). Jess, and the mothers she represents, is not a monster because of the fluidity and multitude of her feelings; rather, she is made to feel this way by patriarchal ideals that presume these qualities to be innate.

Kristeva's work is helpful here insofar as it implies that anyone who experienced a maternal level of change, vulnerability, and interrelatedness would feel similarly wounded and fulfilled. Because mothers must learn to come to terms with the strangeness they feel about themselves after such radical change while still remaining open to the needs and love of an "other," Kristeva suggests that modeling this process may lead to more ethical ways of treating ourselves and others. As Sîan Hawthorne argues, adopting a maternal ethics "offers an alternative to the individualism of paternality that seeks, as we have seen, to establish the primacy of the knowing subject at the expense of the other. . . . The stress in Kristeva's presentation of maternality is on connection, love, nurture, and dialogue with others" (2005, 48).

The creative team's investment in Jess's motherhood as a valuable experience for all readers is evident in at least two ways. The first I hope to have shown above. Through composition and dialogue, Hopeless and Rodriguez approach issue #5 in ways that resonate with Kristeva's essay "Stabat Mater," and in so doing, they invite readers to share some semblance of Jess's maternity. The second comes from the back matter of issue #5, in which executive editor Nick Lowe uses the space that would traditionally hold the letter column to share advice and resources on pregnancy and parenting. While some creative teams may share additional information as a form of worldbuilding, Lowe's list consists of real advice for parents and parents-to-be suggesting that the creative team of *Spider-Woman* sees Jessica's motherhood journey as meaningful beyond its narrative function.

Similarly, in numerous interviews Hopeless has shared that this run of *Spider-Woman* was inspired by his experience as a new father (e.g., Richards 2015), and in the back matter of issue #17, Rodriguez shared that he also had a child during the production of the comic, so the book holds a special place in his heart (Hopeless et al. 2017). Although the three men came to parenthood as fathers, they decided to tell a story about Jessica as a mother, again suggesting that motherhood can be a valuable means of exploring parenthood and superheroism. In fact, following the end of his run, Hopeless tweeted: "For what it's worth, there is a character in our Spider-Woman run with whom I relate a great deal . . . Her name is Jessica Drew" (2017). Therefore, as a subject in process, Jessica's fluidity and complexity as a character not only free her identity as a mother from patriarchal ideals and genre norms, but they also enable a level of relatability that exceeds gender. Whether *Spider-Woman* may also be read as transgressive of gender as a binary social system is also of interest.

JESSICA DREW COULD BE TRANS

If the number of cis women creators and characters at Marvel has been and continues to be disappointingly low, the number of trans creators and characters is markedly worse.[11] Despite the genre's use of magic or futuristic technology to destabilize essentialist gender identities, purposeful representations of the lived realities of trans people have been largely absent from superhero comics (Scott and Kirkpatrick 2015). For example, Chris Gavaler notes that while there are numerous instances of "fantastical gender-switching" in superhero comics that may seem progressive in their explorations of gender fluidity, most ultimately "treat transgender as a temporary plot conflict" (2018, 196–197). According to Thomas Billard and Brian MacAuley, while transgender representations have proliferated in recent years, as of 2015 there were only twenty explicitly identified trans, gender fluid, or nonbinary characters represented in Marvel, DC, and Image comics combined, and only six in Marvel comics specifically (2017). Marvel increased its number significantly in 2022 when it published a short called "LGBT-D" in the one-shot comic *Marvel's Voices: Pride* #1. Written by trans author and comedian Grace Freud with art by Scott Henderson, Lee Townsend, and Brittany Peer, "LGBT-D" brings together a team of characters who work to save an LGBTQIA+ youth center. Six of the characters are trans or nonbinary; four of them are introduced for the first time in the issue (Schlesinger 2022).

Given that the number of trans characters featured by Freud and the rest of the creative team in 2022 equaled the total number of trans characters across Marvel from 1978 to 2015, it is reasonable to suggest that representation of trans lives has numerically improved. But as many critics of (the quality of) LGBTQIA+ representation in superhero comics have noted, it isn't simply about quantity. Superhero stories can be harmful if they do not construct marginalized characters with authenticity and complexity. The need for purposeful stories that celebrate the diversity of trans lives is more pressing than ever. At the time of writing, the ACLU has recorded 420 anti-LGBTQIA+ bills being proposed in state legislatures across the United States. The effects of these bills include denying trans people the right to healthcare or privacy; censoring books, curricula, and performances; denying trans people access to public spaces like bathrooms; ripping trans children away from supportive families; increasing barriers to employment; and putting trans people at greater risk of harassment and violence (2023). Superhero comics are only one small thread in the fabric of US culture, and their importance in combatting trans hate pales in comparison to what legal protections can and absolutely must do. However, in their capacity to celebrate certain lives and hold up particular values as imitable, with more and better stories superhero comics can serve as a site of resistance against transphobia.

Of course, not all superhero comics have failed to trouble binary conceptions of gender in constructive ways, and not all trans readers have found gender-swapping narratives entirely meaningless. In fact,

Jessica Drew's character history reveals one example of a technologically induced gender change that some fans identified as a trans narrative. On the social media site Twitter, an account called Trans Character of the Day used August 30, 2021, to declare, "Today's trans character is Jessica Drew from Ultimate Spider-Man! She is a trans woman!" The tweet shows several panels from *Ultimate Comics Spider-Man* #25, written by Brian Michael Bendis with art by David Marquez (2013); however, this iteration of Jessica made her debut in *Ultimate Spider-Man* #98 (Bendis et al. 2006). Set on Earth 1610 (another part of the multiverse akin to, but different from, Earth 616, where Marvel's heroes traditionally reside), *Ultimate Spider-Man* includes an arc in which an evil scientist has cloned Peter Parker. The various clones resultant from this experiment are all almost identical to Peter with the exception of one or two traits. In this universe, Jessica Drew is one of Peter Parker's clones. When Jessica and Peter are finally able to talk about their relationship in *Ultimate Spider-Man* #105, Jessica says that she needs to leave: "I think I'm going to go elsewhere and start a life and be Jessica Drew and not Peter Parker because I think I kind of already am." Peter responds by saying, "Well, really, the minute you started thinking for yourself you already *became* her" (Bendis et al. 2007).

In *Ultimate Comics Spider-Man* #25, Jessica continues to struggle to understand who she is because, on the one hand, she shares sixteen years of Peter's memories, feelings, and desires as if they were her own; and, on the other, she is aware that she is a clone without a unique past. In a conversation with Miles Morales, the young man who will become Spider-Man, Jessica says: "It's hard to—to process *myself* let alone get you to. I have years of Peter Parker's childhood memories rolling around in my head. . . . And time has gone by, and those memories have faded, and my feelings about my connection to him have faded and—And I've become this *other* thing. I'm *not* Peter Parker. I'm not even a boy. I'm Jessica Drew" (Bendis et al. 2013).

Jessica's difficulty in navigating the past as Peter Parker while knowing that she is the woman Jessica Drew in the present led many fans to read this version of Spider-Woman as trans. Aside from the 175 people who retweeted and the 1,213 people who "liked" the above tweet, other fans posted similar interpretations on Reddit (ramonzer0 2021), Tumblr (heroeswhohappentobewomen 2014), and on various pop-culture websites (Jones 2022; Brigid-Prehn 2022). Jean Brigid-Prehn, for example, writes: "While not at all a one-to-one representation of the trans experience, the idea of a character who was treated as a boy for 16 years of memories before waking up as a girl is one that struck a chord of recognition in me and, anecdotally, several other trans comic readers" (2022). Brigid-Prehn goes on to say that she ultimately found Bendis's depiction of Jess wanting, but a later writer, Michel Fiffe, brought a level of nuance to the character that Brigid-Prehn really appreciated. Even this iteration, however, "lacked the force of outright representation" (2022). M. W. Bychowski similarly notes that the Ultimate Jessica Drew has the potential to be read as a trans-identified character. Like Brigid-Prehn, though, Bychowski argues that this kind of narrative treats trans identity "as the problem to be fixed, resolved, or overcome." More specifically, Bychowski compares Jessica's narrative to that of Sir Tristan in *Camelot 3000*: "In both cases, a male identified character is cloned or reincarnated as a gender they don't claim, as women. The character's trans identification is treated as a problem and their stories cannot move forward until they accept the gender they were given. . . . The trans identity is surrendered" (2016).

Even if these narrative choices disrupt the neatness of binary gender, they overwhelmingly treat trans people as a "mechanism or an object" and do not actually require the reader to "identify with trans subjectivities." What if, Bychowski asks, instead of incorporating trans identity in comics via a cis understanding of the world, "we offer trans and cis readers alike narrations they don't often get to read: looking through the eyes of dysphoria, feeling the touch of sexual play through genitals that have undergone surgery, smelling the scent of perfume perhaps transgressive [sic] purchased or chaffing in clothes dictated by parents or school?" (2016). Like other trans critics and fans, Bychowski is not suggesting that these experiences are universal among all trans people but that engaging with experiences that are widespread may go a long way in creating more authentic characters.

One aspect of Hopeless and Rodriguez's *Spider-Woman* that may speak meaningfully to trans experience is the pressure to hide who one really is from loved ones. In issue #6 Jess finds herself trapped on Earth 65, another part of the multiverse, after a visit to an alternate Spider-Woman goes awry. At one point, with the help of other Spider-women, Jess discovers that her way back to her own reality lies in the hands of her Earth 65 doppelganger, Jesse Drew, who, unfortunately, is not a "good guy." After Jess arrives at her counterpart's stately home in New York, she discovers that Jesse Drew is a man with a wife and two children. Although Jesse is not home when Jess arrives, his wife, Ellen, invites Jess in after Jess tells Ellen that she is Jesse's cousin. Through dialogue and visual similarities, it becomes clear that Jess and Jesse are two versions of the same person. They are so similar, in fact, that Jess can unlock parts of Jesse's office that are accessible only by someone who has Jesse's exact DNA, and one of Jesse's kids remarks that Jess looks just like their dad. Jess eventually reveals to Ellen that Jesse is a spy for an evil corporation, and although Ellen already knew Jesse wasn't an accountant like he claimed, the nature of his job had been kept from her (Hopeless et al. 2016).

Certain aspects of this issue may resonate with trans readers. Popular writer Rachel Stevens suggests that "hiding an important aspect of your identity from the people around you because you can't be sure how they'll handle it" may be particularly relatable to closeted trans people (Scott and Kirkpatrick 2015, 167). If one chooses to read Jess and Jesse's multiverse encounter as a metaphor for trans experience, there are a few other details that may be affirming of trans lives. For example, at the point that Jess finds out that her Earth 65 counterpart is a man, she accepts this reality without comment. There are no remarks about how odd it is to see herself as a man or about how Jesse has the "wrong" body. As an allegory of trans experience, this is arguably a step forward from media that represent the transgender body as "an object of visceral disgust" (Billard and MacAuley 2017, 235), or that "[reduce] transgender experience to being 'born in the wrong body'" (Capuzza and Spencer 2016, 223).[12] That Jesse is in a loving relationship is also notable since, as Billard and MacAuley note, in many media "transgender characters often are not allowed to have (viable) romantic interests" (2017, 235).

Having said that, if Jesse is read as trans, his circumstances may reinforce a kind of "trans-normative" representation that "necessitate[s] whiteness, conventional attractiveness, middle- to upper-class status, heterosexuality, and normative family structure to legitimate trans characters as 'good' transgender people" (Billard and MacAuley 2017, 235).[13] Although Jesse's family life departs from these criteria insofar as his wife and kids are Black, they are otherwise an accurate description of his circumstances. Of course, it is also crucial to note that while Jess and Jesse's arc in *Spider-Woman* does involve cross-gender identification, it is only abstractly related to transgender experience. There is no explicit discussion of being trans in the comic, and as far as I can tell, Hopeless and the rest of the creative team never intentionally set out to depict Jess or Jesse as trans. As such, even if the issues of *Spider-Woman* that feature Jesse include facets that are recognizable to trans readers, they do not constitute a sufficient example of trans representation. What I am interested in here is the purposeful inclusion of a gender-swapping narrative in a book about reproductive rights, pregnancy, and maternity and the potential that represents for a kind of storytelling that illuminates the connections between reproductive justice and trans rights.

On one hand, employing a multiverse plot that involves cross-gender identification may be read as another characteristic of *Spider-Woman* that reinforces how maternal subjectivity as Kristeva defines it can be practiced by anyone, regardless of gender. Jesse, like Jess, is fiercely protective of his family and will go to any lengths to ensure their safety and happiness. And, like Jess, he is both a Spider-man *and* a parent. On the other hand, I argue that by destabilizing biologically essentialist gender identities, *Spider-Woman* enables a discussion of the interrelatedness of trans rights and reproductive rights and points towards the possibility of a feminist superhero who can authentically represent that correlation. In short, Jessica Drew could be trans.

In addition to the examples above that obliquely link Jess and Jesse's multiverse encounter to trans experience, there are a number of other factors that I think warrant this discussion. First, the theme of bodily autonomy is important to both Jessica and Jesse. As discussed previously, Jess's decision to become pregnant and parent outside of a heteronormative relationship is possible because she has access to reproductive technologies. Because of the gains made by reproductive justice movements, women like Jess can decide if and how they become mothers. In issue #7, Jesse realizes that his servitude to a criminal organization is unnecessary when he discovers that the serum his boss injects him with does not actually keep him alive (as he had been led to believe), but instead instills him with Spider-powers. Upon learning the truth, Jesse decides to remove the injection port from his arm. Rather than continue performing in physically extraordinary ways in service of someone else, Jesse chooses to pursue a life without superpowers (Hopeless et al. 2016). Here again, Jesse's narrative may be read as metaphorically related to trans experience. Anne Enke writes that an expansive definition of transgender emphasizes "movement away from culturally specific expectations associated with the sex one is assigned at birth and a movement toward gender self-determination" (2012, 5). Jesse moves away from the expectations set for him as a person with Spider-powers and towards self-determination. In both cases, bodily autonomy is key for

Jess and Jesse, and the fact that these scenarios involve issues of reproduction and embodied identity holds promise.

Second, and relatedly, it is precisely because reproductive rights and trans rights are about bodily autonomy that both are under attack in the United States and merit simultaneous attention. The overlapping waves of political backlash against the gains made by women and the LGBTQIA+ community (among other marginalized groups) are not a coincidence. Educated, healthy, supported, free cis women and trans people pose significant threat to patriarchal cisheteronormative social systems precisely because of their capacity to expose the lie that such systems are "natural" or inevitable. Moreover, because trans women of color are one of the groups made most vulnerable by overlapping systems of oppression, and because trans people also require access to reproductive education, health, and freedom, any intersectional feminist narrative about reproductive justice should necessarily acknowledge this imbrication.[14]

Third, entertaining the possibilities for Jess to be a trans feminist superhero is relevant to this analysis because of the similarities between pregnancy and gender transition. Garbes points towards the work of certified nurse midwife Simon Ellis:

> Ellis believes that there are profound similarities between pregnancy and gender transition—two things that they have direct experience with. Both are temporary states of being that move you towards a future that, in most cases, is desired. Both require that your body be taken over by hormones and changed in ways that are both wondrous and frightening. The way that people look at you as a result of these physical changes will dramatically change, and the way that people interact with you—what they say you are allowed to do or should or should not do—will flip completely. (2018, 138)[15]

Ellis, like other trans-inclusive healthcare providers, emphasizes the need for reproductive and sexual health to be recognized in ways that are not constrained by cisheteronormativity (Ellis, Wojnar, and Pettinato 2015). Trans men can get pregnant and give birth, trans women can be mothers, nonbinary people can choose to start families, or not. There is no reason these realities cannot be reflected in the stories we tell ourselves, superhero or otherwise. Further, in a comic capable of escaping the annihilationist tendencies of binary thinking and complexifying representations of maternity, a trans-inclusive approach could only make it more feminist.

Ultimately, I concur with Brigid-Prehn in suggesting that gender-swap stories involving Jessica Drew have "the makings of a fascinating character, with a queer reading *in potentia* waiting on the sidelines" (2022). The lack of straightforward representation of transgender in *Spider-Woman* constitutes another limitation on the extent to which the book may be read as a feminist superhero comic. However, the already-present theme of bodily autonomy, the real ways reproductive justice is connected to trans rights, and the parallels between pregnancy and transitioning all point to the potential a comic like *Spider-Woman* has.

So, following Bychowski, it seems appropriate to return to a question popular with Marvel creators when they are trying to imagine how things might be otherwise. What if Jessica's storyworld was constructed not by cis men but by trans creators? What if her reproductive choices were indicative of the variety of options available, including the barriers associated with each for cis and trans people alike? What if Jessica and Jesse's agreement to coexist in their respective multiverses was used to expand and diversify pregnancy and parenting narratives? What if, for example, we got parallel stories that explicitly embraced Jessica as a trans woman who becomes a mother and Jesse as a trans man who gives birth? How might these possibilities further strengthen the power subjects in process have to disrupt violent binary systems, celebrate fluidity and dynamism, and model the multidimensionality of maternity?

I am not suggesting that Hopeless and Rodriguez's rendition of Jessica Drew be replaced. I hope to have shown the qualities that make Jessica a feminist superhero and the numerous ways *Spider-Woman* can be read as a feminist text. Nevertheless, as Garbes asserts, "We are still at a point where we lack stories—diverse stories—about pregnancy and motherhood. Only if we tell and hear these stories do we have a chance at understanding the experience, of making progress" (2018, 229).

Further, as Stevens argues, "We need quality *and* quantity. No single trans woman in fiction could encapsulate every single trans woman's experience, nor should she. The same goes for all representation in all fiction and media" (qtd. in Scott and Kirkpatrick 2015, 165). Hopeless and Rodriguez's comic tells the story of one cis white woman, but it also demonstrates the malleability of Jessica as a character and makes it possible to imagine how future iterations might further diversify the superhero genre. Jessica's adaptability is not just evident in her comics history; it can also be observed across forms of media. Her new costume in *Spider-Woman,* for instance, was inspired by a redesign for her introduction as a playable character in the video game *Spider-Man Unlimited* by Gameloft. Similar to the discussion above, Andrew Wheeler notes how this change made Jessica more recognizable as a character with a unique identity, rather than looking "more like a lingerie model than a superhero" (2014).

In terms of how Jessica as a maternal subject in process might facilitate more, and more diverse stories, we can turn to film. The multiverse's tendency to proliferate Spider-people was used to bring Jessica to the big screen in the animated Sony film *Spider-Man: Across the Spider-Verse* (Dos Santos, Powers, and Thompson 2023). Like Hopeless and Rodriguez's iteration, Sony's version of Jessica Drew is a motorcycle-riding momma-to-be; however, this time audiences witnessed what maternity means for Jess as a Black woman.[16] This reimagining of Jess is exciting because, similar to Hopeless and Rodriguez, the filmmakers challenged boundaries of the superhero genre by incorporating pregnancy and maternity, yet by using the multiverse as a plot device, they also added a unique story about a Black woman's experience as a maternal subject.

Aside from lending inspiration to a film that was genre-expanding in its formal innovations, its diverse cast of characters, and its multidimensional storytelling, Hopeless and Rodriguez's *Spider-Woman* can be read as a feminist comic through various lenses. By purposefully featuring Jessica's pregnant body in compositions akin to poetic language, Rodriguez defies the dichotomous gendered logic of the superhero genre. The creative team's treatment of Jess as both a caring mother and a superhero, and their choice to surround her with a support network, further disrupts genre norms that frame superhero mothers as monstrous. Similarly, in making Jess a dynamic character capable of navigating the sometimes-competing experiences of "anger and tenderness," Hopeless and Rodriguez ameliorate harmful patriarchal ideals of motherhood. *Spider-Woman*'s formal and narrative resonances with Kristeva's work on the maternal subject also complexify the representation of maternity in the comic and facilitate reading techniques that emulate the way maternal subjects transgress the divide between self and other. Thus, the parallels between the comic and Kristeva's work serve to demonstrate how the maternal subject in process can be a model imitable by anyone, regardless of gender. Although Hopeless and Rodriguez's use of a gender-swapping narrative arc only allegorically relates to transgender experience, this decision enables an examination of the correlation between reproductive justice and trans rights and highlights the need for more gender-inclusive storytelling. Cumulatively, Jessica's profile as a maternal subject in process and the comic's potential for inspiring more authentic stories about other marginalized subjects make it possible to read *Spider-Woman* as a feminist text.

2 | *AMERICA* AND THE NEW MESTIZA

Punching Star-Shaped Holes through Binaries and Borders

America Chavez was created in 2011 by writer Joe Casey and artist Nick Dragotta. As with many other Blue Age characters, America is technically a legacy character because she originally appeared using the moniker "Miss America," a title previously attached to the white female character Madeline Joyce in the 1940s. Also characteristic of her Blue Age genesis, America was created to reflect changes in US society and culture. Whereas Madeline Joyce, as a white, normatively feminine, heterosexual, nondisabled woman embodied 1940s nationalistic ideals of superheroism, Casey and Dragotta created America as a queer, alien Latina character in an effort to diversify genre norms and in recognition of their multicultural fanbase.

Casey and Dragotta's decision to reflect the multicultural reality of the United States in their character, paired with her superstrength, speed, invulnerability, power of flight, and ability to punch portals through space and time, made America a popular addition to diverse superhero teams such as Young Avengers, A-Force, and the Ultimates. Her introduction also arguably allowed previously marginalized readers to form meaningful connections to the genre. America's capacity to push the superhero genre in more inclusive directions and, as this chapter argues, to embody an intersectional feminist ethos, was more fully realized in 2017 with the publication of her twelve-issue solo series, *America*, written by Gabby Rivera with art by Joe Quinones.[1] In it, America has tired of leading superhero teams and longs for a chance to work on her own growth. So she heads off to Sotomayor University (in another dimension), where she reunites with old friends, gets recruited by the sorority Leelumultipass Phi Theta Betas, and, of course, finds herself having to fight an arch villain and interdimensional monsters, and having to save her ancestral home from pending doom. While this may sound like fairly standard superhero stuff, this chapter demonstrates the significant ways *America* breaks from the mold.

The eponymous comic defies superhero norms not only because it centers on Marvel's first lesbian Latina heroine but also because it emphasizes the importance of solidarity among oppressed people, eschews hyperindividualism, highlights the need for teamwork, champions women's generational knowledge, and is constructively critical of overlapping, xenophobic systems of surveillance, capitalism, and white supremacy that mirror our own. *America* also departs from normative depictions of mainstream superheroes because America Chavez can be read as an example of what Chicana feminist philosopher Gloria Anzaldúa called "the new *mestiza*." That is, America is a subject who exists in the borderlands of culture, who resists and challenges binaries—of gender, of ethnicity, of nationality, even of time and space—a character who embodies and occupies cultures from (at least) two worlds and who has the power to position readers in those same borderlands (for example, by speaking in both Spanish and English).

Finally, to further explore the layers of feminist meaning in *America*, this chapter concludes by shifting from an analysis of America's marginality in the superhero genre (as a queer Latina character written by a queer Latina author) towards her belonging amid other Latinx comics, literature, and media. For instance, in its inclusion of narrative elements like time traveling, magical realms, and *una abuela luchadora* (a grandmother who is a professional fighter), *America* resonates with the *Love and Rockets* comics by the Hernandez brothers, texts that have been linked to the feminist Latin American literary tradition of the mid-twentieth century. In traversing these graphic borders and centering *latinidad* in *America*, Rivera and Quinones provide a powerful counter to the racist, sexist stereotypes of Latina characters in mainstream superhero comics. Therefore, from a feminist perspective, I argue that this iteration of America matters because unlike most of her superhero predecessors, her unabashed mission to fight white supremacy and misogyny is coalitional; as an example of "the new mestiza," she models transcultural understanding that transcends boundaries of language and national identity. In addition, her creators embed her in a storyworld that connects her to other rich, compelling representations of Latinx identity and experience.[2]

CONSTRUCTING A QUEER FEMINIST STORYWORLD

As part of the "Marvel NOW! 2.0" initiative, *America* was one of many titles intended to introduce more diverse creative teams and characters in the hopes of attracting new readers to Marvel comics. According to Frederick Aldama, "Latinx superheroes in mainstream comic book storyworlds (print comics, animation, TV, and film), DC and Marvel universes especially, are few and far between," numbering "somewhere in the fifties . . . in a sea filled with Anglo A- and B-listers" (2017, 3). Esther De Dauw similarly notes that throughout the history of the genre, "only a few superheroes came out as gay," and even by 2021, "gay superheroes remain low in number" (2021, 12). America, as an identifiably lesbian Latina, alien character, is, as Jeffrey Brown writes, "one of Marvel's most obvious departures from the conventional depiction of superheroes as white, male, heterosexual, and American" (2021, 120). The book's writer, Gabby Rivera, also made headlines for being the first lesbian Latina hired at Marvel, and her pairing with artist Quinones made some readers feel like *America* provided an example of better representation rooted in personal experience and care for Latinx stories (Betancourt 2017).

Nevertheless, antidiversity comics fans have argued that giving America Chavez a solo series was nothing more than a virtue-signaling exercise by Marvel; even though America embodies the same intersecting social identities as her writer, they argue that her characterization as a lesbian Latina superhero was a gimmick designed to compensate for a poor-quality book. McKenna James Boeckner, Monica Flegel, and Judith Leggatt show that at the root of these complaints is the belief in the centrality and political neutrality (and therefore goodness) of white heteronormative masculinity (2020). Comics that decenter or call into question whiteness, heteronormativity, and masculinity are, by this logic, deemed as being wrong or bad. However much I disagree with both the premise and conclusion of this stance, what I think antidiversity fans get right is the fact that Rivera and Quinones construct a storyworld, and develop America as a character, in ways that radically depart from the white heteronormative masculinist status quo. In fact, I argue that the traits antidiversity fans identify as "poor" in *America* are indicative of Rivera and Quinones's "willful use of skills and technical devices" to construct a queer feminist storyworld around their lesbian Latina heroine.

The "willful use of skills and technical devices" in the creation of comics "by and about Latinos" is part of what Aldama defines as a creative team's "will to style." He writes that "the will to style is shorthand for identifying the responsibility of the creator (or creators) in understanding well the building blocks of reality that they are reconstructing as well as the degree of presence of a willful use of skills and technical devices to give shape to the making of new pop-cultural phenomena by and about Latinos" (2017, 4). Following this definition, I suggest that throughout *America*, one can observe the responsibility Rivera and Quinones feel in representing intersectional Latinx stories by virtue of the queer feminist narrative and visual devices they employ in America's characterization and in the construction of her storyworld. America herself, for example, is designed and stylized in ways that ameliorate the white supremacist, sexist representational norms for Latinas in superhero comics.

According to Aldama, many early Latina superheroes were beset by racist and sexist stereotypes: they were visualized as hypersexual and exotic, depicted with light skin and Caucasian facial features (2017, 121).[3] Further, like female characters of other ethnicities, Latina superheroes were often clad in tight spandex costumes and drawn in ways that accentuated their breasts and hips. Cumulatively, these representations worked to reinforce stereotypes about "spicy" or "hot" Latina sexuality (Brown 2021, 112). While early appearances of America Chavez arguably perpetuate these stereotypes (her first appearance in Casey and Dragotta's *Vengeance* #1, for instance, is replete with cleavage- and butt-shots), Rivera and Quinones's America productively defies them. From her first appearance in her solo series, America is visualized as unambiguously brown-skinned: she has dark brown curly hair, dark eyes, and prominent eyebrows. She is curvy but also noticeably muscular, embodying what Yvonne Tasker identifies as "musculinity."

Tasker writes that "'musculinity' indicates the extent to which a physical definition of masculinity in terms of a developed musculature is not limited to the male body within representation" (1993, 3). Quinones develops America's musculinity throughout the book in action sequences that highlight her strength and capability and in panels where America is posed so that her musculature becomes a visual focus. On the cover of issue #7, for example, America wears a sports bra and stands with her back to the reader so that the well-developed muscles in her shoulders, arms, and lower back are all visible (Rivera et al. 2017). Her backside is also visible, but because she is wearing denim shorts, it is drawn with subtle curves rather than being explicitly carved into two cheeks in the way drawings of spandex-clad bums often are. America looks back at the reader over her left shoulder with a sly, knowing smile indicating that she is aware that she is being admired, disrupting assumptions about female bodies as passive objects to be looked at (fig. 2.1). In fact, one could read America's posture as deliberately showing off and taking pleasure in occupying the reader's gaze as a muscular Latina. The fact that America is lesbian further divorces the male gaze—as a mechanism for fixing women as objects of heterosexual desire—from the act of looking and the pleasure it induces. Therefore, Quinones's version of America queers or disrupts "binary conceptions of gender identity" (Tasker 1993, 3) and broadens representations of Latinas in comics.

As I have just suggested, America's sartorial choices also depart from stereotypical representations of Latina superheroes. Rather than sexually objectify her, America's superhero outfits are more akin to white male superheroes' uniforms: the use of red, white, and blue with gold stars and eagles affirms a kind of nationalism (Dittmer 2013). Her adoption of cropped jackets and pro-wrestling gear (like lace-up boots and knee pads) also visually aligns her with other Latina comics characters such as those in Steve Ross's *Chesty Sanchez* comics or Jaime Hernandez's *Locas* stories. These are both points I will return to in the sections that follow, but my focus here is the ways America's clothes add depth to her as a queer feminist character.

While America occasionally wears recognizable superhero garb—spandex bodysuits, for instance—she is most often shown pairing such elements with, or completely outfitted in, contemporary streetwear. Cropped tops, denim, high-top sneakers, overalls, athletic gear like thigh-high socks or wristbands, and gold hoop earrings make up the bulk of America's looks throughout the series. Patriotic colors and symbolism visually confirm America's status as an "American hero," but their manifestation as streetwear also reveals something about her personal preferences as a young woman and may make her relatable to readers who embody a similar aesthetic.

These sartorial choices also underscore the importance of Black and Latinx cultural influences in America's storyworld, since US streetwear is popular with many Black and brown working-class youth. Additionally, fashion scholar Michelle Alejandra Mireles draws attention to the "queer potential in streetwear's push back on what is considered fashionable, respectable, and gender appropriate. For example, a more

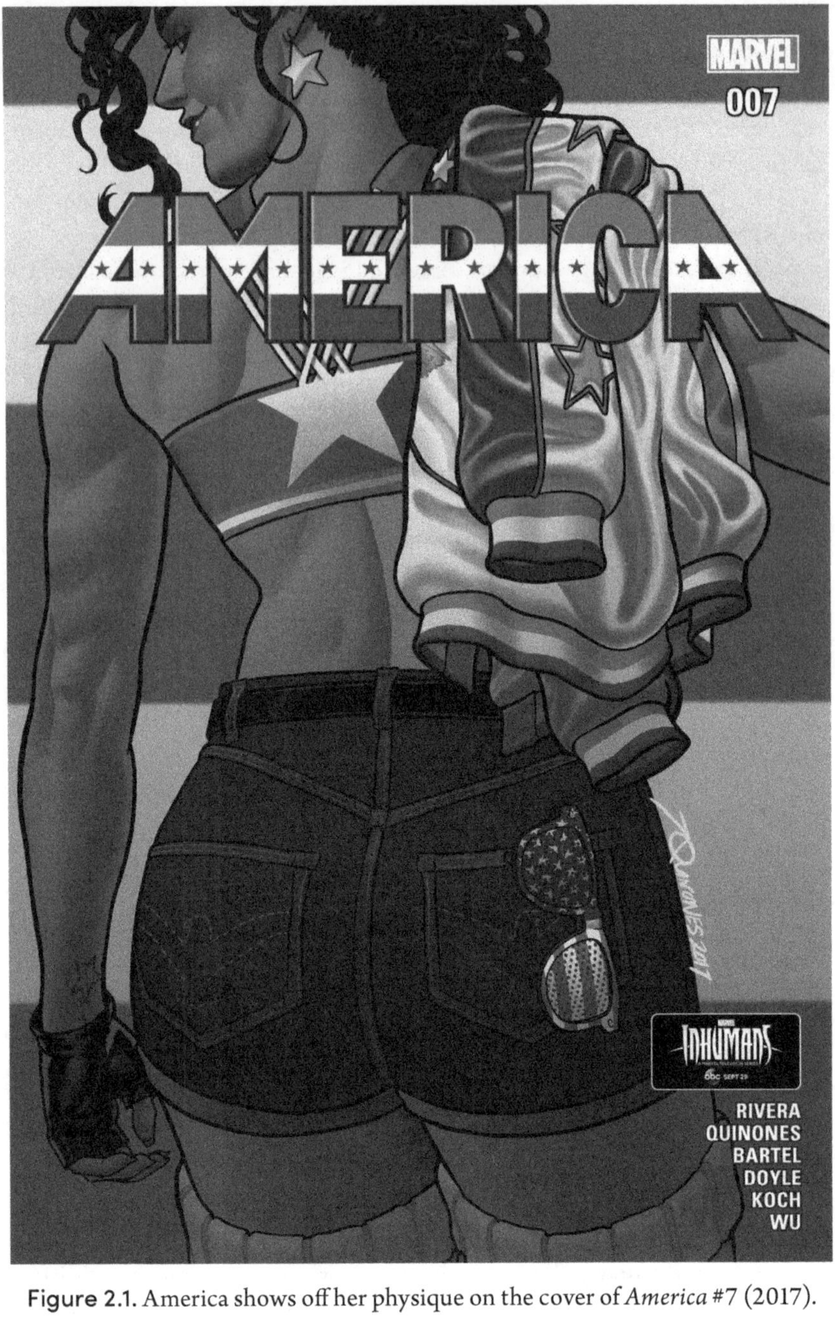

Figure 2.1. America shows off her physique on the cover of *America* #7 (2017).

hip-hop style of dress includes mixing baggy clothes traditionally read as masculine with glamorous jewelry traditionally read as feminine" (2022, 3–4). Towards the end of issue #2 we see America embody this combination in her adoption of baggy overalls, a cropped T-shirt, sneakers, an oversized beanie, and her signature gold hoop earrings (Rivera et al. 2017). As Mireles suggests of streetwear generally, America's look "pushes boundaries by blurring 'gender appropriate' accessories and hybridizing racialized aesthetics" (2022, 4).

America's gold hoop earrings, frequently worn with red lipstick, also connect her to her surroundings and signal a distinctly Latina tradition of fighting for justice. In an interview for *Book Riot,* writer Gabby Rivera explained that the name and design of America's educational institution, Sotomayor University, are an homage to the life and work of US Supreme Court Justice Sonia Sotomayor (Guthertz 2018). A self-described "wise Latina," Sotomayor has donned gold hoops and red lipstick as part of her signature style throughout her career, despite thinly veiled sexist and racist admonishments from political authorities about a lack of professionalism (Tarver 2011). As only the third woman, and the first Latina, to ever be nominated to the Supreme Court, Sotomayor's aesthetic choices are bold reminders of the disruption her nomination brought to a white supremacist, androcentric status quo. Through these visual devices, both Sotomayor University and America herself are thus associated with Justice Sotomayor's tenacity and commitment to changing what justice looks like.

Another example of how America's outfits tie her to real women of color and enrich her depiction as a feminist character appears on the cover of issue #2 (Rivera et al. 2017). Quinones draws America in the center of the page. She wears a broad-rimmed top hat that comes down to the bridge of her nose, gold eagle earrings, necklaces (complete with a large gold eagle pendant) that extend down her neck and across her clavicles, and an off-the-shoulder blue-and-white starred dressed cinched at the waist with a red-and-white striped belt. Behind her stand Carol Danvers as Captain Marvel and Monica Rambeau as Spectrum; although only half of each woman is visible, it is clear that they are both staring intently at the viewer (fig. 2.2).

America's outfit and the composition of the three women allude to pop superstar Beyoncé's music video "Formation," in which she is similarly clad and flanked by two protective-looking people. Ever since she slid onto the stage at the Video Music Awards in 2014, positioning herself in front of a brightly lit sign that read "FEMINIST," Beyoncé has been one of the most popular faces of US feminism and has used her music to affirm that Black women are at the heart of her politics.[4] Because, as Aldama explains, comics artists can use covers to orient readers towards "certain generic paths and expectations" and introduce signposts of "what is to follow within the storyworld" (2017, 88), it is possible to read this cover as indicative of America's status as a feminist figure. Beyoncé's "Formation" video is explicitly critical of state-sanctioned violence against Black people; it celebrates Black womanhood and sexuality; and it carves out space for Black women to flourish in places where they were historically oppressed. It is therefore interesting to note that the video's invocation in America's comportment also works to align Beyoncé's expressions of feminism with heroism. Captain Marvel's and Spectrum's looks of determination and their stances behind America, as if backing her up and committing to her fight, further echo the collective vision Beyoncé develops for women in "Formation" and set expectations for similarly coalitional action in the pages that follow.

The visual allusion to "Formation" may also summon for viewers the larger album of which it is a part, *Lemonade*. According to Black queer "femme-inist" scholar Omise'eke Tinsley, Beyoncé's visual album celebrates Black women's expressions of gender and sexuality, explores motherhood and mothering, centers children in the fight for and vision of a liberated future, cultivates a focus on heritage and ancestral knowledge, depicts Black womanhood as inclusive of trans- and queer women, and showcases the diverse ways Black women support and love each other (2018).

While Rivera and Quinones's depiction of America and her storyworld is inclusive of Black women's experiences, it is not as explicitly focused on Black women's lives as Beyoncé's album. Nevertheless, similar themes run throughout *America* and are core components of what make the superhero and the book queer and feminist. Quinones's "Formation" cover could therefore be read as signposting a storyworld that celebrates Latina womanhood and sexuality, centers motherhood and mentoring, explores children's needs for protection and belonging, is inclusive of queer and nonbinary people, and showcases the many ways America and her found family love and support each other.

Jeffrey Brown observes that upon publication of her solo series, America's "lesbian sexuality garnered more public attention than her ethnicity. This discrepancy is an indication of how more normalized nonwhite superheroes have become in the comics and, conversely, how

Figure 2.2. Carol Danvers, America, and Monica Rambeau "get in formation" on the cover of *America* #2 (2017).

much farther nonheterosexual characters have to go to be normalized" (2021, 119). Brown's assessment is substantiated by the fact that there is nothing particularly sensationalist about Rivera and Quinones's depiction of America's romantic interactions. In issue #1 America concludes a mission with her team, the Ultimates, and travels back to New York City to see her girlfriend Lisa (Rivera et al. 2017). They greet each other on Lisa's stoop, embrace, and eventually America carries Lisa down the hallway to her apartment. On the next page, Lisa and America are in bed together talking, both partially (but modestly) dressed. The implication is that they have been intimate with each other; however, this sequence does not include even a kiss in terms of explicit physical intimacy. Later, in issue #5, America sits with an old flame talking about their mutual childhood crushes on each other; the women lean into one another, and as they begin to kiss, America is betrayed and stabbed with a syringe. While Ramon Villalobos, the penciler and inker on the issue, shows the women as their lips touch, the subsequent panel of the two shifts point of view to a low angle that moves away from their faces and instead draws a focus on the needle with which America is about to be stabbed (Rivera et al. 2017).

All other expressions of America's sexuality are largely confined to the comic's dialogue, in which America occasionally articulates longing for lovers past or uncertainty about her dating future. On the one hand, the lack of explicit physical intimacy between America and other women may be read as one of Marvel's attempts to "portray their LGBTQ superheroes in ways that do not alienate the predominately straight (and male) audience that has long consumed their comics" (Panuska 2020, 129). As Sarah Panuska argues, adding graphic sexual content to comics is not necessarily a guarantee of better queer representation; however, "making LGBTQ sexuality *visible*" remains an important step. So too is "a willingness to accurately reference and reflect real-life LGBTQ community and culture" (Panuska 2020, 131). Panuska writes that "despite its rich metaphor and healthy abundance of characters who can be read as LGBTQ, *America* makes few references to everyday contemporary LGBTQ life and culture" (2020, 145).

On the other hand, the relative lack of sexual content in *America* may be read as a mechanism for achieving Rivera's goals to avoid subsuming America's growth as a person into romantic relationships and to show that pursuing love does not have to be "the quest for a lover" (Guthertz 2018). Further, Brown suggests that Rivera's focus on the emotional aspects of America's relationships, rather than on the erotic or physical, serves to normalize lesbian relationships "for readers of any sexual orientation" and productively disrupts the genre's tendency to sexualize and exploit women's relationships "for the more prurient viewing of male readers" (2021, 120). As with many mainstream comics intended to represent marginalized stories *and* sell to large audiences, these competing aspects of *America* are interrelated and create a paradox that presents readers with an exploration of queer sexuality that errs in its subtlety but that also ameliorates sexist genre trends.

While it does not resolve the tensions just discussed, another element of *America* that adds depth to its celebration of queer female sexuality is America's superhero genealogy. Even for readers unfamiliar with her backstory, issue #1 of *America* makes it clear through caption boxes reflecting America's thoughts that she had two mothers whom she lost (Rivera et al. 2017). Issue #4 of the series begins with a flashback that details their deaths. On the cliffs of the Utopian Parallel, a place that "exists outside time, outside reality," Elena and Amalia, the superpowered mothers of America, stand discussing the impending doom the Parallel faces. The only way they can save their home world is by combining their power and sacrificing themselves to "form a permanent seal" to keep the Parallel safe. Following a panel showing the two women soaring through the sky holding hands with eyes closed, the flashback concludes with a young, pigtailed America waking up in her home and calling out for her mothers, who are now gone (Rivera et al. 2017).

Many superheroes begin their journeys by being orphaned; however, a skeptical reading of this scenario might suggest that the radical move to give America lesbian parents who are then killed constitutes an example of the "bury your gays" trope. According to De Dauw, "In this trope, usually one partner, or sometimes both, in a gay couple is killed. The trope mostly affects women, revealing how female lesbian relationships are less acceptable when lesbianism is not fetishized for male consumption" (2021, 116–117). The frequency with which this trope is employed in popular visual culture (particularly TV and film) further suggests that gay and lesbian characters are seen by creators as more expendable. Elena's and Amalia's absence may also perpetuate the superhero genre's propensity for erasing mothers from the origin stories of women and girls (Stuller 2010, 9).[5] Rivera and Quinones arguably disrupt these toxic heteronormative trends through the use of flashback scenes that allow America's moms to remain visually present throughout *America*. The complexity of Elena and Amalia as characters, and their centrality to America's story, is particularly evident in issue #7. In an effort to find out more about herself and her lineage, America travels to the Ancestral Plane, "a metaphysical place that holds the history" of her people (Rivera et al. 2017). Once there, the sky begins to show America not just the history of her parentage but also her cosmic heritage.

While the scenes America sees in the skies of the Ancestral Plane make her mourn the loss of her mothers, they also cause her to swoon over the romance between women, signaling to readers the joy and excitement of lesbian love. For example, America sees two cosmic female spirits, Berraca and Sanar, fall in love after finding each other across the expanse of the galaxies. Their union results in the creation of Planeta Fuertona, the world where America's mother Amalia was born. As the images unfold, America discovers that Amalia and her mother, Madrimar, had to flee their home world for the safety of the Utopian Parallel, a world inhabited solely by women, including the young girl who would become America's other mother, Elena.

After watching her two moms fall in love, America eventually witnesses the day of her own birth. Amalia and Elena are shown in their home and described in a caption box as "soon to be moms of America Chavez, but first and foremost, two people who've got that real love magic." Amalia is visibly pregnant, but once she begins to go into labor, both women are rushed to "the atrium," or the birthing location. The first image of the newly born America shows both mothers suspended in an orb of light, facing each other and cradling the baby, who is also suspended in a smaller orb between them (fig. 2.3). The repeated circular imagery of the birth page—the baby in an orb that is encompassed by the bodies of her mothers, who float in their own orb of light—echoes the previous image of Berraca and Sanar joining together. Drawn by Jen Bartel, Berraca floats in a descending arc along the left side of the page, while Sanar ascends in an arc along the right, forming a circular image reminiscent of a yin and yang symbol; between them blooms the globe of Planeta Fuertona (fig. 2.4). These images depict women's romantic and erotic relationships as equal, creative, tender, encompassing, and literally life giving. They also explicitly link America's power to her queer, woman-centered parentage and cosmic heritage. As Panuska writes, "The creators of *America* have not only put a new spin on the trope of the superhero origin story but created an entire culture initiated by and supportive of emotional and sexual love between women" (2020, 145).

Figure 2.3. America's mothers, Elena and Amalia, cradle an infant America. *America* #7 (2017).

Figure 2.4. The goddesses Berraca and Sanar create Planeta Fuertona. *America* #7 (2017).

Amalia's and Elena's sacrificial deaths could be read as adhering to the superhero status quo of orphaning heroes, but their depiction as powerful, loving, and luminous women subverts the genre's history of framing lesbian mothers (where they actually appear) as monstrous (Murray 2011). Further, because their memories are a constant presence for America, and their sacrifices form the basis of America's superheroic mission (i.e., she strives to be as heroic, brave, and selfless as her mothers), one could hardly consider them "buried" or absent. Amalia and Elena may not be physically present to mother America, but their motherhood, as it was made possible by "emotional and sexual love between women," is shown to be a core aspect of America's storyworld.

The incorporation of mothering also contributes to America's queer feminist storyworld in that mothering is a practice not limited to Elena and Amalia. In issue #3 America reminisces that after her moms died, she left the Utopian Parallel looking for belonging and family. She landed a star portal in the Bronx, New York. At the Santana family BBQ, Abuela (grandmother) Santana welcomed America as "one of hers. No questions asked." She later found comfort among the Mejia family in Cartagena, Colombia, and then eventually felt a sense of "home" being with her girlfriend Lisa (Rivera et al. 2017). In each of these instances, America finds care, protection, and support; first from women of color when she is a child and from a queer white woman when she is a young adult. Even though America and Lisa break up in issue #1, Lisa's insistence that she cannot follow America to college and that America must find her own path resonates with a radical, queer model of mothering. As Alexis Pauline Gumbs asserts, queer mothering is "an investment in the future that requires a person to change the status quo of their own lives, of their community and of the society as a whole again and again and again in the practice of affirming growing, unpredictable people who deserve a world that is better than what we can even imagine" (2016, 115). Abuela Santana and the Mejias' willingness to change their communities by unconditionally welcoming America into them and Lisa's belief in America's future regardless of the change it means for their relationship status both help to affirm America and enable her growth.

Aside from America's mothers, the character who perhaps most embodies this kind of mothering is Madrimar, Amalia's mother and America's abuela. In the first three issues Madrimar is little more than a cloaked figure lurking in the background of America's story. By issue

#4 she reveals herself to America and explains that she has been guiding America across the multiverse to help her better understand her powers and how to control them. Like America, Madrimar can fly and open star portals, but despite their parallel powers and Madrimar's claims that she knew America's mothers, America initially rejects Madrimar from her life (Rivera et al. 2017). It is not until issue #6, when Madrimar swoops in to help America defeat a gang of villains, that America is willing to hear her out. Amid America's repeated attempts to shut the conversation down, Madrimar finally catches her by surprise saying, "*Oye*, if you weren't my granddaughter, I might have a hard time liking you, America Chavez" (Rivera et al. 2017).

As discussed above, in issue #7 Madrimar takes America to the Ancestral Plane and explains that they are from Planeta Fuertona and that their gifts as "starlings" (i.e., those who can create star portals) come from the cosmic spirit Berraca. Madrimar goes on to explain that she left America and her mothers on the day of America's birth because she was called by the spirits to protect her planet and to keep America hidden from enemies who were tracking all Fuertonas. In other words, while Madrimar kept her physical distance from America to prevent their enemies from tracking them both, she nevertheless tried to show her love through guiding America, giving her access to her ancestry, and reintroducing America to her "home" world.

America muses in issue #8 that of the changes Madrimar brought to her life, she gave her "Planeta Fuertona and pieces of my moms I've never had before. I have stories greater than me! *Soy Fuertona. Soy Latina. Soy America.* And I'm not alone anymore." Later, America admits that while she is hurt that Madrimar left their family, she still thinks "Madrimar is epic. Tough, gentle, mysterious and stuff—like the *abuela* of my dreams" (Rivera et al. 2017).

Madrimar's mothering can be read as queer because her investment in America's future is so strong that she was willing to disrupt the status quo of her life, the lives of her daughters, and America's life to help build a better world for America to call home. Further, Madrimar's model of mothering may be read as feminist because it not only affirms America's path forward but also reinforces America's woman-centered ancestry and helps her understand her power in terms of that lineage. The creative team's treatment of mothering as a practice not tied solely to biological relationships brings more women into America's storyworld and thus ameliorates the superhero genre's tendency to erase mother figures from female characters' lives.

Madrimar's mothering also facilitates the introduction of female mentors for America. Similar to the treatment of mothers in the superhero genre, superwomen have been overwhelmingly guided by male mentors. Jennifer Stuller argues that "women mentoring women . . . is invaluable because when all we see are images of superwomen—even extremely talented and capable ones—receiving their training from only male teachers, gurus, sensei, and sages, it assumes that intellectual and physical power is masculine and that female knowledge has no value" (2010, 9).

To help guide America through her journey of self-discovery, Madrimar employs the aid of three women who all have important lessons to teach America about being a superhero. Professor Douglas, teacher of Intergalactic Indigenous Revolutionaries at Sotomayor University, guides America both inside and outside of the classroom. On the first day of classes, America enters Professor Douglas's "Intergalactic Revolutionaries & You" course late, and, in an attempt to compensate for being unprepared, reverts to trying to punch her way through a tricky learning simulation. Professor Douglas reminds America that she must be accountable for her actions and "that no one is better than the work" (Rivera et al. 2017).

Although America does not find out until later, Professor Douglas is also Madrimar's primary aid in communicating with America's other mentors across space and time. In fact, during America's first attempt to use a star portal to travel back in time for her class project, she finds herself in Germany on the battlefields of World War II. As much as America is surprised to see Agent Peggy Carter,[6] Professor Douglas's communications prepare Peggy to take America's appearance in stride. Even amid an ongoing battle and, thanks to America, a botched tactical operation, Peggy is able to convey to America the importance of having a plan beyond "punch first, ask questions later."

America's next attempt at multiverse travel is also redirected by Madrimar and Professor Douglas to introduce America to her third mentor, the X-Men leader Storm in the 1980s. Despite America's discomfort, Storm helps America to be open to the possibility that her powers may exceed what she knows and to center her mind even in the heat of battle. The lessons these women teach America not only prove invaluable as she continues to expand her powers; they also help her to mature as a person. Further, as Enrique García notes: "These scenes are an attractive endorsement of America as the new queer Latina superheroine by the previous heteronormative white and ethnic superheroines that have opened the path for her. This portrayal thus links her to a bigger feminist movement that is fighting for inclusivity" (2018, 176).

America's creative team also underscores the importance of mentorship in their feminist storyworld by making America a mentor as well. In issue #1 America and the Ultimates battle an unknown entity attacking the planet Maltixa. After America helps to save the day, some local nonbinary femme teens begin to idolize her and form themselves into the Chavez Guerrillas.[7] Although America encourages them to follow her on social media, she subsequently ignores their attempts to connect, and it is not until they kidnap her ex-girlfriend Lisa that America must reckon with her role as a mentor. As America sets off to rescue Lisa, she summons the lessons she has learned from her mentor Peggy and recalls her own needs as a child:

> Okay, Chavez, don't do that thing where you run off and mess everything up. Remember what Peggy told you—you need a **plan.** And the Maltixans who took Lisa are just kids. You can't go punching a bunch of kids in the face. Remember, you were once that kid looking for someone, **anyone** to connect to. That's still you. (Rivera et al. 2017)

After her unexpected detour to Storm's oasis, America finally reaches Maltixa, where she realizes that the Guerillas' attempts to contact her were not done simply in admiration but because they needed her protection and guidance. The weight of her responsibility to the kids comes to bear as the same entity from the beginning of the series begins to attack Maltixa again. At one point, as America prepares to fly into a portal, Imani (a young Maltixan) yells after her: "You flew off last time, too. Is this what you do? You dive into people's lives, sprinkle a little super-hero junk everywhere and then run off when things get real?" (Rivera et al. 2017). This jibe is, on one level, aimed at America's previous faulty assumptions that the only requirements for saving the day were her two fists. On another level, Imani's comments act as a critique of generic norms for superheroes who seem to stand apart from or above the communities they supposedly save. What Imani and the Guerillas want from America is guidance on how best to protect their home from future threats and assurance that their community matters to America beyond just another chance to declare "mission accomplished." Only by applying everything she learned from her mentors—accountability, strategy, and listening—is America able to provide the kind of safety she initially promised the Chavez Guerillas.

The Maltixan teens are not passive in this scenario, however; they are emboldened by America, who works with them to save the planet. If, as García argues, Peggy and Storm acting as mentors to America serves as an endorsement and links them all to a feminist legacy, then America's mentorship of the Guerillas may be similarly understood as purposefully embracing femme nonbinary teens (and the various constituent groups they represent) as part of that movement. Moreover, the creative team's choice to make nonbinary femmes so central to America's storyworld is confirmation of their commitment to *intersectional* feminism and an important amendment of the virtual invisibility of nonbinary characters in the superhero genre (Cowling and Cray 2022, 210–211).

The Chavez Guerillas are not the only characters to join America in protecting Maltixa. At Sotomayor University America's closest friend is self-described Blerd (Black nerd) David Alleyne, a.k.a. Prodigy. A former Young Avengers teammate, David is exceptionally intelligent, adept at technology, and a fierce friend who does not hesitate to call America in when she becomes impulsive. X'andria, leader of the female-femme student group Leelumultipass Phi Theta Betas (LLMPPTB), also becomes a close friend of America's and is characterized in issue #2 as someone who can challenge America and help her reach "goals-level greatness" (Rivera et al. 2017).

When America first hears of Lisa's abduction and flies off, David and X'andria are concerned that her anger will get the best of her, leaving them with little choice but to go after her. Once on Maltixa, they find America, Lisa, and the Guerillas struggling to fight off the attacks of the unknown entity, so David, X'andria, and the rest of LLMPPTB jump into the fray. Through a combination of skills—manipulating radio waves, dance fighting, and piloting—the Guerillas, LLMPPTB, and David are able to buy America the space and time she needs to put all the lessons she learned from her mentors into action in order to trap the entity (Rivera et al. 2017).

The Maltixan battle is important for a number of reasons: first, it is one of many instances that underscore the collaborative nature of the model of heroism developed in *America*. Second, this particular story arc is notable because it brings together the diverse cast of characters that occupy central roles throughout the book. Far from making these characters token inclusions, Rivera, Quinones, and the rest of the creative team are attentive to the lives of their Black, brown, and queer cast to the extent that each main character is portrayed with some level of complexity. Readers become aware, for example, that Imani sometimes suffers from panic attacks and needs their friend Zu to calm her down; David was born a mutant, and although he is depowered, he is still a genius who values education; X'andria has aspirations to be class president and comes from a matrilineal line of women who have done the same.[8] These details add depth to each character and confirm that as unique individuals, they matter to America and her storyworld beyond their capacity to diversify the pages of superhero comics.

Finally, the team up on Maltixa also serves as the basis for this cast of characters to become a found family. Found or chosen families are distinctly queer forms of kinship because they eschew heteronormative ideals of the biological nuclear family and instead are defined by people bonded through experiences, shared understandings, and various forms of emotional, psychological, and intimate connection. Therefore, in line with Rivera's desires to demonstrate the ways one can find love outside of sexual, romantic relationships, America's found family allows her to experience intimacy, interdependency, and mutual understanding even in the absence of her mothers or lovers. Once America proves that she will not abandon Maltixa again, for instance, she and Imani share a warm embrace. At the end of issue #4, America stands with the Guerillas and LLMPPTB silhouetted behind her and, in response to a perceived adversary, states, "What you're not going to do is cause me and my people any more pain," while pointing at herself and those behind her (Rivera et al. 2017).

After leaving Maltixa, America travels to visit her best friend, fellow superhero Kate Bishop (a.k.a. "the real Hawkeye"); while not a Sotomayor student or member of the Chavez Guerillas, Kate is also part of America's chosen family. In fact, America uses her spring break to go to Kate's in order to recuperate and feel more like herself. In caption boxes over panels of their past adventures and current pizza pig-out, the text reads: "There are those connections that remain constant no matter what dimensions you're in. When everything is swirling with danger and chaos, be brave together. Slay monsters, the patriarchy, and extra-large pizzas" (Rivera et al. 2017). By the end of their spring break (mis)adventures, America embraces her friend saying, "You're my ride or die, Kate Bishop." Kate responds, "How about we're each other's ride and survive?" America agrees, "Yes, forever that" (Rivera et al. 2017).

Once America returns to university after her adventures with Kate and her trip to the Ancestral Plane with Madrimar, she decides to stop living alone and becomes roommates with David, who is now described in a caption box as "possible platonic life partner of America Chavez." As she stands in their new room, America says to David, "Bio family, chosen family and a room not in my van. Maybe it's all gonna be okay" (Rivera et al. 2017). Lastly, following another collaborative battle against a villainous university dean, America, David, and X'andria walk through campus with their arms around each other, and America says, "Prodigy, X'andria . . . you two have my heart. You saved my life. **Loved** me. Like, damn" (Rivera et al. 2018). All of these examples contribute to the queer feminist storyworld of *America*. Specifically, they work to redress the ways women's relationships in superhero comics have been overdetermined by heteronormative romance. They celebrate the ways marginalized people support and love each other in social contexts that may otherwise prohibit or exclude them from being recognized as worthy of love. And, like the incorporation of mothering and mentoring, the depictions of America's found family constructively work against hyperindividualist genre norms that distract from the need for intersectional, coalitional justice.

AMERICA AS THE NEW MESTIZA

Interwoven with the aforementioned aspects of America's queer feminist storyworld and her identity as a Latina superhero is the work of Chicana feminist philosopher Gloria Anzaldúa. Just as Rivera, Quinones, and the rest of the creative team willfully use "building blocks of reality" that connect America to real women of color and evoke queer forms of relationality, so too does their will to style echo Anzaldúa's borderlands thinking. Like the works of other borderlands theorists such as Américo Paredes and Rodolfo Acuña, Anzaldúa's foundational text, *Borderlands/La Frontera: The New Mestiza* ([1987] 1999), explores the impact of the formation and enforcement of the US-Mexico geopolitical border on the lives of Chicanx people. Further, similar to the French feminist philosophers discussed in the previous chapter, Anzaldúa's work is concerned with disrupting patriarchal binaries and deconstructing essentialist categories. Together, these aspects made *Borderlands* a revolutionary text. Because it was anchored in Anzaldúa's experiences as a queer Chicana and *tejana*,[9] *Borderlands* introduced a distinctly feminist approach to Border studies and a distinctly Chicana approach to transnational feminism. Anzaldúa aimed to center the experiences and epistemologies of those who straddle two or more cultures and value systems and to combine them with her mission to transcend harmful patriarchal dualities. This amalgam forms the basis of a "New Mestiza Consciousness" that is demonstrated throughout Marvel's *America*. In fact, as Ande Davis asserts, "America Chavez is, whether by design or happenstance, a considerably Anzaldúan character, navigating multiple identities, borders, and (*des*) *conocimientos* in her role as a superhero" (2021, 73).

More specifically, through their character design and backstory, Rivera, Quinones, and the rest of the creative team transcend national boundaries and evoke Anzaldúa's ideas of latinidad.[10] In their fluid use of both English and Spanish in the dialogue and back matter, the creative team disrupts the Anglocentric norms of the superhero genre and invites readers to traverse linguistic boundaries in ways that emulate Anzaldúa's writing. Similarly, the narrative choice to frame one of America's central conflicts as arising from a need for translation and a willingness to cross historical and cultural boundaries resonates with Anzaldúa's call for *nepantleras* ("those who facilitate passages between worlds") (Anzaldúa 2002, 1). Lastly, America's explicit battle against white supremacy, racism, and xenophobia as they manifest on her college campus not only echoes Anzaldúa's theories of borderlands subjectivity but also references the work of other border studies scholars concerned with the combined dangers of high-tech surveillance, nationalist policymaking, and border policing. Just as Anzaldúa saw mestiza consciousness as a fundamentally feminist perspective, so too do these qualities add depth to *America* as a feminist text.

According to Jason Dittmer, a nationalist superhero is one who "explicitly identifies himself or herself as representative and defender of a specific nation-state, often through his or her name, uniform, and mission" (2013, 7). Nationalist superheroes embody nation-states and become a symbol of a nation's ideals and norms. Consequently, in terms of the United States, nationalist heroes have been overwhelmingly white and male—Captain America is the most recognizable example. The original Miss America, Madeline Joyce, defied the tendency for nationalist superheroes to be male; however, as Dittmer notes, her presence did not really disrupt the white, androcentric status quo: "In many ways Miss America can be held as the icon of classically feminine nationalist superhero—subordinate to, and understandable in relation to, the men in her life" (2013, 31).

As discussed at the beginning of the chapter, Joe Casey and Nick Dragotta's decision to reinvent Miss America as Latina was undertaken to specifically address how they perceived American norms and ideals to have changed. While still draped in red, white, and blue and named for the nation-state she is presumed to embody, America Chavez is intended to represent a more multicultural nation (Brown 2021, 117). Her disruptive potential becomes obvious in issue #1 of Rivera and Quinones's book when, during her accidental field trip to a World War II battlefield, America steps in front of Captain America in order to knock Hitler's lights out (2017). This moment is an homage to the cover of the first issue of the Captain America comic (1941), on which Cap is depicted punching Hitler, signifying the idealized American commitment to fighting fascism. Yet Rivera and Quinones's page also subverts this legacy by demonstrating that there is nothing inevitable about the whiteness or maleness of that fight.

The true Anzaldúan nature of America's character design goes beyond the exchange of one set of identity categories for another, however. Grace Martin writes that "dressing a queer Latinx superhero in the US flag and calling her 'America' is rebellious, but not without a cause. She wears major symbols of US patriotism while simultaneously vesting them with new meaning that is relevant and representative of a nation of many ethnicities, many immigrant cultural legacies, and a significant Latinx population" (2020, 40). We can see this in America's attire. The repeated use of red, white, and blue, complete with white stars and gold eagle imagery, certainly summons the US flag and the country's national bird. However, the variations the creative team adopts to combine these elements also evoke the flags of other parts of the Americas. Flags that also combine red, white, and blue with white stars include Latin American countries such as Puerto Rico, Cuba, and Chile. Eagles are displayed on the flags of Mexico, Bolivia, Ecuador, and the US Virgin Islands. In incorporating symbols that represent parts of South America, the United States, and two US territories, America's costuming troubles ideological borders intended to restrict what is "American" to the contiguous United States, while also representing the diversity of Latinx people within the United States.

Further, these countries and territories, although distinct, share histories of European colonialism, Indigenous displacement and genocide, and participation in the transatlantic slave trade. As a result, their populations are indeed multiethnic and multicultural, and for Chicanas like Anzaldúa, this kind of *mestizaje* (mixing) does not threaten the integrity of one's identity but rather expands it, even if in fraught ways. Anzaldúa writes that la mestiza—the woman who accepts "this racial, ideological, cultural and biological cross-pollinization" in her own heritage—has "a plural personality, she operates in a pluralistic mode[;] nothing is thrust out, the good the bad and the ugly, nothing rejected, nothing abandoned. Not only does she sustain contradictions, she turns the ambivalence into something else" (1999, 99–101).

Beyond America's appearance, her backstory and subsequent discovery of her ancestry make this kind of mestiza consciousness clear. As discussed above, issue #3 of *America* explores how, as a child from an alien world, America found solace and belonging among various Latinx communities, including Puerto Rican New Yorkers and a family in Colombia. Nevertheless, as she reflects on her past, America thinks, "Still, I was a tourist everywhere. Lifting language and culture from the love of people who weren't my kin but held me as their own" (Rivera et al. 2017). Again, this seeming contradiction—of feeling both a part of and apart from particular Latinx communities—is, according to Anzaldúa, inherent to the mestiza experience. Moreover, as Melissa Castillo Planas argues, America's search for her roots across borders of ethnicity, culture, and nationality reflects "the realities of diasporic identities that are colored by non-nation-specific hybrid mixtures that are becoming more common in the United States" (2021, 8).

Once America works through the pain of losing her mothers and discovering the reason for Madrimar's absence, she is able to embrace her Planeta Fuertona heritage. Crucially, discovering this new layer of her identity does not cause America to abandon all the ways she came to understand herself as a Latina American. In simultaneously declaring, "*Soy Fuertona. Soy Latina. Soy America*," America embodies the kind of multicultural subject Anzaldúa describes. This plurality allows America to connect to something greater than herself, or, as Anzaldúa writes, to turn her "ambivalence into something else" (1999, 101). On the last pages of issue #12, America explains to Madrimar that she can feel a new level of untapped power and that she is ready to explore the extent of her connection to the universe. As America soars into the stars, drawn with her face turned upwards in a blissful expression, Madrimar states, "As a starling, you have the power to create **new worlds**," and a caption box reads, "Remember that you are both the galaxy and all the worlds still unknown" (Rivera et al. 2018). This page resonates with Anzaldúa's observation that the mestiza tolerance of contradiction and plurality can evolve into a heightened awareness and joy. She writes, "Living on borders and in margins, keeping intact one's shifting and multiple identities and integrity, is like trying to swim in a new element, an 'alien' element. There is exhilaration in being a participant in the further evolution of humankind, in being 'worked' on. I have the sense that certain 'faculties'—not just in me but in every border resident, colored or non-colored—and dormant areas of consciousness are being activated, awakened" (1999, 19).

Just as Anzaldúa begins to feel new parts of herself activate after learning to traverse her shifting, multiple identities, America too awakens to "Sanar and Berraca-level power" at the conclusion of her journey of self-discovery. For America, like Anzaldúa, the work required to synthesize all the paradigms that inform who she is also enables her to open up, to evolve, to "be the supernova" (Rivera et al. 2018). These parallels between Anzaldúa's experiences as a mestiza and America's superhero journey lend weight to Castillo Planas's assertion that America's "ultimate superpower" is her "Latinx identity" (2021, 2). If, as Dittmer suggests, superheroes are "co-constitutive elements" in American identity (2013, 3), then the creators of *America* have constructed their Latina character to highlight and celebrate the notion that American identity need not be defined by purity, stasis, and homogeneity but rather in terms of hybridity, malleability, and plurality.

America's adoption of hybridity and plurality also plays out in her speech and is another quality indicative of "the mestiza way." Anzaldúa writes that the mestiza, "being tricultural, monolingual, bilingual, or multilingual, [speaks] a patois" (1999, 100). Martin notes that similar to Anzaldúa's use of Chicana Spanish, which "challenges and bends the rules of proper Spanish and English to produce a unique identity marker," America's dialogue also features "non-standard code-switching" (2020, 45). In issue #2, for example, Agent Carter shuts down another agent who attempts to detain America; in response, America asks, "Need a little ***vivaporū*** for that burn?" (Rivera et al. 2017). As Enrique García explains, "vivaporū" is Caribbean Latino slang for Vicks VapoRub, and its use acts as a linguistic marker linking America to a Newyorican-Caribbean identity (2018, 174).

Martin similarly notes that the Spanish dialogue used by and among the inhabitants of Planeta Fuertona resembles "the heritage language of a hybrid, diasporic Latinx community" (2020, 45). The use of borderlands language adds complexity to the book's representation of Latinx culture and language by disrupting the assumption that Spanish is linguistically homogenous. The way language is printed in *America* also disrupts strict boundaries, encourages fluidity, and resonates with Anzaldúa's work. As Aldama demonstrates, the overwhelming trend in superhero comics featuring Latinx characters has been to designate Spanish through the use of asterisks or brackets and yet still print the text in English, or to include Spanish but immediately follow it up with an English translation (2017). In both instances English is presumed to be the norm, both for superheroes and their readers. It privileges those who are native or fluent English speakers, and despite giving the appearance of inclusivity, it never actually requires monolingual readers to extend themselves beyond what is presumed to be the default mode of communication.

America, however, makes use of Spanish without translation or typographical approximation. As previously discussed, America herself speaks in both Spanish and English, switching back and forth between the two, often in the same speech balloon, therefore disrupting the assumption that English is the norm for superheroes. Native and fluent Spanish-speaking readers who have long been marginalized linguistically in comics are brought from the margins to the center with this book. And for readers who are not fluent in Spanish, to truly engage with the book requires navigating between the taken-for-granted position of English as a default and a position of investigating, learning, and extending outside and beyond oneself to understand. In this, the book mirrors Anzaldúa's writing—it fluidly employs multiple languages. Sonia Saldívar-Hull asserts that in her efforts to establish "political, feminist social awareness," Anzaldúa writes so that "Spanish appears as casually as English," and her texts do "not easily admit those who refuse full engagement with the linguistic demands of Border language. . . . Anzaldúa mixes Nahuatl, English and vernacular Spanish as a larger cultural critique of how the dominant group enforces domination through language" (qtd. in Anzaldúa 1999, 8).

Rivera's similar use of Spanish and English throws into relief the ways representations of Latinx superheroes have been forcibly assimilated through language. Moreover, the creative team's use of borderlands language reclaims superhero comics as a space in which, and through which, readers may see the richness of their linguistic heritage come to fore, or they may venture across linguistic borders and deepen the co-creative reading process.

Even as a bilingual character, America still runs into linguistic trouble by the end of the book, a scenario the creative team uses to model the work one must do to bridge the divide between self and other. Throughout her time with Madrimar, America comes to learn that the reason Planeta Fuertona had to be evacuated was because alien invaders called La Legion "inhaled and annihilated the life force" of the planet (Rivera et al. 2017). Although the planet was put into an ice age to stop the advancement of La Legion, their eventual reawakening poses a threat that America must help address. During a fight with the aliens, Madrimar is taken into "the Red Haze" where La Legion congregate. Despite warnings from other Fuertonas, America goes to the power source of the planet, a sentient crystal called Uzam, to get a boost before pursuing La Legion. She is told that "La Legion isn't what they seem," and to stop the battle between species, America must discover the truth about the source of the conflict (Rivera et al. 2018). Her only choice is to fly into the amorphous, floating clouds of La Legion, a space she and the other Fuertonas know little about but perceive as a threat. In short, America must cross into a space Anzaldúa would call *nepantla*: "This in-between space, an unstable, unpredictable, precarious, always-in-transition space lacking clear boundaries" (2002, 1).

Once inside the cloud, America finds a liminal world where for the first time she can comprehend the language of La Legion, who explain that they were once allies of Uzam. Because the languages of La Legion and the Fuertonas were "at odds," La Legion could not explain their presence nor clarify that their consumption of the planet was merely what they needed to survive. America realizes that the pain La Legion and the Fuertonas have caused each other is rooted in ignorance and an inability to communicate. Thus, the red clouds also act as nepantla because, as Anzaldúa writes, nepantlas can be associated "with states of mind that question old ideas and beliefs, acquire new perspectives, change worldviews, and shift from one world to another." In her vow to resolve the conflict and make the situation right, America takes on the role of a *nepantlera*, one who can "facilitate passages between worlds" (Anzaldúa 2002, 1).

Although America's powers always give her the ability to travel in between and across dimensions of time and space, this sequence in particular is perhaps most indicative of the ways her characterization echoes Anzaldúa's theories of nepantlism. America's willingness to enter an in-between space enables a reevaluation of taken-for-granted ideas and beliefs, allowing America, La Legion, and the Fuertonas to relate to each other and shift towards an interconnected existence. Unlike many superhero comics wherein heroes actively work to police the borders between the supposedly disparate categories of good and evil, us and them, nepantleras like America "[honor] people's otherness," and lay the groundwork for "an alliance between 'us' and 'others'" (Anzaldúa 2002, 570). Of course, hot pink insect-like aliens like La Legion may stand in for any number of "others," and America's willingness and ability to facilitate peace in this context may seem too metaphorical to speak to real-world conflict. However, scholars like Davis also see in America's nepantlism the potential for concurrent "White supremacist 'othering' to be examined in full view" (2021, 71).

Although Anzaldúa deals with the psychological, sexual, and spiritual borderlands "present wherever two or more cultures edge each other," her work also begins with and is rooted in her lived experiences as "a border woman" who spent her life along the border that extends between the southwestern United States and Mexico (1999, 19). As such, her work is as much about exposing and critiquing the white supremacist patriarchal violence that upholds borders as it is about how mestiza consciousness has the power to subvert and traverse them.

The creative team behind *America* similarly explores borders, not only in terms of the cultural work required to cross them but also via the institutional power and violence invested in maintaining them. In issue #8 Dr. Billie Brightly, a thin, white woman wearing business attire, arrives at Sotomayor University as the new dean of students. Brightly cites an attack on the school and the absence of Professor Douglas as justification for imposing a curfew, increasing surveillance, and banning the use of powers that "disrupt dimensional borders" or, in Anzaldúan terms, nepantlism. She brings in a private security team to safeguard the new protocol and to keep Sotomayor "safe." Brightly's attempts to justify the revocation of students' rights to movement and privacy, as well as her use of force to "secure" the borders of the school, echo the discourse generated by American political leaders who point towards the need for national security as a means of validating the seizure of land, the disregard of citizens' concerns, increased militarization, and the violation of migrants' rights (Díaz-Barriga and Dorsey 2020).

As Anzaldúa notes, the threat to security is discursively constructed through racist rhetoric about borderlands people as being "the squint-eyed, the perverse, the queer, the troublesome, the mongrel, the mulato, the half-breed, the half dead; in short, those who cross over, pass over, or go through the confines of 'normal'" (1999, 25). Border studies scholars Miguel Díaz-Barriga and Margaret Dorsey give an example of this kind of constructed threat by noting how, in 2009, the Department of Homeland Security secretary described the border wall along the southwestern border of the United States as a tool to mitigate "the crossing of unauthorized persons, smugglers, and terrorists" (2020, 11). And, of course, more recently, the 45th president of the United States characterized the people of Mexico (i.e., those who threaten to cross the US border) as "drug dealers, criminals, and rapists" (BBC 2016). The reality, according to Díaz-Barriga and Dorsey, is that "border cities on the US side are among the safest in the nation," yet US policy makers persist in conceptualizing "the southwestern border region as a war zone" and the people "as a class apart" (2020, 3). As her primary target, Brightly uses similar rhetoric to describe America by first suggesting that she was "raised quite ferally" and then describing America's rising anger as the result of "the nature of [her] people to resort to violence" (Rivera et al. 2017).

While many of America's classmates are horrified by Brightly's treatment of America, others are emboldened by the dean's racist rhetoric and willingness to employ violence to ensure control. In issue #10 a group of white students carrying torches attempts to stop LLMPPTB from rescuing America. The leader, a decidedly angry young white man who goes by the handle @altgeekpepe online, says, "There's a new dean in town. We're taking our school ***back*** from you freaks," and describes America as Prodigy's "***illegal*** friend" (Rivera et al. 2017).

The layering of visual and narrative referents to the rise of fascism in the United States in the first decades of the twenty-first century is clear. On August 11, 2017, a group of white nationalists marched on the University of Virginia campus bearing torches, performing Nazi salutes, and shouting slogans like "White Lives Matter" and "You will not replace us" (Lind 2017). These sentiments are explicitly white supremacist and reveal a sense of entitlement to power. They are also indicative of ultraconservative ideologies that are fundamentally opposed to ethnic and religious diversity, as well as racial and gender equity. Like the white students at Sotomayor who were encouraged by the presence of Brightly, the white nationalists at Charlottesville were almost certainly emboldened by the 45th president, who refused to condemn their actions and instead concluded that among them, there were "some very fine people" (Phelps 2019). The online handle of the white supremacist Sotomayor student points towards the spread of these toxic ideologies throughout popular culture. The beginning of the handle refers to the "alt-right," or alternative right, adherents of a political ideology fundamentally opposed to multiculturalism, egalitarianism, and open immigration. The word "geek" summons the various online movements among "geek culture" that adopted alt-right ideology in their often-violent rejections of increased diversity in video games and comics. "Pepe" references a green cartoon frog that became an internet meme popular among alt-right groups (Woods and Hahner 2019).

The choice of *America*'s creative team to include these references to US alt-right movements in their depiction of students who align themselves with and in support of the implementation of racist and authoritarian institutional policies—against which America and her chosen family must fight—acts as a definitive condemnation. While the torch-bearing students, and their real-world counterparts, demonstrate particularly egregious forms of bigotry, Rivera and the rest of the creative team work to make clear how these groups are enabled by the institutionalized othering of marginalized groups. Further, by couching Brightly's villainy in safety protocols and a rhetoric of protection, the creative team of *America* shows how white supremacy actively works against fictional and real-world nepantlism. As Castillo Planas notes, in "uniting the theme of the oppressive system with that of the construction of the hybrid Latina identity, the comic reflects a reality that today is very present in the life of the Latinx: hatred and racism towards migrants, a constriction of options in the name of protection" (2021, 11).

The revelation of Dr. Brightly's alter ego and her evil plan to achieve global domination also highlights how white supremacist, capitalist systems simultaneously attempt to prevent and exploit the movement of borderlands subjects. In *Borderlands*, Anzaldúa details how migrants in search of better economic conditions who make it across the US border without documents are "caught between being treated as criminals and being able to eat, between resistance and deportation." More specifically, although it is illegal for undocumented migrants to work without green cards, many US industries actively exploit these circumstances: "Big farming combines, farm bosses and smugglers who bring them in make money off the 'wetbacks' labor—they don't have to pay federal minimum wages, or ensure adequate housing or sanitary conditions." Anzaldúa further notes how Mexican women who risk the journey are subject to sexual abuse along the way, and if they avoid prostitution, they often wind up in domestic labor, the garment industry, or doing hotel work for less than a livable wage (1999, 34).

These conditions are possible because, as Kristy Ulibarri explains, one of the functions of the border is to determine who is a "legitimate" citizen of the United States and who is not. When a migrant crosses the border without legal sanction, their status becomes "illegitimate," precarious, and unprotected. By deeming undocumented migrants as "illegal," US systems deny them the rights that make them recognizable as citizens and as human beings. In short, within the US security framework, migrants become invisible and thus expendable. Therefore, despite the racist rhetoric US policy makers use to frame Latinx migrants and borderlands subjects as dangerous and undesirable, migrants' needs for economic improvement combined with their invisible status allow entire US industries to profit from their exploited labor (Ulibarri 2022).

This dual strategy to uphold white supremacy and expand capitalist power plays out in issue #10 of *America,* when Brightly's safety protocols target America directly. America's refusal to abide by the new restrictions positions her as a supposed threat to the school and is used to justify her arrest, even though she was using her powers in an attempt to locate Professor Douglas. As a "violator" of the laws supposedly intended to keep the university safe, America is taken out of sight of her fellow students and is detained so that she cannot pose any further "danger." Once America is secured, Brightly reveals herself to be Exterminatrix, arch villain and CEO of the global Midas Corporation. Exterminatrix does not simply want to get rid of America; she has stolen America's DNA to make a cyborg army capable of employing America's powers in the service of conquering the multiverse for Midas.

In other words, by first framing America as a criminal, Exterminatrix is able to remove her from the population and then exploit America's abilities in the hopes of maximizing Midas's power and capitalistic gains. Because Exterminatrix is the primary villain for the first ten issues of the book, it is not difficult to see how *America*'s creative team intends to critique the disciplining and control of borderlands subjects.

Exterminatrix's character design adds another layer of meaning to her villainy that is important from an intersectional feminist perspective. As a white woman, Brightly/Exterminatrix demonstrates how gender is not in and of itself a basis for solidarity and shows how white women can be complicit in racist, capitalist systems of oppression. Her appearance (she is dressed head to toe in black latex) and name allude to the figure of the dominatrix—a woman who takes the dominant role in certain kinds of sexual encounters. Again, stylizing Exterminatrix in this way can be read as a critique of postfeminist assumptions that women who achieve power and dominance and who are unabashed about their sexuality are free from, or above, oppressive social systems.

Moreover, the means by which Exterminatrix is defeated underscores how coalitional Anzaldúan action can act as an anecdote to the politics of exclusion she represents. America is freed by the combined efforts of her Black and brown, queer chosen family. Hovering near death, she portals herself to the Ancestral Plane (an in-between space) where the cosmic spirits Berraca and Sanar offer her healing, and a vision of Madrimar reminds America that her power cannot be contained or diminished by her enemies. Once America regains consciousness, she uses the knowledge she has gained from her ancestors and mentors to defeat Exterminatrix and her cyborg army.

On the final page of issue #10, America explains that her ability to break free of Exterminatrix's control stems from the people she loves who give her strength to recognize her own power and worth (Rivera et al. 2017). This sequence echoes Anzaldúa's assertions that the role of the queer mestiza "is to link people with each other—the Blacks with Jews with Indians with Asians with whites with extraterrestrials. It is to transfer ideas and information from one culture to another" (1999, 106–107). To resist "the dominant white culture," marginalized people must come to know their own histories of resistance, as well as each other's, and work to "meet on a broader communal ground" (Anzaldúa 1999, 108–109). Describing the vision she has for Chicanas free of "the fictions of white supremacy," Anzaldúa writes, "I seek our woman's face, our true features, the positive and the negative seen clearly, free of the tainted biases of male dominance. I seek new images of identity, new beliefs about ourselves, our humanity and worth no longer in question" (1999, 109). America Chavez fulfils Anzaldúa's feminist aspirations insofar as she demonstrates the hybrid, multicultural nature of Latina identity specifically and American identity generally. Through her coalitions and bonds of friendship and family, America acts as a bridge between generations, races, genders, nations, and ethnicities.

The creative team of *America* does not construct these alliances in order to ignore or erase differences but rather to highlight how new connections can change worldviews. In imagining America as a new mestiza and focusing on her role as nepantlera, Rivera, Quinones, and the rest of the creative team can redress racist, sexist norms for nationalist superheroes; expand linguistic genre conventions; critique exploitative white supremacist politics of exclusion; and highlight transcultural feminist praxis.

CROSSING GRAPHIC BORDERS

America (along with several other titles centered on women, people of color, and the only other queer character to get a solo title at the time [Iceman]) was canceled after a relatively short run. Marvel chief creative officer Joe Quesada insisted that despite appearances, the cancellations were purely a result of low sales and claimed that readers "decide what survives" (Polo 2017). The implication, of course, is that because only a minority of readers purchased *America*, Marvel saw no benefit in publishing the title further. Combined with the fact that Rivera was the only queer Latina writer at Marvel, and America herself represents the intersection of several marginalized identities, it would be easy to reduce *America* to being a minor exception to the superhero rule. But to draw such a conclusion is to adopt a perspective that reinforces white supremacist, patriarchal, heteronormative, nationalist characters as being the most definitive of the genre. That perspective also ignores how meaning has long been and continues to be made in the margins. In this final section, I shift the focus from America's marginality relative to the white, straight, male majority to her place among other complex Latinx characters in the superhero genre and beyond. By examining the elements that align *America* with the tradition of other Latinx superheroes, I show how the character America Chavez is part of a larger legacy of superheroes fighting social injustice that extends beyond the borders of whiteness.

Understanding the feminist nature of this legacy becomes possible by observing how *America* echoes the character traits and storyworlds of prior Latina superheroes specifically, as well as how the book invokes feminist Latina comic book characters more generally. Exploring *America*'s Latinx feminist genealogy also affirms how Anzaldúa's work has crossed graphic borders and how comics centered on Latina heroines fit into a larger feminist literary tradition.

According to Aldama, taking this approach is not simply informative: "The more we familiarize (schematize) ourselves with the Latino ingredients that make up the whole pie, the greater the cognitive and emotive pay off for the reader-viewer" (2009, 81). I close by briefly discussing examples of America's presence in other types of media and merchandise, "free of the confines of the comic book pages (and the niche audience that reads them)" (Brown 2021, 122), and I conclude that America's potential to make meaning as a feminist superhero cannot be reduced to the ill fate of her solo title.

Aldama begins *Latinx Superheroes in Mainstream Comics* (2017) with an initial typology of Latinx superheroes that is illuminative of some of the criteria that America fits within a broader tradition of Latinx characters. He writes, "Whereas Anglo superheroes (often characterized as recast Manifest Destiny cowboy types injected with invincibility) tend to defend the nation but are somehow apart from it, Latino superheroes tend to be linked to the community" (7). On one level, this is true of America. Despite her patriotic garb, America's battles are never to defend the United States as a nation but instead are waged to protect her chosen family, her school, or her home planet. As discussed above, Imani, a young Maltixan, even makes a subtle critique of (Anglo) superheroes who stand apart from the communities they are meant to save. On another level, however, the alignment of Latinx heroes with their communities is complicated for America by the fact that she is an alien—an identity that, nevertheless, she also shares with many Latinx superheroes.

According to Mauricio Espinoza, superhero comics published since 1993 mirror the tendency of US horror and science fiction narratives to feature Latinx characters who are monsters, mutants, or aliens. This trend tends to problematically perpetuate negative depictions of Latinx people as "others" or invaders. For Espinoza, however, appropriation of "the alien-monster-threat distortion formula" has allowed Latinx superhero comics to subvert these harmful stereotypes in two important ways: as "resistance against the forces of cultural assimilation" and as "superheroic activism aimed at cultural empowerment and self-determination" (2016, 184). America's creators defy assimilationist tendencies by imbuing her with characteristics of the new mestiza. As Espinoza notes, cultural hybridity and "identities that are fluid, complex, and ambivalent . . . negate any attempts at stereotyping, simplifying, or essentializing" (2016, 184). Like other alien Latinx superheroes, America also "battles against radical, discriminatory forces that seek to oppress" her in her fight against Exterminatrix (2016, 192). Thus, while America does not belong to a singular Latinx community in the way that Bonita Juarez as Firebird does, she still acts as a metaphor "of Latino/a power and agency" and reflects some of "the ongoing real-life struggles and aspirations of the ethnic and cultural communities" that she represents (2016, 184).

The creators of *America* arguably improve on the next aspect of Aldama's typology: the tendency for Latinx superheroes "to be identified more with their bodies and emotions (usually raw and out of control) than minds" (2017, 7). Although America begins the book all fists and fury, her relationships with her mentors—Madrimar, Professor Douglas, Agent Carter, and Storm—help her to realize that knowing more about her ancestors, carefully planning her next move, and centering her mind are all crucial to being the kind of woman and superhero she wants to be. Like her white counterparts, this balance between body and mind allows America to evolve into a more well-rounded character. Similarly, whereas Aldama writes that white superheroes tend to be born special and Latinx characters more often must "*learn* to become and *work at* becoming superheroes," America's creators combine these qualities (2017, 7).

As a starling, America is born of and with extraordinary powers. Even at the beginning of *America,* it is clear that America has long been an active member of various superhero teams. However, she must also learn about her heritage, and she has to work at harnessing her full power. Maintaining these aspects of Latinx superhero narratives enables Rivera, Quinones, and the rest of the creative team to rectify the paucity of women mentors in the genre and to move away from hyperindividualistic models of heroism.

One final way America reflects the larger Latinx superhero community according to Aldama is through her costume: "Latino superheroes tend to accessorize in ways that root them in pre-Columbian histories and the Latino community" (2017, 7). Again, although America's costumes do convey some level of US patriotism, they also invoke the flags of several Latin American countries in their combination of colors and symbols. Further, in their adoption of street clothes and Sotomayor-esque accessories, America's creators root her aesthetic in contemporary Latinx culture. These commonalities help to shift the focus away from America as an anomaly and to anchor her in a larger tradition of Latinx superheroes.

Examining *America* in relation to other Latinx superhero comics also affirms its feminist legacy. As discussed previously, America's appearance and costuming add depth to her as a queer, Latina

American superhero; however, these attributes may also be read as a link to other feminist Latina characters. In her first appearance in *Vengeance* #1, America wears a bustier with a cropped jacket and tight, low-slung pants with a metal-studded belt (Casey and Dragotta 2011). This combination strongly resembles the superhero costume of Steve Ross's character Maria Sanchez, a.k.a. Chesty Sanchez, the star of his eponymous title *Chesty Sanchez* (1995). Maria's costume includes a bejeweled bra or bikini top worn under a short mariachi jacket. Her tight, hip-hugging pants are accessorized by a bullet harness that forms an x across her hips. Although America's outfits in her solo title are less reminiscent of Maria's, her donning of cropped tops and jackets emulates Maria's costume insofar as it "reveals her ripped abs" (Aldama 2009, 57). This is particularly apparent in issue #8, for example, when America stands up from her seat in the audience to address Brightly on stage. Quinones composes the page so that America stands in the center and draws the most focus. She wears a cropped, sleeveless hoodie and jacket with short denim shorts that make her chiseled abdominal muscles visible (Rivera et al. 2017). Like Maria, America is also tall (they are 6′3″ and 6′, respectively), with extraordinary strength; as Aldama says of Maria, "She packs a punch" (2009, 57). As an ex-luchadora (ring fighter), Maria's fighting style is informed by her abilities as a wrestler, a style America also adopts in issue #6 when Madrimar teaches her the power stomp (Rivera et al. 2017). Both Maria and America exhibit a combination of brains, brawn, and wit; maintain a focus on "family and cultural roots"; and use their powers to fight "exploitative capitalists" (Aldama 2009, 57–58).

America also shares similarities with another Latina superhero comic, Laura Molina's *Cihualyaomiquiz, The Jaguar* (1996). Specifically, both books center on Latina women who decide to attend university to further their personal journeys. While there, both America and Linda Rivera (the hero of *The Jaguar*) draw on their ancestral roots to wage battles against "local neo-Nazi villains" (Aldama 2009, 58). Regardless of her minority status among Marvel superheroes, America's similarities to other Latina superheroes point towards a rich body of literature that celebrates the power and worth of Latina experiences and stories.

The parallels between *America* and other female-led Latinx comics outside the superhero genre further align the book with a feminist tradition of storytelling. For example, America's occasional adoption of wrestling gear (like knee pads or lace-up wrestling boots) and

Madrimar's luchadora costume and performance evoke several of the female character's in Jaime Hernandez's *Love and Rockets* comics.[11] And similar to the way America admires and is saved by Madrimar, one of Jaime's main characters, Maggie, also looks up to and is frequently saved by wrestling phenom Rena Titañon. Enrique García notes that just as America displaces Captain America in clobbering Hitler on the battlefields of World War II, so too does Jaime's character Penny Century "deconstruct superhero masculinity" through her fantasies of becoming a superhero (2018, 175–176).

Most of the cast of characters in the comics of both Jaime Hernandez and his brother Gilbert are women, and like in *America,* they vary in race, sexuality, and embodiment. One of the primary locations of Gilbert's *Love and Rockets* comics is a fictional town called Palomar, which Brittany Tullis describes as "thoroughly matriarchal in structure, and the mythical forces surrounding the village seem intent on preserving and protecting this legacy of female power" (2018, 258). One could easily use this description in discussing America's all-women home world in the Utopian Parallel or her ancestral home Planeta Fuertona, created and protected by the love between two female cosmic spirits. Tullis's analysis of the language used in *Love and Rockets* also resonates. She suggests that Gilbert's use of Spanish and English in his Palomar stories makes the reader "aware of the ways in which interacting with the world in a second language can result in a transformation of perceived subjectivity" (2018, 263). As discussed above, *America* also explores this subjective transformation through the La Legion storyline, as well as in presenting its non-Spanish-speaking readers with the task of translation. Tullis similarly sees Anzaldúan influences in the *Love and Rockets* comics not only because, like *America,* they speak "to borderlands theorizations of US Latinx identity," but also because "the series itself can be linked to the process of *mestizaje* that Anzaldúa describes in *Borderlands/La frontera,* the product of transcultural fusion that in many ways shapes Latinx identity" (2018, 264).

Importantly, *America*'s resonances with *Love and Rockets* not only reinforce the book's place among other feminist Latinx comics; they also connect the title to a broader tradition of feminist Latin American literature. Tullis argues that *Love and Rockets* combines matriarchal social structures with "mythical, magical forces" in "the feminist vein of the fantastic established by Latin American women writers including María Luisa Bombal, Elena Garro, Rosario Ferré, and Isabel

Allende" (2018, 259). While all superhero comics contain fantastical elements, I suggest that *America*'s construction of women-centric worlds sustained by cosmic feminine power and its investment in ancestral knowledge, magic, and healing are distinctly feminist. I argue that like *Love and Rockets, America,* too, uses visual and narrative elements that "hearken back to the connections that can be drawn between femininity, the supernatural, and the subversion of patriarchal power, as evinced in the aforementioned literary tradition of feminist Latin American women writers of the mid-twentieth century" (Tullis 2018, 259). These parallels imbue *America* with more complex layers of feminist meaning. Further, the book's similarities to other Latinx comics and literature that have long sought to diversify representations of Latinx people help to diminish cynical reductions of *America*'s intersectional politics to nothing more than marketing.

As a character, America has also crossed over graphic borders into other kinds of media like animation, merchandising, and film. Brown points towards the impact America may have on younger audiences, in particular. Animated television shows like *Marvel Rising* (2017–present) show a version of the character that does not ignore her sexuality, "but it is also not emphasized. Conversely, her ethnicity is always front and center." America is framed "as a Latinx hero to be admired and identified with" (2021, 121–122). America also appears in merchandise aimed at children, including as a doll modeled on her appearance in *Marvel Rising.* Brown recognizes that "while the marketing logic of America Chavez merchandise may be driven by corporate profitability, the fact remains that America Chavez is helping normalize a belief in diverse superheroes" (2021, 122).

America's first appearance in the MCU was in *Doctor Strange in the Multiverse of Madness* (Raimi 2022), where she is played by Mexican American teen actress Xochitl Gomez. While there are differences between Rivera and Quinones's America and the one who appears on film, certain aspects of the comic do manifest. For example, the period of America's life depicted in the movie is her early teen years (but set prior to when the plot of *America* begins). As a result, America has far less control over her powers and is in greater need of protection from the adults around her who, in this case, are not Latinx people. In fact, Dr. Stephen Strange, a white man, becomes her primary protector, working in concert with the Sorcerer Supreme (Wong, an Asian man) and with an alternate-reality Christine Palmer, a white woman scientist. Because this version of the character is framed primarily by the danger she is in, much of what makes her a feminist superhero is lost, including any reference to her sexuality (save for a pride flag patch on her jean jacket) or what it means to her to be Latina. That said, the movie does not ignore America's queer Latina heritage entirely. In a scene where America and Dr. Strange are traveling through an alternate universe, they find stepping stones that depict a person's memories; when America steps on the stone, a vision of her two mothers plays on screen.

America's linguistic fluidity is also highlighted, and even Anzaldúa's sentiment that one must do the work of crossing linguistic borders to engage mestiza consciousness is hinted at. In a scene where America is seated with Dr. Strange and Wong in a diner, America speaks with Wong in Spanish, and the two note the absurdity of Strange's ability to travel the multiverse yet remain monolingual. The film also concludes with a scene in which Strange relinquishes control and encourages America to believe in her abilities. Like in the comic, it is America's recognition of her own power and worth that saves the day by the end of the film.

Although not the most complex appearance of her character, America's role in this first film paved the way for her future in the MCU. It is my hope that more of what makes *America* a feminist text crosses with her character as she continues to appear in other media: namely, the creative team's willful use of visual and narrative devices to construct a queer, feminist storyworld that is populated by a diverse cast of characters, expands norms for representing women's relationships, connects America to real women of color, and highlights coalitional forms of justice. Equally important to America's feminist characterization is her embodiment of mestiza consciousness. Rooted in Chicana women's experiences and ways of knowing, Anzaldúa's theories of mestiza consciousness and nepantlism enable America to defy essentialist categories, constructively transcend national boundaries, celebrate hybridity, and critique white supremacist, patriarchal systems in her own storyworld and beyond. Lastly, America's resonances with other Latinx superheroes and feminist characters help to widen the myopic view of her character beyond her marginal status among mainstream superheroes and point towards a complex, feminist tradition of representing Latinx people and their stories. In its ability to defy stereotypes, disrupt essentialist binaries, and break through exclusionary borders, *America* demonstrates an intersectional feminist politics that celebrates Latina empowerment and invites readers to expand their worldview.

3 | THE UNSTOPPABLE WASP

Diversifying Superhero Teams with Queer Science and Feminist Friendship

Traditionally, Marvel superhero teams have been male dominated. Multimember teams like the Avengers, the Fantastic Four, Guardians of the Galaxy, and the X-Men have been composed historically of more men than women, and when human or human-approximate, more white characters than characters of color (Cocca 2016, 14). Marvel superhero teams often are organized in paternalistic hierarchies that justify the sustained leadership of individual male superheroes who act as the "head." Even when male characters inflict violence on teammates or wreak havoc in the pursuit of safety and freedom, they are still often framed as though their continued leadership is natural and inevitable. While some recent titles have defied these norms, this chapter argues that few have offered as radical a departure as *The Unstoppable Wasp*. The book debuted in 2017 but, like other female-led Blue Age comics, it was canceled after eight issues.[1] However, the title was so meaningful to readers that a campaign was started to purchase the trades and vocalize demand for future issues.

Encouraged by writer Jeremy Whitley and editor Alanna Smith, readers and fans were so vociferous in their desires to see the comic continue that Marvel hired Whitley to restart the book in 2018. Now complete after an additional ten issues,[2] the book centers on Nadia who, after escaping the Red Room (a brainwashing and training program designed to turn young women into elite assassins) and discovering that her father, former Ant-Man Hank Pym has died, sets to work on forming a super-genius girl group.[3]

In its mission and membership, Nadia's team offers a powerful critique of the homogeneity of some superhero teams. Expanding the criteria for superhero teams, Nadia gathers brilliant young minds historically overlooked because of gender, race, class, sexuality, and disability to form G.I.R.L. (Genius In action Research Labs). However, what makes *The Unstoppable Wasp* different—and renders it a necessary intervention in Marvel superhero team comics—are the elements of its storyworld that make it a feminist text. The inclusion of a diverse cast of characters is crucial, yes, but "all new, all different" does not necessarily a feminist comic make. As scholars like Lillian Robinson have argued, many contemporary superhero comics have increased the numbers of powerful women in their pages but have generally done so while ignoring ongoing, real-world gender inequity, racism, and heteronormativity, making these "inclusive" comics postfeminist at best (2004).

The creative team of *The Unstoppable Wasp*, which achieved gender parity throughout the book's run, not only populates the book with an almost entirely female roster of characters; they also construct a storyworld with identifiable intersectional failings that can only be improved through feminist forms of justice. Writer Jeremy Whitley[4] kicks off Nadia's mission to recruit for G.I.R.L. with dialogue that explicitly recognizes the historical sexism of superhero teams and that critiques androcentric assumptions about intellectual prowess, heroism, and leadership. The purposeful expansion of who counts as a hero in relation to race, gender, sexuality, class, and disability also acts as an explicit corrective of superhero homogeneity. The choice to give each girl or woman in the book STEM-related acumen, and the inclusion of STEM-focused pedagogical features, also serves multiple purposes: one, dialogue makes clear the difficulties women face in science professions; two, the back matter of the book concretely combats this marginalization by highlighting real women scientists; and three, the choice to focus on girls and women in science effectively "queers" science in terms of ideal practitioners and methods.

Finally, through exploring intergenerational and cross-racial friendships among girls and women by posing complex, dynamic, and sometimes difficult situations, the book models the kinds of friendship feminist theorists have argued are crucial for collective liberation. Therefore, using feminist philosophies of androcentrism, queer feminist science studies, and philosophies of feminist friendship as interpretive tools, this chapter will center on a close textual reading of *The Unstoppable Wasp* in conjunction with analysis of contemporary discourses of identity to explore those elements that let us read the comic as a feminist text.

ADMITTING THE PROBLEM

While numerous scholars concerned with the representation of gender in superhero comics have explored the various problems resultant from overlapping systems of social oppression, far fewer superhero comics themselves have expressly done the same. Impressively, within the very first issue, *The Unstoppable Wasp* identifies and critiques one of the most pervasive (if sometimes elusive) problems of patriarchy—androcentrism. After being escorted to the immigration office in Manhattan by Ms. Marvel, a.k.a. Kamala Khan, Nadia suddenly finds herself fighting in a team-up with Ms. Marvel and Mockingbird, a.k.a. Bobbi Morse.

After they beat the baddie, Bobbi treats the girls to smoothies and discovers that Nadia is Hank and Maria Pym's daughter. Bobbi explains to Nadia that she is a longtime acquaintance of Hank's and that they used to work together on scientific research projects. After Bobbi clarifies that her full name is Barbara Morse, Nadia excitedly recites Bobbi's own research and superhero resume back to her, declaring that she admires and aspires to be like Bobbi. The composition of the panel in the middle row to the right of the page uses a close-up to focus the reader on Bobbi's face. This is reinforced by Nadia, who is drawn in profile in the lower left-hand corner of the panel facing inward towards Bobbi. Her downward glance and the tear slowly running down one cheek indicate that Bobbi is overcome with emotion. She admits to Nadia that no one "has ever said that I inspire them. And . . . people don't remember that I'm a scientist. They just remember that I used to be married to Hawkeye and I hit things with sticks. So that means a lot" (Whitley et al. 2017). The invisibility Bobbi experienced as a result of her association with her husband, and the collapsing of all of her talents into being "married to Hawkeye," is a classic example of androcentrism. While Whitley does not use the word itself, feminist theorists like Charlotte Perkins Gilman (1911) and Dale Spender (1998) have argued that androcentrism refers to a system of thought in which men are assumed to be universal subjects and male experience is assumed to be most representative of human experience. Because it posits male subjects and perspectives as the "norm" and other subjects and perspectives as derivative, or *abnormal,* the genderedness of this worldview is elided. Part of Bobbi's reaction to Nadia surely stems from having someone see her, *all* of her, for who she is rather than because of her relationships with men like Hank Pym or Clint Barton (Hawkeye).

Janet van Dyne, the original Wasp and Nadia's stepmom, also has plenty of experience with this problem: in issue #7 she says that "fake fanboys like to talk about how I'm only a super hero because I happened to be Hank's wife. [. . .] After that, the worse one is that I'm some kind of *team mom.*" Janet's "favorite misconception," however, "is that [she] doesn't have any useful powers. That [she] was somehow redundant on the Avengers" (Whitley et al. 2018). Here, as with Bobbi above, Janet describes the androcentrism at the heart of people's misconceptions of her: that she is only knowable and useful in relation to men, as a wife or a mother, and that nothing she did was of her own volition but rather to cater to men's interests.[5]

Whitley draws attention to the sexism inherent in these views by attributing them to "fake fanboys," and redresses the situation by interrupting Janet's numerous phone calls "to get things done" with an unexpected fight with two villains—proving not only that Janet can make real, positive change as a powerful businesswoman but also that she kicks ass as a superhero and does so for herself and for the benefit of other girls and women.

The prevalence of androcentrism in the Marvel Universe is also spelled out in another conversation between Nadia and Bobbi. In issue #1, as Nadia shows Bobbi around her lab, Bobbi begins to reflect on "the list." Compiled by S.H.I.E.L.D. (a worldwide law-enforcement organization), the list supposedly records the smartest people in the world. As Bobbi explains, the first woman on the list is way down at number 27! Nadia's alarm and disbelief are intended to convey the absurdity of this state of affairs, but Whitley gives Bobbi the dialogue to make the nature of this problem even more apparent. Lunella Lafayette, a.k.a. Moon Girl, recently disrupted the presumed accuracy of the list by taking a test left behind by super-genius scientist Bruce Banner, thus proving that she is the smartest person in the Marvel Universe, despite not having been previously recognized by S.H.I.E.L.D. Bobbi says that Lunella's new status helped her to realize the nature of the problem: "It got me thinking about who *made* these lists, right? Other guys, other SHIELD Agents, other super heroes. All these guys have known each other forever. They don't seek out new people." She goes on to say, "We gotta start looking for *our* people. We've gotta start looking for *girl geniuses*" (Whitley et al. 2017).

What Bobbi articulates here is a direct critique of androcentric assumptions about intelligence and heroism: if the measures for such qualities are determined by white men who assume the criteria are universally applicable to all types of people (when in reality they arise from white men's specific experiences and ways of knowing), then clearly only other white men will make the cut. The existence of such a list is further critiqued by Nadia, who says, "I'm not sure I believe in a test like that. Sure it can measure raw intelligence, but what about creativity? Knowing things doesn't save the world, inventing things does" (Whitley et al. 2017). This sentiment echoes the substantial critiques of real-world IQ tests, which have proven to be far more limited than they purport and have a history of racial and cultural biases (Sternberg 2015). Nadia acts on her knowledge about the list in issue #2 when she begins to recruit other girl geniuses who have been ignored, erased, or overlooked. In her first pitch, to roboticist Taina Miranda, Nadia plays a hologram presentation to explain her motives:

> The Avengers, S.H.I.E.L.D., A.I.M., nameless cabals, super-teams and illuminati. The greatest heroes and villains in the world. Also widely regarded as the smartest and most formidable minds in the world. Also, seventy-five to ninety percent male. Recently, a young girl named Lunella Lafayette was revealed to be the smartest person in the world. If she hadn't proved it all on her own, they never would have known. Because they're not looking for us. Even now, they put Lunella at the top of the list, but the rest of the list remains the same. That's where we come in. G.I.R.L. Genius In action Research Labs is dedicated to finding the brilliant girls and women who will not just save the world, but change it. (Whitley et al. 2017)

The problem Nadia articulates operates on two levels: first, it serves the narrative purpose of recognizing how the issue of sexism affects Nadia's world and acknowledging that something needs to be done to address it; second, Nadia's presentation also acts as a metacritique of mainstream superhero comics, which are indeed centered on male characters and made by male creators about 85 percent of the time (Cocca 2021, 7). Nadia's recruitment efforts are important from a feminist perspective not only because they drive the narrative around building a more diverse superhero team but also because they demonstrate the actions necessary to address this androcentric inequity. Rather than assume that supposedly universal or neutral parameters of intelligence, leadership, and technological acumen are enough to illuminate talent, Nadia begins with the recognition that such parameters have been overdetermined by one demographic and thus are incomplete.

Nadia's starting point for recruitment is what makes her mission equitable. Echoing S.H.I.E.L.D.'s recruitment methods, she selects members of G.I.R.L. based on acumen each candidate displays in their research, but because she made a point of first looking at research by young women (a group historically ignored), the composition of her lab is both more inclusive and more reflective of the various iterations of human genius (fig. 3.1).

In contrast to the comics analyzed by Robinson, *The Unstoppable Wasp* does not center on postfeminist "girl power" (which swaps female strength and visibility for collective and systematic justice), but instead embraces feminist critiques of structural inequities and models the types of action necessary to redress such issues.

Having said that, true to the norms of the genre, *The Unstoppable Wasp* does rely on female superheroic strength and action in many instances of conflict. As I discussed in the introduction, the debates around whether violence is mutually exclusive to feminist storytelling are complex and ongoing. If a society's problems are defined by overlapping systems of structural oppression, what good do flying, punching, and blasting really do? Does violent combat really count as feminist just because girls or women are doing the fighting? While it would be disingenuous to argue that *The Unstoppable Wasp* is entirely free from these tensions, its use of defensive physical fighting does depart from, and actively disrupt, the "fists first" strategy of most androcentric superhero comics.

Specifically, Nadia's active desire to avoid doing harm means that she employs alternative strategies—like deflection, dialogue, and humor—before ever resorting to fighting, which in her case is overwhelmingly defensive. The dialogue or narration supplied by Whitley throughout the book explicitly addresses structural issues of violence against women but never implies that "a punch to one white man's jaw" is a substitute for collective nonviolent action. Further, the frank way the comic deals with the cost of violence—physically, psychologically, and socially—productively disrupts charges about gratuitous or sensationalist violence in superhero comics.

Perhaps the most obvious example of these departures from the status quo takes place in issue #4. As Nadia tries to recruit botanist Priya Aggarwal at her family's Times Square souvenir shop, former pro wrestler and criminal-for-hire Poundcakes barges in demanding "protection money" from the Aggarwals. Instead of immediately donning her suit and initiating a fight, Nadia first attempts to talk her nemesis

Figure 3.1. Nadia explains her motivations for forming G.I.R.L. *The Unstoppable Wasp* #2 (2017).

down; she expresses admiration for Poundcakes's former career and empathy with the economic hard times that have befallen the wrestler. Nadia saves Priya's mother, Vandana, without throwing a single punch. Violence ensues only when Poundcakes's "former tag-team partner" and "current partner in crime" Letha discovers Avengers-butler (and Nadia's surrogate father) Jarvis outside the shop. Believing that they are about to be apprehended by the Avengers, Poundcakes and Letha go on the attack. Even as the situation escalates, Nadia attempts to dissuade the two wrestlers from using violence: "You don't have to hit me," she tells Poundcakes. Letha and Poundcakes choose to ignore Nadia and respond violently (Whitley et al. 2017).

The sequence depicting Nadia's response pairs detailed illustrations of the damage she inflicts with captions in which she describes her technique. As she explains the theory behind Krav Maga, the form of self-defense she employs, she asserts, "The most important thing to remember about Krav Maga is that it's about survival. It's designed to help a woman take down a man twice her size" (Whitley et al. 2017). Figure 3.2 shows how artist Elsa Charretier composed the panels in different shapes and sizes, most at a diagonal angle, which gives the viewer a sense of movement and encapsulates the action of the fight. Onomatopoeic words like SNAP!, KRAK!, and SMACK! all emphasize the impact of Nadia's strikes, as each mimics the sounds a body would make as it is punched or kicked. While Nadia devastates her opponents, these scenes arguably constitute what Henry Giroux characterized as "symbolic violence": a representation that "'attempts to combine the visceral with the reflective' as a means of incorporating elements of social critique" (qtd. in Mickwitz, Horton, and Hague 2020, 6). In this instance, Nadia's inner monologue makes readers aware of the need for a self-defense system designed specifically to help women escape violence from men, thus acting as a feminist critique of patriarchal culture.

Indeed, as scholar Martha McCaughey argues, women's defensive fighting and aggression may work to disrupt the sexist assumptions about women's bodies as passive, as objects to be acted upon, that contribute to cultural apathy in relation to violence against women (1997). That said, Nadia knows that violence is not a catchall solution and that unjust circumstances (like those faced by Poundcakes and Letha) are often what drive people to crime. In issue #8 we see Nadia and Janet visit Poundcakes and Letha in jail, where they have an honest dialogue about their uses of violence, about rehabilitation, and about the

Figure 3.2. Nadia explains her fighting techniques as she battles two villains. *The Unstoppable Wasp* #4 (2017).

implications of economic instability (Whitley et al. 2018). Their discussion, paired with Janet's decision to fully employ Poundcakes and Letha as security guards, undermines traditional superhero conventions that suggest villains are "unambiguously evil";[6] recruiting the "villains" may even be read as a kind of abolitionist feminist praxis.[7]

The sequence that begins with Nadia's attempts to recruit Priya and ends with Janet and Nadia visiting Poundcakes and Letha in jail is also indicative of the various departures from genre convention *The Unstoppable Wasp* makes by demonstrating the consequences of violence. Chris Gavaler writes that many mainstream superhero comics, like *Superman*, *Batman*, and *Spider-Man*, evolved to portray superheroes "ostensibly motivated to protect society, [who] appear to relish combat itself" (2018, 26). Further, while combat is almost ubiquitous throughout superhero comics, the effects of violence were initially seldom seen: When Superman threw a plane from the sky, where did it go? When Batman threw a man off a roof, what was the outcome? As Gavaler notes, "Though most superhero violence is non-lethal, even the broken noses and bloodied lips that would result from real-world punches often go undepicted." The cumulative result was "an oxymoronic genre of sanitized hyperviolence" (2018, 28). From a feminist perspective, this matters: "Most of these media have historically starred white, cisgender, heterosexual men, and through repetition have collapsed these four categories into a singular demographic profile and imbued it with the attributes of 'masculine,' 'American,' 'exceptional,' and 'violent'" (Cocca 2021, 26).

To perpetuate this trend of violence-without-consequences, therefore, is arguably androcentric; conversely, to depart from these conventions may be read as feminist. Combined with the fact that Nadia prefers to use violence as a last resort, the semirealistic depictions of the effects of combat throughout *The Unstoppable Wasp* push against the tendency for "sanitized hyperviolence." In the sequence discussed above, every punch, kick, and chop is shown—some in close-up—drawing attention to the pain, blood, tears, and crunching bones of the characters involved. Even Nadia, who is the superior fighter and who has advanced tech at her disposal, suffers from the fight and is shown in profile with blood dripping from her mouth and nose. These scenes are representative of almost all fight scenes throughout the book. Hash marks show up where scrapes and bruises would realistically appear, skin and muscles crinkle as punches or kicks land, and red trails leak from broken noses. Other physiological effects are also clear. For example, as Nadia and Janet visit Poundcakes, the wrestler complains that the injuries she's sustained may be career-ending, and Nadia is frequently shown falling asleep from the sheer exhaustion that comes from superheroic combat.

Of course, the costs of violence are not only physical. Nadia's early years in the Red Room caused trauma, and we see how the aftereffects take their toll on her and those close to her. In issue #7, for instance, Nadia is under extreme stress after her lab is attacked and her best friend is rushed to the hospital. In her panic, Nadia punches Janet in the face; this compounds Nadia's feelings of guilt, inadequacy, and trauma. And, well, Janet is left with a broken nose (Whitley et al. 2018). Similarly, in issue #4 of the relaunch, Nadia experiences a manic episode that is exacerbated by a lack of sleep and immense stress. When her friend and G.I.R.L. teammate Shay tries to stop her rampage, Nadia throws Shay across the room into a wall, spurring Alexis and Ying to try to stop Nadia; the scene ends with Nadia having assaulted both young women (Whitley and Gurihiru 2019). Once again, Nadia is overwrought and the strain her outburst places on the team almost brings them to a breaking point.

The intergenerational bonds at the heart of *The Unstoppable Wasp* also play a role in illuminating the lasting effects of violence. In issue #8 Nadia overhears a conversation that alludes to Hank Pym's past abuse of Janet. Nadia, who had no prior knowledge of these events, does what any teen would do and turns to the internet to verify what she's heard; what she finds isn't pretty. When she confronts Janet, Nadia is visibly upset. It isn't just that her paradigm surrounding her father is being torn apart (How can he be a great man if he abused his wife?), it is also that someone she loves, Janet, has suffered. Janet explains to Nadia that it has taken her a long time to process what happened and to find a way to live her life without letting the abuse she suffered determine her way forward (Whitley et al. 2018). Superhero violence in these instances is directly linked to trauma and is shown to be harmful to all those involved.

It's not to say that Nadia never relishes the chance to engage in combat.[8] However, throughout the comic, violence is largely reserved for defense; it is never framed as the primary or best way to solve problems, and honest depictions of physical, psychological, and social consequences of violence subvert androcentric superhero norms. As noted above, scholars like McCaughey even go so far as to argue that accepting women's use of defensive fighting and aggression can change "what it means to be a woman" and "throws open for critique the gender ideologies to which we have all become more or less habituated" (1997, 3). Like Nadia's mission for recruitment and the critiques articulated by Bobbi and Janet, depictions of violence in *The Unstoppable Wasp* call attention to the illusory universality of superhero norms (which are in fact rooted in male experiences and expectations), thus subverting them as a feminist critique.

Further, because the characters of the comic actively seek to redress these androcentric norms, *The Unstoppable Wasp* also avoids the postfeminist tendencies of many previous female-led superhero comics. These aspects of the book productively trouble superhero conventions and make it possible to read the comic as feminist. How the comic "queers" norms around science, technology, engineering, and math underscores the book's intersectional feminist politics.

QUEER FEMINIST SCIENCE AND QUEER FEMINIST SCIENTISTS

Feminist philosophers of science have long sought to dispel myths of pure objectivity and to illuminate deeply entrenched biases relating to scientific methods. As Cyd Cipolla, Kristina Gupta, David Rubin, and Angela Willey argue, "Science is not a static or unchanging object of analysis. Nor is it the nom de plume of objectivity. Rather, science is dynamic and changing, and it is always political" (2017, 6). The politics of science extends, of course, to determining who is considered knowledgeable or credible enough to conduct scientific research, and like the superhero genre, the normative face of Western science has overwhelmingly been that of white men. The Draw-a-Scientist Test shows that these stereotypes are socialized from an early age. The test had its origins in a pilot study from 1957 in which high school students were asked to describe their image of a scientist. Subsequent research from the 1960s onwards has charted a timeline of the age at which this image becomes cemented in young people. The research finds that children in kindergarten and the first grade are less likely to draw a stereotypical scientist: that is, a white man with facial hair, who wears a lab coat and glasses and who is exclaiming something like "Eureka!" while surrounded by lab equipment, formulae, and books. By the second grade, however, the stereotype begins to cement; how schools teach science combines with media images, social ideas, and expectations that children pick up from parents, teachers, and other influences. By the fifth grade, the stereotype is overwhelmingly fixed. A review of fifty years' worth of international research on the Draw-a-Scientist Test demonstrates that, across cultures, the stereotype of scientists being male has largely endured since the advent of the test in 1957. More specifically, the research shows that in Western cultures, students draw a white male—even minority students. However, children exposed to female scientists via a combination of classroom visits by women scientists and talks and readings about women's contributions to science and about their careers are more likely to draw both women and men as scientists (Steinke et al. 2007).[9] Thus, the composition of G.I.R.L. in *The Unstoppable Wasp* has immense potential to queer the normative ideals demonstrated by the DAST and to contribute to more equitable representations of scientists.

Cipolla, Gupta, Rubin, and Willey explain that to queer the sciences is to "unsettle some of our cherished givens"; it is to "trouble, disrupt, and reconfigure assumptions about nature, difference, species, and worldliness" (2017, 5). Scholar Mel Gibson similarly suggests that comics as a medium can disrupt the status quo: "Comics are able to present a queer space in which cohesive and diverse groups exist that are not dominated by representations of white, affluent, able-bodied, Western heteronormative girlhood" (2020, 2). Indeed, G.I.R.L.'s composition boldly disrupts identity-based assumptions about both scientific prowess and superheroism. More specifically, the girls differ in their histories, heritages, embodiments, and cultural values, but they share acumen for science, technology, engineering, and math, thereby reconfiguring the face of science as well as the standard for superhero teams.

Puerto Rican sisters Tai and Lexi live with their abuela in Washington Heights, New York—a neighborhood with a majority Latinx population from Puerto Rico, Cuba, and the Dominican Republic. Lexi is a fierce athlete and a budding entrepreneur with a need for speed. Her younger sister Tai is an exceptional roboticist and engineer who uses "scrap metal and cast-offs" to construct everything from elevators to robotic goalies. Born with cerebral palsy, Taina uses crutches and a wheelchair for mobility, further unsettling superhero norms that assume, as Charlotte Johanne Fabricius has argued, that "a superhero's agency—their identity, even—is based on the expectation of their bodily capability" (2020, 87). As is evident by the end of the book, Taina's use of mobility aids does not detract from her heroism and in fact enables her to save the day on more than one occasion.

Priya is a first-generation East Indian American from Queens, a botanist, a fashionista, and, at the beginning of the book, a closeted scientist who wants nothing more than a "nice, normal life" and "a boyfriend with a cool beard and big shoulders." After joining G.I.R.L. and being exposed to chemical gas, Priya develops the power to communicate with and manipulate plants, eventually inspiring her to begin training to become a full-time superhero. African American Priscilla LaShayla Smith (also known as Shay) is a physicist from Brownsville, Brooklyn, where she lives with her father and frequently destroys his apartment with her explosive experiments. Shay's intelligence and unique sense of style (strongly reminiscent of singer and artist Janelle Monáe) certainly make her a Black Girl Nerd,[10] but unfortunately these qualities also make it difficult for her to fit in at school. For Shay, joining G.I.R.L. means forming strong friendship bonds and even finding love.

Like Nadia, Ying "Last Name Unknown" was raised in the Red Room, and although she knows she was born in China, she has no memory of her family beyond that. She is also a trained assassin, has a weird sense of humor, and is a biochemist. Ying has Nadia and the rest of G.I.R.L. to thank for saving her life after a Red Room villain planted a bomb at the base of her skull that was expertly disabled by the team.

Finally, Nadia is a young white woman with Russian and American heritage who, after being raised in the Red Room, is adept at engineering, physics, chemistry, and biology, as well as various means of being an assassin. While Nadia is aware of her parents' identities, she never knew them, so in addition to building G.I.R.L. to correct discriminatory norms, Nadia also longs for a sense of family. Like Tai, Nadia lives with a disability. From the beginning of the comic, readers are made aware of the past trauma from which Nadia is recovering, but not until issues #4 and 5 of the relaunch does it become clear she has also inherited bipolar disorder from her father, making her a rare example of a superhero (as opposed to a villain)[11] with an official diagnosis of a mental disability (Alaniz 2014). Whitley and the rest of the creative team further queer the genre with Nadia's diagnosis by virtue of how issues #4–10 of the relaunch disrupt and blur supposed distinctions between "deviancy" and "normalcy." Like Taina, Nadia's disability does not preclude her from performing as a scientist or a superhero; rather, by learning to reorient her own understanding of what it means to "live" and by making use of resources like medication and therapy, Nadia redefines what "normal" can be for a super-scientist-hero.

Another aspect of the team that further queers both the superhero genre as well as representations of scientists in popular culture is the inclusion of varying sexualities as a meaningful part of the girls' identities. Anna Peppard describes how the establishment of the Comics Code Authority made explicit explorations of sex and sexuality in mainstream superhero comics virtually impossible until the late 1980s. Unfortunately, much of the content created after the waning of the code "had a decidedly misogynistic or homophobic flair" (2020, 6). Even now, as dominant discourses on sexuality have begun to diversify, Peppard argues that "the mainstream embrace of sexuality as a meaningful aspect of superheroic identity remains decidedly tentative" (2020, 6).

Popular representations of female scientists (in film, for instance) have also been problematic. As Holly Hassel has argued, a readily observable trope in action films is the "babe scientist" who serves as "a romantic interest or buddy, or a combination of the two" for a male protagonist (2008, 191). Echoing Hassel, Jeffrey Brown notes that "the young and sexy female scientists in films . . . explain complex plot devices and help the hero achieve his goals," giving her the appearance of having equal significance to her male counterpart. Brown further suggests, however, that "the authority granted female characters with PhDs is really a chimera as the films typically show her as 'too bookish' and ultimately she needs to be saved by the more impulsive hero who survives on gut instincts" (2015, 68). In short, where female scientists appear, they are characterized as heteronormative objects of desire for male protagonists, and while they initially seem to be valued for their work, their credentials are frequently subsumed under their sexiness, helplessness, or both.

Refreshingly, throughout *The Unstoppable Wasp,* readers are given clear indications of many characters' sexualities in ways that neither objectify them nor reduce their capacity as hero-scientists. While some of the characters in *The Unstoppable Wasp* do exhibit heterosexual desire, they are not framed as the only or most important sexual subjects. In issue #7, for example, we see Janet spending her "me time" in a bubble bath reading "muscle magazines" featuring male superheroes like the Hulk and Thor, with words like "hot," "hottest," and "hunky" visible on the covers (Whitley et al. 2018). As mentioned above, Priya states in issue #3 that her desires are for "a boyfriend with a cool beard and big shoulders" (Whitley et al. 2017). And in issue #10 of the relaunch, Taina is shown berating her new boyfriend for the (mechanical) "disaster" she finds under his hood (Whitley et al. 2019).[12] Each of these examples appears in single panels on multipanel pages, suggesting that they are not more important than anything else that appears on the page. These scenes give us further insight into the characters in question, but they are not remarked on or called attention to, freeing the characters from being overdetermined by their sexualities and avoiding undue focus on heterosexuality, in particular.

In fact, the most central romantic relationship in the comic is established through the mutual desire between Shay and Ying.[13] Beginning in issue #8 with an awkward hug and then a date night dancing, Shay's and Ying's attraction is clear. In issue #1 of the relaunch, readers are presented with a full-page spread of Shay watching Ying sing and dance as she writes on a white board. The third horizontal panel on the page is particularly evocative of Shay's feelings, as it provides a close-up of Shay resting her head in her hand with hearts in her eyes and hearts on either side of her head as she muses about whether she should make the next move. By the conclusion of the scene, Priya has arrived to tell both girls they are needed and calls Ying Shay's "little girlfriend" (Whitley et al. 2019). Ying herself uses the word "girlfriend" to describe Shay later in issue #3, a choice Shay reacts to once again with big glistening eyes, and in a speech balloon filled with pink hearts she remarks, "She called me her girlfriend!" A few pages later there is another full-page spread of Shay and Ying discussing the use of the word, clarifying their desires, and ending with Shay kissing Ying on the cheek (Whitley et al. 2019).

In issue #6 of the relaunch, nine of the twenty pages are devoted to Shay and Ying's relationship as they meet Shay's mother and Shay attempts to come out as lesbian. While Shay's mother reacts unsupportively and reveals herself to be homophobic, Shay and Ying are still able to strengthen their relationship. The last page of the issue is composed of three panels, the top one of which takes up two-thirds of the page and encapsulates Ying and Shay's first kiss against a background of what are commonly known in shojo manga as love bubbles (Whitley et al. 2019).[14] The amount of space devoted to Ying and Shay's relationship radically centers girls' queer desires, disrupting the status quo of positioning young women as objects of male desire. Other members of G.I.R.L. are excited for the relationship and affirm Ying and Shay's attraction to each other.[15] In this way, the comic queers mainstream superhero comics not only by creating a focus on a lesbian couple but also by doing so in a celebratory way.

As Ross Murray has demonstrated, being able to identify lesbian relationships in superhero comics was often a tenuous task, and even when sapphic couples like X-Men's Mystique and Destiny were introduced, the "deviancy" of lesbianism was eradicated with one woman's demise (2011). In addition to Ying's and Shay's existence, and the fact that both girls live and thrive as lesbians, the quality of the representation of their relationship also departs from genre norms. Sarah Panuska notes that even as mainstream publishers have slowly increased the number of LGBTQIA+ characters, "expressions of intimacy are rare, as are direct references to contemporary or historical LGBTQ culture" (2020, 130). Kisses, hugs, and holding hands are, as noted above, an observable part of Shay and Ying's relationship.

As a couple, they also evoke contemporary LGBTQIA+ culture. Shay's character design, for instance, visually evokes Janelle Monáe, a queer Black singer, actor, and artist whose style is informed by dandyism and tuxedo pieces largely in black and white. Moreover, Monáe's creative ethos evokes Afrofuturism, a movement that mobilizes imagination to resist and invert normative thinking (Szaniawska 2019). Thus, Shay's presentation queers heteronormative expectations of girls' embodiment and signals Black liberation.[16] Another example can be found in the scene discussed above in which Ying sings along to music; her speech balloons contain the lyrics to a song called "Closer" by Canadian singers Tegan and Sara, both of whom are openly gay women. Finally, it is also important to note how Ying's and Shay's sexualities disrupt "babe scientist" stereotypes. While they become subjects of desire for each other, theirs is a mutual attraction that does not strip either of her agency, her abilities as a scientist, or her role as an active member of their team.

As the titular hero, Nadia also disrupts norms of representation—Whitley characterizes her as asexual and aromantic. Nicholas Miller writes that even as mainstream superhero comics attempt to broaden representations of identities, representations of asexuality have been sparse at best and pathologizing at worst. Even when asexual characters are identified in comics, sex-normative views of the world[17] often perpetuate stereotypes of asexuality as abnormal or as a disorder. More specifically, asexuality is often framed as a "lack" or "deficit," and asexual characters are often depicted as entirely passionless (Miller 2017). Writer Jeremy Whitley took to Twitter to explain why it is important that Nadia is both very passionate, and asexual and aromantic: "[I] was thinking about Nadia being an ace character and how I think it's important because she's a character who's shown to be caring and passionate, not playing into the stereotype that aces are robotic and don't feel" (Whitley 2021c). He goes on to say that being "ace" (shorthand for asexual) does not stop Nadia from engaging in physical affection:

> Obvs she's a hugger, a snuggler, and somebody who is actually very hungry for the physical contact often associated with a romantic relationship but . . . I do also see her as aromantic or perhaps more specifically Quoiromantic. She loves a lot of people platonically and affectionately in a way that might be mistaken by others as romantic, but doesn't have much interest in pursuing those relationships as romantic. (Whitley 2021a; 2021b)

Whitley's desire to push back at stereotypes is admirable, but whether it is immediately obvious to readers of *The Unstoppable Wasp* that Nadia is asexual and aromantic is perhaps debatable. The first indication that she is ace appears in issue #2 when Jarvis questions whether her time might be better spent engaging in "normal" dating activities like "kissing boys." Nadia sticks her tongue out in disgust and says, "Jarvis . . . *Ewww.*" Jarvis asks whether Nadia is still afraid of cooties, to which she responds, "No! It's not cooties, I'm just not——you know what? I'll let you know when I start being more interested in kissing someone than quantum physics, okay?" (Whitley et al. 2017). There is no other dialogue explicit to this effect throughout the rest of the book,[18] calling into question how visible this identity actually is.

However, one could argue that Nadia's asexuality is observable in alternative ways that expand norms for representation. Whereas the other girls express romantic or sexual desires or form nonplatonic relationships, Nadia instead exhibits excitement about her work, affection for her friends, and invests in her own flourishing. Despite Jarvis's initial teasing, no one pressures Nadia to engage in sexual or romantic pursuits, and she is never characterized as "deviant" because her interests diverge from sexual or romantic connection. To echo Miller, the creative choice to give Nadia "visible passions and pleasures helps push back against pathologized narratives of asexuality as a disorder, and opens up liberatory possibilities for what asexual lives and asexual experiences might look like in popular culture" (2017, 371). Does Nadia's asexuality add to representations of queer superheroes? Miller warns against uncritically collapsing asexuality and aromanticism into LGBTQIA+ identity structures in relation to comics. That said, from the perspective of queer feminist science studies, Nadia's asexuality and aromanticism do productively reconfigure representations of "normalcy" by calling into question taken-for-granted assumptions about human sexual desire, thus still making it feasible to claim that she queers the genre.

By returning to an understanding of queering as disrupting and reconfiguring norms, it is possible to observe one final way the comic resonates with the aims of queer feminist science studies. Cipolla, Gupta, Rubin, and Willey argue that "the ubiquity of scientific narratives and their power in shaping the parameters of what we think about the distinctions between nature and artifice, biology and culture, time and space, and mind and body, and other vital issues means that science studies must roam far beyond institutions of sciences" (2017, 5). *The Unstoppable Wasp* embraces this directive by inviting readers to engage in science studies within its pages. Throughout each issue, various scenes feature captions displaying Nadia's science facts. Rather than detailing the fictitious science behind objects like the Tesseract, Nadia's science facts give basic explanations of real-world objects and processes, helping to educate readers in the same STEM areas in which G.I.R.L. is so invested.

In issue #1, for example, artist Elsa Charretier and colorist Megan Wilson include two circular panels that, through their content and coloring, evoke x-rays of the joints of a giant, evil robot. Adjacent to both x-ray panels are narrative captions containing "Nadia's neat science facts," which explain the real-world differences between "r-joints" and "v-joints" and why each is advantageous for robotics (fig. 3.3) (Whitley et al. 2017). While several of Nadia's science facts are humorous (e.g., "Holograms are awesome"), most are also truly informative and range from discussing static electricity to energy consumption to road friction, allowing readers to learn about the science of their own world in accessible, entertaining ways.

Perhaps even more impactful is the back matter in each book. Scrapping the traditional letter column, Whitley and the various artists on the book elected to create an end section, titled "Agents of G.I.R.L.," that profiles real women scientists (fig. 3.4). As discussed previously, these inclusions have immense potential to disrupt socialized biases about scientists. Across eighteen issues, twenty-five cis and trans women scientists of differing ages, ethnicities, sexualities, and backgrounds are interviewed about their specialties and why it's important for young women to be involved in STEM fields; about which feminist

Figure 3.3. Nadia's fun science facts include details about real-world technology like "r-joints" and "v-joints." *The Unstoppable Wasp* #1 (2017).

AGENTS OF G.I.R.L.

Oh my gosh, what a cliffhanger! Hey, new friends, it's Nadia! I'm so glad to see you again. You look great! Winter must really agree with you! Don't worry, Team Wasp will be back next month to bring you another chapter of our story, but in the meantime, I have some more really special lady scientists to share with you. These new Agents of G.I.R.L. are extra amazing, so please check out what new recruits Jin Kim Montclare (@jkmontclare) and Raychelle Burks, Ph.D. (@DrRubidium) had to say!

WHAT KIND OF WORK DO YOU DO?

Jin: I am a professor of chemical and biomolecular engineering, and I work on engineering new types of proteins. Proteins are important biomolecules that exist in foods such as eggs, milk and meat as well as in all living organisms--including humans. My research focuses on creating a protein that can detoxify toxic nerve agents such as pesticides as well as creating new protein biomaterials that can deliver important therapies to treat human disorders.

Raychelle: I'm a chemistry professor and spend my time teaching and doing research. My area of focus is analytical chemistry, specifically designing detection techniques for compounds of forensic interest (drugs, explosives, chemical or biological weapons, etc.). My research group is currently focused on using color image analysis as a stand-in for colorimetry--and we're using cell phones to do it!

WHAT EXCITES YOU ABOUT YOUR WORK?

Jin: Two things really excite me: that I get to 1) work on research that can ultimately help people (by removing toxins or treating diseases) and 2) interact with a wonderful group of young aspiring engineers and scientists making exciting advances in research.

Raychelle: I love the challenge of coming up with low-tech, affordable, reliable and portable detection schemes. It gives me and my students an opportunity to play super-science MacGyver!

WHY ARE YOU PASSIONATE ABOUT YOUNG WOMEN GETTING INTO SCIENCE?

Jin: Being a woman in STEM, I feel fortunate to be doing what I love to do as an educator and researcher! My path was made possible through the support of my mentors from K-12 to now, so I do my part by encouraging other young women to pursue STEM. More than half the students I mentor directly at NYU are women, and I am quite proud of it! I have also actively engaged in mentoring programs including STEM Women on Fire as part of the Ultimate Mentor Adventure Contest! I work with science teachers at local K-12 schools to help effectively convey scienctific ideas and make them exciting. In fact, in collaboration with InSchoolApps, we made an app called LewisDots for kids to make chemical structures and learn about bonding!

Raychelle: As a black female scientist, I am familiar with the historical and current barriers to our access and advancement in STEM career fields. Margot Lee Shetterly's great book *Hidden Figures* (now a feature film) speaks to such struggles. While gains have been made in accessibility, we have a long way to go in making STEM careers equally within reach for woman of color and other under-represented minorities.

WHAT FEMALE SCIENTISTS (REAL OR FICTIONAL) HAVE INSPIRED YOU IN YOUR WORK?

Jin: When I was little, my hero was Marie Curie. She not only won a Nobel Prize in Physics, but years later, she was awarded the prize in Chemistry, too! Very few individuals are awarded the Nobel Prize, so to earn two in two different fields is AMAZING! In terms of inspiration for my work, my graduate advisor Alanna Schepartz has mentored me through my own dissertation work on miniature proteins at Yale while serving as an incredible role model. Finally, the Nobel Laureate Ada Yonath, who was responsible for determining a high-resolution structure of the ribosome (a gigantic complex that helps decode DNA into protein), is an amazing source of inspiration because my group employs the insights from such structures to make cool proteins in the lab.

Raychelle: When I was little, I didn't know of any female scientists--talk about hidden figures! It wasn't until I was a senior in high school that I discovered Dr. Mae Jemison, medical doctor and NASA astronaut. Before that, I looked to my favorite fictional super-brain, Agatha Christie's Miss Marple, for inspiration. She is one hell of a quantitative thinker! When I'm in need of inspiration, I look to Jeannette Brown's *African American Woman Chemists*. I am also inspired by my science friends: Dr. Danielle Lee, Dr. Stephanie Page, Dr. Kate Clancy and Dr. Malika Jeffries-El.

DO YOU HAVE A FAVORITE EXAMPLE OF CLEVER/UNUSUAL/OR NONSENSICAL USE OF SCIENCE IN COMICS?

Jin: I thought it was clever that the characters from X-Men had super-powers due to mutations. It made absolute sense to me since mutations in DNA can cause changes in living things in order to adapt (like a giraffe's neck to allow them to reach the treetops for food).

Raychelle: I'm a sucker for super-hero-by-vampirism. Okay, that sounds splashier than super-hero-by-blood transfusion. She-Hulk fits the bill! Hulking out is a bit like a blood-borne disease? It almost makes sense, except...it totally doesn't! I love these sci-fi stretches!

HOW LONG HAVE YOU BEEN READING COMICS AND WAT WAS YOUR FIRST COMIC BOOK?

Jin: I started reading comics when I was in elementary school with *Archie Comics*, but my favorites have been *Sandman* and *Lucifer*...and of course *Rocket Girl* and most recently MOON GIRL & DEVIL DINOSAUR! For MG & DD, I love that the protagonist is a girl STEM genius and I even get consulted on it for inspirational scientist/engineer quotes (because my husband, Brandon Montclare, is writing it)!

Raychelle: I started reading comic books in high school, jumping into the Wonder Woman reboot by George Pérez when I stumbled across in my local public library. It caught my eye because I grew up watching reruns of Linda Carter's *Woman Woman!*

Please send all of your suggestions for girl, lady or lady-identifying geniuses in science and technology to us at MHEROES@MARVEL.COM and mark your letters "Okay to Print"! You can also tweet at us using the hashtag #AgentsOfGIRL.

Until next month, *do svidaniya!*

Nadia

Figure 3.4. The back matter of the comic includes the "Agents of G.I.R.L.," which features interviews with real women scientists. *The Unstoppable Wasp* #2 (2017).

scientists (both real and fictional) inspire them; and about their relationships to comic books. The women interviewed range professionally across STEM, representing fields such as engineering (environmental, chemical, electrical, materials, nuclear, aerospace), astrophysics, and biology. They discuss the real hurdles they have faced individually as well as the stereotypes that challenge women in STEM generally. They are also all passionate about making STEM and representations of scientists in popular culture more inclusive both for the benefit of girls and women and with the mission of conducting better science. As trans, queer activist and environmental engineer Julie Johnston states, "Science is all about thinking outside of the box and exploring interactions and diversity in the natural world. We need women, non-binary folks and every other underrepresented group to be a part of this exploration. Our unique perspectives in the world change the way we perceive and approach our scientific curiosity. In these subtle moments, the diversity of personal identity shines and reshapes scientific investigation" (Whitley et al. 2019). The "Agents of G.I.R.L." interviews demonstrate the variety of ways science is being done both within formal institutions and beyond; they queer normative expectations for who can do science, and how; and they invite readers, particularly girls and women, to participate in scientific discussions. This final element also powerfully queers characterizations of the readership of superhero comics who have been historically framed as young, white, and male.

Cumulatively, the inclusion of real-world science facts, the choice to construct a diverse team of characters, and the use of the letters page to actively combat women's marginalization in STEM lend further weight to a feminist reading of *The Unstoppable Wasp*. Like queer feminist science studies more broadly, the comic actively calls into question "a) what counts as legitimate scientific knowledge; and b) which kinds of people, bodies, and institutions can conduct scientific research in the first place" (Cipolla et al. 2017, 6). In doing so, *The Unstoppable Wasp* contributes to much-needed shifts in how science and scientists are represented while also carving out more space for girls and women in mainstream superhero comics, both on and in front of the page.

FEMINIST FRIENDSHIP

Despite being a titular comic, and thus drawing more attention to Nadia's character arc, *The Unstoppable Wasp* nonetheless cultivates a thorough focus on what it means for G.I.R.L. to be a team. As discussed above, not only does G.I.R.L. depart from superhero team norms in its diversity, but its inclusion of intergenerational mentoring, alternative kinship bonds, and feminist friendships also radically bends genre conventions. Jennifer Stuller writes: "Generally, teams of male heroes are brought together by chance (The A-Team) or because of convenience (The Justice League of America). They participate in missions together, simply because it's pragmatic to combine their skills. But women's desire for companionship . . . and tendency to support and nourish the skills of those around them has raised the status of cohorts, teammates, and sidekicks" (2010, 8). Shared scientific interests and a desire for companionship do draw the characters of G.I.R.L. together, but what bonds them—such that they support and nourish each other's growth—is the honest, and sometimes fraught, work of establishing truly feminist friendships. A large part of that process involves the presence of Janet and Bobbi, who act as mentors to the girls, again marking a departure from superhero norms. Stuller explains that superwomen are often raised by fathers or stepfathers or male mentors; whereas mothers are more prevalent in the origin stories of male superheroes, they are overwhelmingly absent in the stories of girls and women (2010, 9). Including Janet and Bobbi as integral to the success and flourishing of the members of G.I.R.L. once again rectifies androcentric genre norms and pushes back against wider cultural trends of erasing older women(s knowledge).

The marginalization and erasure of older women are noticeable in film, for instance. Anne Lincoln and Michael Allen suggest that older women in the film industry face a kind of "double jeopardy": that is, the combination of their age and gender overwhelmingly works against them in gaining substantial roles or critical acclaim after a certain age (2004). Jeffrey Brown confirms that the invisibility of older women is observable in action films specifically (2015, 12–15). "Casting" Janet and Bobbi (whose ages are not specified but who are likely meant to be in their 40s) as active superheroes who care for and mentor younger women thus disrupts these ageist trends in action-oriented popular culture.

Moreover, Whitley's narrative framing of Janet and Bobbi as supportive mentors does not revolve around their supposed inherent maternal instincts. While it is the case that mother-daughter relationships are underrepresented in superhero and action media, it is also true that Western popular culture exhibits a dearth of intergenerational female relationships that do not require the older woman to exhibit normative traits of maternality. As Rosemary Gillespie notes, "In Western societies, pronatalist cultural discourses establish a template of femininity, whereby motherhood is perceived to be the cornerstone of adult femininity and the desire for motherhood and the role of mothering central to what it means to be a woman" (2003, 123–124). Narrative captions and dialogue make it clear that neither Janet nor Bobbi feels that desire. In issue #7 captions reveal Janet's thoughts on the matter: "I've never been the maternal type. I never had kids. I was always doing my own thing." Even by the end of issue #8, after Janet has told Nadia that she loves her, captions again reveal Janet's stance on motherhood: "I never really wanted a kid and I still don't. But I meant what I told Nadia. I love her. She gives me hope" (Whitley et al. 2018). Similarly, in issue #2 of the relaunch, we see Bobbi hugging Ying as she wonders what it would be like to have a mother; Bobbi replies, "Look, I'd make a terrible mom and I'm probably not the most dependable mentor. But I'm great at gathering information, and if there's any information out there about where you come from, I'm gonna find it" (Whitley et al. 2019).

Janet's and Bobbi's articulations of having no desire to be mothers, and the contexts in which they make these statements, are important for at least two reasons. First, Gillespie points out that "women who choose to be childfree are frequently seen by others as unfortunate or psychologically flawed, selfish, and deviant" (2003, 124). Even though both women state that they do not desire to be mothers, they do so in scenes where they are also offering the girls guidance, support, affirmation, affection, and immense amounts of time. There is nothing selfish about Janet and Bobbi's behavior; in fact, they are incredibly devoted to the well-being of each member of G.I.R.L., and they articulate their willingness to do whatever they can to support their mentees. Second, neither woman is characterized as psychologically flawed, nor is her childlessness framed as deviant. Throughout the book both Janet and Bobbi discuss the challenges they've faced and the trauma they've endured, but they do so openly, honestly, and in terms that are never tied to reproductive capacity. Whereas Black Widow calls herself a "monster" in reference to her sterility in the Marvel film *Avengers: Age of Ultron* (Whedon 2015), neither Janet nor Bobbi is ever made to appear "unnatural" because of their childfree statuses. From a feminist perspective, the choice to include childfree women as mentors to teen girls is important because it represents "a positive feminine identity separate from motherhood," thus broadening representations of women (Gillespie 2003, 133).[19] However, familial dynamics are not entirely absent from the relationships that inform G.I.R.L.

In fact, in issue #6 of the relaunch, as Janet and Bobbi watch Shay and Ying use a teleporter to transport themselves to Los Angeles, Bobbi jokes, "They grow up so fast." Janet retorts, "How did I end up co-parenting two super-genius assassins with you again?" (Whitley et al. 2019). While Janet and Bobbi choose not to be biological mothers, and while they are not in a romantic relationship together, they do love each other and operate as partners as well as best friends. Further, because they are helping to mentor, protect, and care for girls, it is entirely appropriate to call what they do parenting.

Jarvis, too, takes parental interest in supporting G.I.R.L. and is especially protective towards Nadia. From issue #1, Jarvis accompanies and looks after Nadia in notably caring ways. The relationship that forms between them eventually leads to Nadia using the term "*dedushka*" to address him and his use of "*vnuchka*" to address her in return—Russian terms of endearment for "grandfather" and "granddaughter." Even Matt Murdock, a.k.a. Daredevil, acts as surrogate guardian when he helps Nadia navigate obtaining citizenship—and when he surreptitiously helps to protect all of the girls from an ambush of villains.

Nadia describes these relationships as choosing her family in issue #8 of the first run (Whitley et al. 2018), and in issue #8 of the relaunch she notes that she has "real support from this family I've made for myself" (Whitley et al. 2019). Thus, similar to Darieck Scott and Ramzi Fawaz's reading of the 90s X-Men comics, I argue that the main characters of *The Unstoppable Wasp* are bound by "distinctly queer attachments . . . grounded in the terms of alternative intimacy, kinship, and belonging" (2018, 209).

This is perhaps nowhere more obvious than in issue #7 of the relaunch, when all of Nadia's "family" attend her birthday party. In addition to her G.I.R.L. teammates and mentors, Nadia is introduced to her other superhero family by Viv Vision, the synthezoid daughter of Vision. The family tree Viv displays is based on Hank Pym's relationships and creations: Ultron (a robot created by Hank) is listed as Nadia's "brother," and Vision (a synthezoid created by Ultron) is listed as Nadia's "nephew." Throughout the party Nadia is introduced to myriad robots, mutants, gods, aliens, and superheroes who, according to the Pym genealogy, are half-brothers, nieces, and great-nephews, even though most are characters Nadia has never met before (Whitley et al. 2019).

This "screwed-up family," as party guest Tigra describes them, humorously calls into question the supposed "naturalness" and "normalcy" of patrilineality and demonstrates that real, caring connections can be made in ways that defy normative kinship frameworks. Nadia's "family" and teammates exhibit the kinds of bonds philosopher Marilyn Friedman associates with liberatory forms of friendships:

> Friendship is more likely than many other close personal relationships to provide social support for people who are idiosyncratic, whose unconventional values and deviant life-styles make them victims of intolerance from family members and others who are unwillingly related to them. In this regard, friendship has socially disruptive possibilities, for out of the unconventional living which it helps to sustain there often arise influential forces for social change. (1989, 286–287)

The attendees at Nadia's party are there because they genuinely care for her and because they want to support her as a superhero and as a young woman, regardless of supposed bloodlines. They also represent a group of characters who have experienced isolation, rejection, and intolerance because of their origins, their sexualities, their pasts, or some combination of these things. In choosing to align themselves as family, the characters who attend Nadia's party demonstrate the value of bonds forged in unconventional ways in their support of each other and in their ability to work together. Further, feminist friendship bonds manifest in observable ways when we analyze the relationships among the members of G.I.R.L.

Some readers might be tempted to assume that by virtue of being established between young women, the friendships formed by the members of G.I.R.L. are inherently feminist. More specifically, because as "scholars of the long philosophical discourse on friendship in the West note . . . in classical thought, friendship was characterized as ethical, public, exclusively masculine, and elite"; thus, female friendships might appear "by definition 'dissident' in relation to the predominant discourse" (Schweitzer 2016, 337–338). However, as philosopher Ivy Schweitzer explains, girls and women who enter into relationships that are modeled on the same ideals from which they have been historically excluded "may not change or subvert that order" (2016, 348).

For instance, many white first- and second-wave feminists adopted traditional Western (white supremacist) ideals of friendship that conflated mutuality and equality with sameness. This meant that early white activists and thinkers tended to romanticize female friendships such that they ignored differences between women and instead assumed solidarity based on the differences between women and men (Davis 1981). Not only did this fail to result in actual solidarity among women, but it also perpetuated intersectional oppressions.[20]

In addition to exacerbating the difficulties experienced between women, patriarchal discourses devalued women's friendship experiences more broadly. As Schweitzer notes, well into the 1970s "women's friendship 'was systematically ignored, derogated and trivialized within a very wide variety of traditions (including history, anthropology, sociology and psychology).' Scholars tended to dismiss friendships between women as trivial or gossipy, or as an immature stage in 'normal' female psychosexual development whose goal they assumed to be heterosexual attachment" (2016, 352). This discursive degradation resonates with some of the tropes born of the portrayal of women's relationships in superhero comics. In fact, Peppard has argued that from the 1970s onwards, Marvel comics, like most pop culture of the time, had to confront the changes brought about by feminism, although it did so in contradictory ways. Female friendships and sisterhood in particular became more observable as narrative devices and yet were often framed as delusional and as weapons aimed at the destruction of men. The repeated attempts of female superheroes like Spider-Woman to make friends with villains heavily implied that female friendships were inherently antagonistic and doomed to fail. Following a brief historical survey of female friendships in Marvel comics, Peppard concludes: "We're told that sisterhood might be powerful, if it wasn't a delusion; and that the greatest threat to female empowerment is not patriarchy, but other women offering the false promise of beautiful revolutions" (2019).

Historically, the presence and collaboration of many women did not automatically result in friendship, let alone in friendships that were feminist. Moreover, dominant discursive and pop-culture trends characterized female friendships as fleeting, delusional, and even deadly. In response, scholars like Audre Lorde, Adrienne Rich, María Lugones, and Elizabeth Spelman (among others) argued for the need to reconceptualize friendship. According to Schweitzer, Lorde developed philosophies of friendship that evoked "a form of political and social alliance and solidarity that embraces change, struggle, and pain" (2016, 357). Lorde advocated for a version of vulnerability that would allow women to constructively critique one another as well as identify oppressive thinking within themselves; in short, friendships that would lead to radical social change. Moreover, Lugones advocated for models of friendship wherein "her friend is not a double, thereby rejecting the slippage towards sameness we saw in classical friendship discourse." Instead, friendship should be plural, it should involve "doing justice to an other's realities, and to our own," and it should allow for "the shifting multiplicity and specific logics of the locations we all move through" (Schweitzer 2016, 362).

Building on these insights, then, feminist friendships between women and girls in comics would necessarily involve change, struggle, vulnerability, self-critique, plurality, multiplicity, and transformation. The friendships between the members of G.I.R.L. arguably meet all of these criteria, thus eschewing androcentric "lone wolf" tendencies that erase the importance of friendships in superhero comics as well as avoiding sexist depictions of female friendships that pit women against each other.

The diversity of the team is, as previously discussed, an important part of what sets G.I.R.L. apart from many other superhero teams, but it is also a crucial aspect of what makes their bonds feminist. For scholars and activists invested in intersectional justice, all women must achieve liberation for any women to achieve liberation; however, reaching this goal cannot be a matter of homogenizing or flattening women's experiences. Unfortunately, various US feminisms have been slow to embrace this realization. Even recent events like the Million Women's March in 2017, which was organized under the banners of intersectionality and inclusion, was embroiled in controversy as Black women and women of color articulated their experiences of erasure and exclusion (Duster 2019). Thinkers like Lorde and Lugones argue that intersectional justice necessarily involves coalitions between women of varying identities, but coalitions cannot be forged in such a way that they eradicate difference.

Cross-racial and cross-ethnic relationships among women, for example, must allow for each individual's experiences and ways of knowing to be recognized, even as this kind of diversity requires the simultaneous negotiation of disparate needs alongside shared goals. As I have argued above, *The Unstoppable Wasp* maintains each girl's unique circumstances in conjunction with the team's aims. Readers are made aware of, for example, the challenges Priya faces navigating her desires to be a "normal" American teen as well as being a member of her Indian family; Shay struggles with normative social expectations at school and with homophobia from her mother; Tai and Alexis have faced hardships related to the loss of their parents and to Tai's disability; Ying struggles to recover from Red Room–induced trauma and with the loss of her familial and cultural identity; Nadia, of course, also must heal from trauma, navigate parental loss, and learn to live with her disability. Together, the girls work to establish their lab, to collaborate on new research, and to fight evil.

What's important is that at no point are any of their individual circumstances made to seem less important than their collective work with G.I.R.L., and their friendship bonds do not form *despite* different realities but often *because* of them. Crucially, the comic makes clear that forming friendships under these circumstances is not always a comfortable process, nor should it be. Nadia's manic episode, and the ramifications that follow, illustrates the challenges as well as the liberatory potential of feminist friendships.

On one level, Shay, Alexis, and Ying's willingness to physically fight Nadia demonstrates a deep commitment to their friendships and to doing what is right for Nadia, regardless of the literal danger it poses. Priya's decision to pursue Nadia into her micro-lab after the rest of the team has left also shows the pain that can come with what Jean Keller describes as "an unexpected tear in the fabric of friendship that must be repaired" (2008, 165). On another level, though, it is difficult not to see uncomfortable resonances with racist tropes that require sacrifices from characters of color in order to save the white protagonist.

As Nadia begins to describe the suicidal ideation she is experiencing, Priya interjects by assuring Nadia that the world would be a poorer place without her in it (Whitley et al. 2019). Priya's intervention risks being read as a derivation of "the magical Negro" trope—a stereotypical role generally assigned to Black characters whose actions are relegated to assisting white protagonists in discovering their strength and worth (Glenn and Cunningham 2009). In her insistence that Nadia is "the single best person" she's ever known and that Nadia is "kind and caring and smart," Priya's dialogue is reminiscent of a line from the highly criticized film *The Help* (Taylor 2011), spoken by Viola Davis in her affirmation of a young white girl: "You is smart, you is kind, you is important." Writer Helen Gould argues that what makes such lines "frustrating is that they are so rarely said to people of colour, particularly black people." Instead, Black people and people of color are "forced, in reality and in fiction, to constantly provide support to others" (Gould 2019).

However, I would suggest that while seemingly similar, Priya's role in issue #5 of the relaunch departs from racist tropes like "the magical Negro" in important ways. First, Priya, Tai, Alexis, Ying, and Shay all have their own backstories and narrative trajectories that are established independent of their relationships to Nadia or her success. Second, while Priya does step in to save Nadia (which is arguably the only ethical response in such a situation), it is not solely for Nadia's sake that she does so; Priya's motivations are also driven by her own desire to assuage her guilt over her brother's death by suicide. Third, throughout the comic, each member of G.I.R.L. is regularly affirmed and supported by Nadia, Janet, Bobbi, or the other members of the team. Finally, while it is the case that it is the Black girl and the girls of color who suffer from trying to save the white protagonist, Nadia is held accountable for the harm she causes. In other words, the pain endured by Shay, Ying, Tai, Alexis, and Priya is never framed as a necessary sacrifice to bolster Nadia; it is clear that Nadia's behavior is harmful, and she must face the consequences of that behavior.

In issue #6 of the relaunch, for example, Nadia travels to Alexis and Taina's apartment to try to make amends. During her manic episode, Nadia had made a list of the ways she would "help" the members of G.I.R.L.; her entry for Taina suggested that Nadia wanted to "fix" her. Her overinflated ego led her to go so far as to call Taina's doctors, constituting an egregious breach of privacy. When Nadia tries to apologize to Tai, she makes a further mistake in insinuating that Tai will be incapable of continuing her engineering if she doesn't have access to the resources Nadia has provided. Taina responds by saying, "*Listen* to you! Even your *apology* is some privileged ableist nonsense! I was building robots out of *junk* before you showed up here. Making 'em out of titanium instead of tin ain't worth sharing lab space with somebody who thinks she needs to 'fix' me!" (Whitley et al. 2019).

Even if Nadia's assumptions about Taina being "broken" arose in part because of her own struggles with bipolar disorder, she is still confronted with how acting through her own privilege and desire to "help" perpetuates ableism (which reduces people with disabilities to their limitations) and classism (which assumes ingenuity and skill are the remit of those with ample resources). Taina's initial response—to slam the door in Nadia's face—is not unreasonable according to Lugones and Spelman. Because white women who have tried to "save the day" for all women have historically done more harm than good, Lugones and Spelman argue that it should only ever be out of a true sense of friendship that white women engage in dialogue with women of color. That said, to truly develop feminist friendships, white women must be prepared to do the hard work of unlearning oppressive ideologies and must not expect to be embraced without hesitation. Lugones and Spelman write:

> So you need to learn to become unintrusive, unimportant, patient to the point of tears, while at the same time open to learning any possible lessons. You will also have to come to terms with the sense of alienation, of not belonging, of having your world thoroughly disrupted, having it criticized and scrutinized from the point of view of those who have been harmed by it, having important concepts central to it dismissed, being viewed with mistrust, being seen as of no consequence except as an object of mistrust. (1983, 580)

Taina's initial reaction, followed by her subsequent conversation with Nadia, conveys to readers how reductive Nadia's thinking had been. Nadia not only apologizes but also comes to terms with being wrong. She listens to Taina's perspective on what it means to live with a disability and has to confront her own internalized ableism. By issue #8 of the relaunch, we see Nadia starting to learn to "become unintrusive [and] unimportant" as she elects not to showcase her own research at the G.I.R.L. Young Scientists Expo and instead plays host by welcoming people and introducing the work of her teammates. Issue #10 concludes with captions in which Nadia muses, "This isn't just my story, this is the story of a whole community of amazing women" (Whitley et al. 2019).

For the members of G.I.R.L., developing their friendships involves "openness . . . sensitivity, concentration, self-questioning, [and] circumspection," making them feminist in nature (Lugones and Spelman 1983, 581). Each girl struggles with her own circumstances and must reevaluate what she wants from her own life and from her relationships with others, while at the same time the members of G.I.R.L. work together to establish a community for girls and women in STEM. The fact that Nadia's final lesson is about realizing that "saving the world all at once" is less important than embracing the complexity of life and establishing bonds with other girls and women is notable. Not only does it disrupt androcentric, white-as-universal genre conventions that suggest that superheroes must adopt universal, selfless missions (Coogan 2013), but it also emphasizes the interconnectedness of feminist friendships and collective liberation for girls and women.

Like the other Blue Age versions of characters analyzed in this book, Nadia's presence extends across media. As a regular member of the superhero team the Champions, she frequently appears in the titular comic as well as in other Marvel titles. Nadia is a playable character in the video game *Marvel Future Fight*, and in 2020, author Sam Maggs published a YA novel focused on Nadia and the rest of G.I.R.L. called *The Unstoppable Wasp: Built on Hope*. In the Marvel Cinematic Universe (MCU), Hank Pym and Janet van Dyne remain together and are parents to Hope, a character whose name in Russian would be Nadia and who may be intended to be an alternate universe version of the Nadia discussed here. As other superhero media continue to inspire fans to seek out the comic book source material, the potential for superheroes to make meaning across media expands. This includes Nadia, whose appearance across media may inspire audiences to seek her out in *The Unstoppable Wasp*.

Moreover, while Nadia as a female superhero (and G.I.R.L. as an all-girl team) may still be numerically marginal, the character's impact cannot be so easily reduced. In its clear identification and critique of androcentrism in the Marvel Universe, *The Unstoppable Wasp* adopts an explicitly feminist approach to superhero comics. Rather than taking for granted that women and men are equal, the comic reflects our own real-world gender inequities and, most importantly, demonstrates that collective action is necessary to address them. Nadia's recruitment mission redresses exclusionary measures of recognizing talent, superheroic and otherwise. Part of what allows Nadia to assemble such a diverse team is her willingness to question social and scientific norms that have historically been taken for granted; in other words, it is through queering science that Nadia initiates G.I.R.L.

The comic book also enacts something akin to queer feminist science studies in its inclusion of real-world science facts in fun, accessible ways. These features bring science out of formal institutions and make it possible for anyone to engage in STEM-based learning. The back matter of the book also powerfully queers normative representations of science insofar as it features real cis and trans women of all ages, backgrounds, sexualities, and specialties in STEM, thus further inviting readers to learn more about and aspire to participate in the sciences. The members of G.I.R.L. also powerfully queer representations of scientists, as well as typical superhero teams, by being drawn from different ethnicities, backgrounds, and sexualities. This diverse representation has the potential to upset decades of real, socialized biases about who can do science and how. That the bonds amongst the members of G.I.R.L. are intergenerational, cross-racial, and feminist also queers superhero norms for teams formed based on chance or convenience.

Including older, child-free women as mentors to teen girls counteracts wider pop-culture trends steeped in ageism; it also pushes back at dominant discourses of femininity that problematically align maternality with "woman." The book's focus on alternative kinship bonds and chosen family pushes back at assumptions about the "normalcy" of patrilineality and offers relationship models that are often more nourishing for marginalized people.

Finally, in its acceptance of the complex and even difficult ways cross-racial friendships between girls and women manifest, *The Unstoppable Wasp* points towards the importance of truly feminist friendships for liberatory communities. These qualities do not exist in place of traditional superhero comics conventions but rather alongside them, proving that there is nothing inevitable or inherent about the genre with respect to gender, race, sexuality, disability, or age.

From a feminist perspective, *The Unstoppable Wasp* is an exceptional comic not only because it pushes the superhero genre in more progressive directions but also because it puts its feminist ethos into practice by centering girls and women on the page, opening opportunities for real women in STEM to reach girls and women beyond formal settings, and modeling forms of friendship that are integral for intersectional justice.

4 | SAMPLING *IRONHEART*

Black Feminist Thought, Superhero Ethics, and Afrofuturism

Like other Blue Age characters, Riri Williams, also known as Ironheart, made her first appearance in the 2010s. Created by Brian Michael Bendis and Mike Deodato, fifteen-year-old engineering genius Riri Williams was introduced in 2016 in *Invincible Iron Man* #9[1] as an aspiring superhero who made use of her MIT scholarship to build her own Iron Man suit. Eventually, with Tony Stark's endorsement, Riri perfected her tech, stepped out of Iron Man's shadow, and fully took on the mantle of Ironheart. Despite diversifying Marvel's cast of superheroes by introducing a Black teen girl, these early depictions of Riri also entailed various intersectional failures related to the character's background and visual presentation, to certain narrative choices, and to her reception by readers. Further, as with most other Marvel titles, Riri's team of creators were overwhelmingly white men. However, following a successful fan-led campaign on Twitter, combined with a Change.org petition, poet and scholar Eve Ewing was eventually hired by Marvel to write a new solo series in 2018 (Rockett 2018).

As one of only four Black women writing for Marvel at the time she was hired (joining Nnedi Okorafor, Roxane Gay, and Yona Harvey), Ewing's inclusion was a cause for both celebration and concern. For many fans and scholars, it was simultaneously disappointing to be reminded of how exceptional Ewing's hiring was, yet thrilling to think that a genuine shift might be taking place (Sage 2018). In addition to the astonishing paucity of diversity among creators, fan concerns around new Blue Age titles were also informed by a history of superhero comics that "[espoused] platitudes of diversity while actually obscuring any signs of racial difference" (Singer 2002, 107). Despite these circumstances, I argue that together with Kevin Libranda, Luciano Vecchio, Geoffo, Matt Milla, and Clayton Cowles, Ewing created a book that not only mitigated many earlier problems but also pushed against norms of the superhero genre in truly progressive ways. In fact, as this chapter demonstrates, when analyzed through the prism of intersectionality, *Ironheart* provides a strong example of a feminist superhero comic.[2]

As discussed in previous chapters in this book, intersectional feminist philosophies are employed as a lens through which to conduct a close reading of the text (as well as relevant paratextual material) and to analyze contemporary dominant discourses of identity. I use them here to show how this iteration of Riri Williams draws attention to and acts to combat overlapping systems of oppression. Contrary to analyses that paint the US superhero genre as persistently and inescapably white supremacist, heteronormative, sexist, ableist, neoliberal, and nationalist, I echo Ramzi Fawaz in asserting that comics like *Ironheart* serve "as sites of political world-making where the presence of diverse actors in expansive fictional universes of encounter, conflict, and negotiation . . . provide substantive creative responses to social difference" (2016, 22). Specifically, in making changes that actively avoid (and repair) previous androcentric and anti-Black narrative and visual design choices around Riri, *Ironheart* decenters numerous problematic ideals of superheroism. Further, by drawing on, by sampling, Black music, culture, and history, the creative team powerfully remixes, or reinterprets, Riri's origin story (in particular), while also decentering certain aspects of the superhero genre more generally.

Finally, while there is no denying Riri's minority status (as a Black teen girl superhero) within Marvel comics, I echo numerous scholars of Black superhero comics who argue that analyses of such characters must necessarily extend beyond this obvious fact. By reframing my examination of *Ironheart* away from its marginal status within the superhero genre and instead turning my focus towards reading it as an Afrofuturist text, I endeavor to clarify how this comic is indeed part of a recognizable, meaningful cultural change. Riri is not the only superhero who enacts intersectional justice, and thus, like the other female characters examined in this book, her character may be read as feminist. I hope to demonstrate that she is absolutely one we need.

THE ARMOR ISN'T THE ONLY THING THAT CHANGED

The creation and treatment of Black female superheroes in mainstream comics has often been fraught. As numerous scholars of Black superheroes have observed, superhero comics—created overwhelmingly by white men—have, at times, produced empowering ideals of Black women's heroism while also frequently reinforcing racist, sexist stereotypes (Brown 2001; 2013b; carrington 2016; Gateward and Jennings 2015; Howard and Jackson 2013; Nama 2011; Singer 2002; Whaley 2015). The original iteration of Riri Williams is no exception. Black superheroines have frequently been presented as hypersexual in mainstream comics, making it relatively unsurprising that an early cover for Riri's solo run in *Invincible Iron Man* garnered negative attention for its portrayal of the teen hero. Despite Riri's youth, J. Scott Campbell created a variant cover for Midtown Comics that depicts not a fifteen-year-old girl but a highly sexualized woman. Riri stands in the middle of the cover with her Iron Man helmet under her right arm and her left arm stretched forward in a "Halt!" pose (fig. 4.1). She stands with her feet shoulder-width apart, but her right knee is slightly bent into a lunge, putting her hips at a slant, accentuating the curves of both her chest and her behind. She wears a snug, sleeveless crop top that clearly shows the shape of her breasts and tight, low-cut black pants that leave the majority of her torso exposed, highlighting details of her stomach muscles as they meet her hips.[3] Her eyes look forward to meet the gaze of the reader, but her chin is turned to her left and tilted downward, giving her a rather coy facial expression, one that Campbell himself described as "sassy" (Flood 2016).[4]

In response to such images, journalist Clio Chang notes: "Black girls also aren't simply allowed to be girls. It's a phenomenon that [Monique] Morris describes as 'age compression,' in which black girlhood is conflated with black womanhood. The reasons for this are complex, but Morris notes that the hypersexualization of black females has been a constant, dating back to historic stereotyping of black women as 'jezebels' with loose morals, an idea that was once used to justify the rape of slaves" (2016). Far from being unique to comics, however, this type of depiction demonstrates a prominent representational trend. In a recorded conversation with Melissa Harris-Perry, bell hooks asserts that within dominant Western popular culture, "black children no matter their age are always seen as miniature adults" (2013).

Figure 4.1. J. Scott Campbell's variant cover of *Invincible Iron Man* #1 (2016) received criticism for the way it portrayed Riri.

The social media response to Campbell's cover was swift and thoroughly damning of the hypersexualization of Riri, and as a result, the cover was withdrawn. Bendis also expressed relief that the cover was recalled (Flood 2016), and thankfully, Deodato's subsequent illustrations of Riri avoided both hypersexualization and age compression. That said, the fact that Campbell's cover was approved for publication in the first place and the amount of attention it attracted cannot be overlooked. As McKenna Boeckner, Monica Flegel, and Judith Leggatt note, Riri's depiction on the cover in question was one of the main elements antidiversity fans seized on to justify their rejection of Riri, vilifying and (inaccurately) reducing her to a "black lesbian sexualized teenager" (2020, 189–190). In perpetuating these problematic trends, Campbell's cover constituted an intersectional failure: that is, while it included an image of a Black female character—a traditionally excluded identity in the superhero genre—it relied on misogynoirist[5] stereotypes that perpetuate overlapping systems of oppression related to race, gender, and sexuality.

Kevin Libranda and Luciano Vecchio's art[6] throughout *Ironheart* redresses problematic representations of Black teenhood. Riri is consistently drawn with youthful facial features like big, bright eyes, and her body is more realistically stylized for a fifteen-year-old girl. When not in her armor, Riri wears comfortable yet trendy clothing like high-top sneakers, T-shirts, and cropped leather jackets, and her hair is styled in a fauxhawk with an undercut, making her recognizable as a contemporary Black girl. As Blair Davis notes, comics creators have long used "such elements as dress, accessories, weaponry, and the like . . . [to] convey particular representations of black culture, identity, and/or history" (2015, 195). However, as I have previously discussed, the overrepresentation of white men on creative teams meant that those representations of Black culture were often rendered via a "[white] comic book gaze" (B. Davis 2015, 200).

Thus, depictions of Riri in *Ironheart* are important from an intersectional feminist perspective because they are informed by writer Eve Ewing's own experiences as a Black woman. To echo andré carrington, the progressiveness of these depictions of Riri is rooted in the fact that a Black woman's "lived and historical experiences and ongoing creativity are the conditions of possibility" for the character; rather than simply acting as "a figment of the normative imagination," this version of Riri represents a model of Black girlhood that is constituted by a Black woman herself (2016, 91–92). The visual focus on and variety of Riri's affect displays, or facial expressions, are also important aspects of *Ironheart* when analyzed within an intersectional feminist framework. From one panel to the next, her facial expressions transform from wonderment, incredulity, fear, pride, determination, and love, depending on context. Layouts frequently include panels that show a close-up of Riri's face, making the complexity of her feelings and reactions clear, and when not in her armor, Riri appears most often from the waist up.

These artistic decisions act to counter misogynoirist traditions of representation in several ways. First, in depicting the dynamism and fluidity of Riri's emotions, *Ironheart* defies the history of Black female characters in comics being rendered as one-dimensional (Whaley

2015, 7). Moreover, Harris-Perry, echoing Patricia Hill Collins (1991), argues that popular stereotypes and representations of Black women often reduce them to three tropes: the hypersexualized Jezebel; the angry, emasculating Sapphire; or the subservient Mammy (2011, 31). While Riri's reactions to her circumstances vary—including affects that can be read as sassy, witty, angry, or caring—she is always reacting *to something*. Riri's demonstrations of wit or anger are only a few of myriad emotional displays, and they arise in relevant contexts (e.g., when Riri is verbally sparring with a peer or when she perceives a true injustice). Thus, they cannot be read as inherent to her "Blackness" or as the sum total of who she is.

The focus on Riri's face and upper body (which, again, is always modestly clothed for comfort and style) also disrupts racist, sexist trends of representation in comics because it shifts the viewer's gaze. Blair Davis describes how earlier Black superhero comics featuring characters like Luke Cage, Cyborg, Storm, and Vixen cultivated a problematic "compulsive gaze" through regular narration that invited viewers to "look closely" or "study" characters; crucially, "varying degrees of exposed flesh factor into the visual design" of each one. He argues that Black superhero costumes that display bare backs, thighs, shoulders, and chests uncomfortably evoke the historical reality of slave auctions, where the bodies of Black men and women were closely scrutinized by white slave owners. Superhero characters are subject to this "particularly when readers are spurred by a narrator to scrutinize the black flesh that has been so blatantly put on display" (2015, 209–211).

By composing so many panels using close-up angles, the artists on *Ironheart* invite readers to see what Riri sees (e.g., the data display in her helmet) or to share in her reactions. When she is out of her armor, medium-view panels show Riri from the waist up to varying degrees, rarely revealing exposed flesh beyond what is normal for T-shirts. On the few occasions where Riri wears sleeveless tops, her arms are always visibly a part of her whole, active body; the panels do not visually dissect her such that her bare arms become objects of scrutiny, and there are never narrative directives to "look closely." This is an important remediation not only of the problems outlined by Davis but also of other contemporary media tendencies that have equally troubling historical roots.

Analyzing mainstream media reactions to another notable Black female Chicagoan, Michelle Obama, Harris-Perry describes how magazine and newspaper op-eds "dissected" the First Lady by fixating on parts of her body, such as her arms. "The public dissection of Michelle Obama into body parts—first her butt and then her arms—is reminiscent of the treatment of Saartjie Baartman, the so-called Hottentot Venus . . . a Khoikhoi woman from southern Africa who became an exhibit in London's Piccadilly Circus" (Harris-Perry 2011, 279). This treatment was uniquely public because of Michelle Obama's political status, but Harris-Perry argues that it is nevertheless emblematic of how distorting images of Black women impacts their ability to occupy positions as full subjects and citizens. While synecdoche is common in comics,[7] Vecchio and Libranda's panel compositions avoid isolating body parts like the thighs, chest, or arms, and when Riri's bare arms are visible, point of view and angle are used to consistently portray Riri as a complex subject rather than as an object "to be looked at."

For example, a page in issue #7 of *Ironheart* depicts a series of panels encapsulating a video call between Riri and her mother; as is clear in the top left panel, Riri wears a jumpsuit with a sleeveless tank top (fig. 4.2). However, even in the middle panels, where her bare arms are most visible, a medium view is used so that Riri is seen from the rib cage up. Her face is centered in the panel, presenting an eye-level view, an angle Randy Duncan and Matthew J. Smith argue creates "an identification with the characters and a sense of involvement in the action" (2009, 143). Indeed, Riri's face is shown in enough detail that tears are visible in her eyes, and her line of sight (angled down and to the bottom right corner of the panel) draws the viewer's gaze to the projected screen on which she is focused, demonstrating her feelings of concern for her mother, who is on the other end of the call. The next panel shifts the point of view to focus on Riri's mom, Ronnie; she is drawn from her shoulders up, her affect is one of concern, and a small rectangle in the upper-right-hand corner shows an image of Riri's face. Color artist Matt Milla's work here is key: the panel is colored in varying shades of blue to depict the projected screen of Riri's video call, therefore positioning the reader *as* Riri, making clear the worry that's passing between mother and daughter and directly involving the reader in the action on the page (Ewing et al. 2020). Thus, while Riri's bare arms are visible, the visual design of the page makes a problematic "compulsive gaze" virtually impossible. Instead, it is Riri's perspective that is privileged, emphasizing the wholeness of her person and the importance of her relationship with Ronnie. Far from being an exception, this example is indicative

Figure 4.2. Riri is shown on a video call with her mother. *Ironheart* #7 (2020).

of the progressive ways layout and composition are used throughout *Ironheart*.

The redesign of Riri's armor and how she is drawn while wearing it add another layer of meaning to the book when read through an intersectional feminist lens. In issue #9 of *Invincible Iron Man*, when Riri first reverse-engineered her own Iron Man armor, she used outdated plans and stolen material from MIT (Bendis et al. 2016). The result was a large, silver-grey metal suit visually reminiscent of the armor Tony Stark builds in captivity in the first *Iron Man* film (Favreau 2008). After her first successful attempt at stopping a moving vehicle, the suit falls apart, leaving Riri with the task of building a new one. Her second suit, along with her use of the mantle Iron Man, debuts in issue #3 of the relaunched *Invincible Iron Man* and is drawn in the characteristic red and gold of Stark's armor (Bendis et al. 2017). Notably, this suit comes with an AI version of Tony Stark, who had previously uploaded his consciousness before falling into a battle-induced coma.

Again, while it may have seemed to Bendis that there was true potential in having a teenage Black girl step into the role of Iron Man, this progression proved to be intersectionally weak from a feminist perspective.[8] This weakness stems, in part, from the history of "racially remixed" legacy heroes. As Adilifu Nama observes, it has traditionally been quite difficult for Black superheroes who take up the former mantle of white characters to be seen as anything other than derivative. Writing about the relationship between War Machine/James Rhodes and Tony Stark in particular, Nama says that despite taking on his own missions and developing a suit that eventually departed from Tony's designs, "War Machine remained fundamentally derivative of Tony Stark's super-science and was overshadowed by his superhero persona. The armored outfit is such a signature feature of the *Iron Man* comic it is hard to imagine anyone that dons a metallic suit as anything but a knock-off of the original" (2011, 81).

The shift in genders from an originally male character to a female character in *Ironheart* compounds this problem. As Boeckner, Flegel, and Leggatt have shown, many white male fans feel a sense of ownership over characters like Iron Man; they reacted with dismay to Riri's occupation of the title, arguing that focusing on a Black teen girl was a disingenuous "box-ticking" exercise designed to cater to women and people of color at their expense (2020). Tony Stark's continued presence in the form of AI only added to the androcentrism of giving Riri two sets of armor visually resonant of his. There to "mentor" Riri, AI Tony supervised the building of her second suit to the extent that she felt as though he was breathing down her neck. The outcome, of course, was a suit literally made in Tony's image. Once Riri finally began to feel ready to be her own superhero, rather than another version of her mentor, it was AI Tony who gave her the moniker Ironheart (Bendis et al. 2017).[9] A few issues later, in *Invincible Iron Man* #6, Riri was also offered Tony's lab in his absence (Bendis et al. 2017).

The continued visual reference to Tony via the suits, the choice to center him as the guiding "voice" for Riri's evolution as a superhero, the narrative choice to make Tony the originator of the alias "Ironheart," and Riri's adoption of his lab all undermine the significance of Riri Williams as a unique Black teen character. The effect of these combined visual design and narrative choices arguably perpetuated androcentric, whiteness-as-universal modes[10] of superhero comics creation. In other words, the continued centering of Tony visually and narratively (even in Riri's origin story) worked to affirm him—as a white male character—as the natural or normal version of Iron Man and as the embodiment of what is universally true about Iron Man. These story choices positioned Riri as secondary, derivative, and atypical. There is no denying that Tony Stark was the first to wear the suit, but if Iron Man is a position, a title held by others (which Marvel heavily implies with the creation of legacy heroes), then there should be nothing inevitable about his involvement. In handing the mantle over to Riri exactly as it was embodied by Stark, Bendis and the rest of the creative team maintained the status quo of marginalizing Black women, even if inadvertently.[11] Stefano Caselli's redesign of the armor, which debuted on the cover of issue #22 of *Champions*, was an important step in establishing Riri as a superhero in her own right (Zub et al. 2018).

Writer Jim Zub and artist Emilio Laiso brought about the destruction of Riri's second set of armor in *Infinity Countdown: Champions* issue #2, when the villain Thanos almost took Riri's life. Refreshingly, Riri began to plan her new armor in conversation with another female character, Viv Vision (Zub et al. 2018). Inspired by the armor of an alien warrior race, the Chitauri, Riri built her new armor to be lighter, faster, more flexible, and more evocative of her own identity. Blair Davis notes that while white characters like Superman, Batman, and Captain America all donned "chest symbols" and wear color schemes that proved "highly memorable" and that played "an ongoing role in the characterization of each hero," the costumes of many Black superheroes tell us very little about them as characters (2015, 211). Moreover, Anna Peppard observes that the traditional "one-size-fits-all sexualization" that so often informed the creation of female superheroes—and that worked to undermine the individuality of women characters—extended to their costumes: "More often than not, they [were] clothed in costumes that [neglected] specifics of character in favor of a generic sexiness that privileges objecthood above subjecthood" (2018, 159–160).

Riri's self-designed armor ameliorates these raced, gendered pitfalls while enhancing her abilities as a superhero and conveying more about her as a character. The Ironheart suit Riri creates uses lightweight, imbricated plates that slide into each other, allowing for fluidity of movement and full flexibility. While it is more form-fitting than her previous Iron Man suit, throughout *Ironheart* Vecchio and Libranda emphasize the utility of Riri's new armor: the majority of panels of her in it are drawn as action scenes in which she kicks, flies, and punches. The suit's colors—fuchsia, gold, and black—are not commented on, so we may assume that they are meant to convey something about Riri's tastes.

Like the costumes of Superman, Batman, and Captain America, the Ironheart suit displays a chest symbol emblematic of its wearer; on the left side of the chest plate there is an illuminated, slightly angular shape evocative of a heart. Further, the face shield on Riri's helmet constitutes something of a heart shape, as does the light that sits just above it on the crest of the helmet.

In addition to the collaborator for her new suit being another female character, the AI Riri develops for the Ironheart suit is also more reflective of who she is and what she needs. Early in issue #1 of *Ironheart*, we see Riri at her desk tinkering with a piece of faulty equipment when she is alerted by the lab computer about possible danger nearby. We learn that this "disembodied Hal voice" is not the real AI Riri intends to use because hers is still in development. Riri explains to a lab visitor that she is "running analytics" on her own behaviors, weaknesses, dreams, and memories in order to "synthesize an AI system that will serve as a complement" to herself. The last page of the issue is a splash page surprise reveal of the AI program Riri has created as it flickers into being in the form of an aged-up hologram of Natalie, the childhood best friend Riri lost to gun violence (Ewing et al. 2020). The name Natalie is also an acronym for "Neuro-Autonomous Technical Assistant and Laboratory Intelligence Entity," and unlike the AI version of Tony Stark who accompanied Riri as Iron Man, the introduction of NATALIE by Ewing, Libranda, and Vecchio suggests that it is Riri herself and the people who love her who truly know what is best. As a compilation of her behaviors, memories, dreams, and weaknesses, NATALIE can be read as a representation of Riri's consciousness. Thus, by incorporating NATALIE as a key character, *Ironheart* deprioritizes white male knowledge and radically moves Black women's consciousness from the margins to the center.

Patricia Hill Collins describes how Black women's consciousness, or "'inside' ideas that allow Black women to cope with and, in most cases, transcend the confines of race, class, and gender oppression," has often had to remain hidden in white supremacist society. Central to Black feminist thought, then, is "finding a voice to express a self-defined Black women's standpoint" (1991, 92–93). This process of discovery often involves Black women's relationships with each other, most especially between mothers and daughters and among "women as sisters and friends." Collins writes, "For African-American women the listener most able to move beyond the invisibility created by objectification as the Other in order to see and hear the fully human Black woman is another Black woman" (1991, 97–98). By replacing a white male AI Tony Stark with an AI formed from Riri's own consciousness and from her relationship with another Black teen girl, *Ironheart* enacts a shift that affirms Black girls' and women's "humanity, specialness, and right to exist," making the book stronger from an intersectional feminist perspective (Collins 1991, 97).[12]

Similar changes are made to almost all of Riri's most important relationships in *Ironheart*; specifically, they are overwhelmingly with other Black people, a majority of whom are women. Rather than entirely isolating Riri or only giving her white mentors like Tony Stark, Mary Jane Watson, or Pepper Potts, *Ironheart* demonstrates how vital and nourishing it is for Riri to be part of a Black community. As mentioned previously, Riri's relationship with her mother, Ronnie, is undeniably the most important, followed by her rekindled friendships with her neighborhood friend Xavier and her high school friend Daija. Ewing also makes the narrative choice in issue #6 to draw Riri closer to her former Champions teammate Miles Morales. Although we are told that Miles and Riri did not always get along in the past, Riri still searches Miles out after he has gone missing and helps to free him from an interdimensional villain.

In issue #9 we also see Riri initially struggle to get along with Shuri, Princess of Wakanda. However, by the end of the book, Riri has found true solidarity with Shuri and the other Black women who joined their fight, Silhouette and Okoye (Ewing et al. 2020). These relationships are important for at least two reasons: first, narrative captions and thought bubbles throughout the book confirm that Riri struggles to connect meaningfully with others, but they also clarify that much of her discomfort arises from her feelings of isolation, of not fitting in. Rebecca Wanzo analyzes the history of representations of Black superheroes and asserts that even in comics created by Black authors or artists a degree of melancholia is sometimes observable; melancholia "is about a subject's attempt to deal with invisibility and his or her status as an object, as well as the loss of a desired object" (2015, 326). I would argue that in portraying Riri's ongoing struggles, Ewing is similarly evoking melancholia to constructively critique previous manifestations of Riri that objectified and marginalized her as a young Black woman, while also trying to reconcile how those early depictions paved the way for her own version of Riri to rise.

Second, while it does not always come easy for her, Riri does recognize the necessity of strong relationships and of having a community, values which push back at hyperindividualistic, postfeminist models of superheroism. In issue #5, for example, we discover that Riri not only intends to use her new lab to conduct her work free of corporate pressures but also to provide a safe learning environment for underserved kids in her neighborhood. In issue #9, after Riri and Shuri have stopped an attack on Wakanda, we see a full-page spread of the two young women working together to repair damage and assist the injured. By the conclusion of the book, what thrills Riri the most is not being awarded Wakanda's highest honor, the Circlet of Bast, but rather Shuri's declaration that Riri will always have a home in Wakanda. Similarly, on the last page of issue #12, Riri explains to Xavier and Daija that it isn't flying in and of itself that is special—it's who is waiting down on the ground that matters (Ewing et al. 2020). The collaborative, community-oriented nature of relationships in *Ironheart* evokes what Angela Y. Davis has argued is one of the most empowering and efficacious strategies used by Black women in their fight for liberation: "We must strive to 'lift as we climb.' In other words, we must climb in such a way as to guarantee that all of our sisters, regardless of social class, and indeed all of our brothers, climb with us" (1990, 5). Riri's connection to other Black girls and women and her concern for the well-being of her community resonate strongly with Black feminist thought, thus adding to the ways *Ironheart* acts as an intersectional feminist heuristic text.

The final reimagined relationship that merits attention is the one Riri has to the city of Chicago. In an interview with *Time*, Bendis described his motivations for creating Riri by stating that he was struck by "the amount of chaos and violence" he noticed while working in Chicago: "This story of this brilliant, young woman whose life was marred by tragedy that could have easily ended her life—just random street violence—and went off to college was very inspiring to me. I thought that was the most modern version of a superhero or superheroine story I had ever heard" (Dockterman 2016).

While it may be that Bendis's intentions were good, this "origin story" arguably works to perpetuate stereotypes about Chicago as a place inherently or irredeemably violent. Further, by connecting Riri and her family to Chicago largely through gun violence, this statement may also reinforce racist associations of Blackness with violence. In addition, Bendis's reference to the story of the young woman who went off to college could be interpreted as playing into problematic "individualistic personal transformation" (Cocca 2021, 4) superhero tropes; in framing the woman's success with the "chaos and violence" he perceived to be the standard in Chicago, Bendis's statements obscure how the young woman's strengths were a product of the very same community to which she was seemingly an exception. While it's true that Black Chicagoans suffer from high rates of violence, without an acknowledgment of how those experiences are rooted in the city's history of systemic racism (Fleisher 2019), in a lack of resources (Ewing 2018), and in overpolicing (Goodwin and Grayson 2020), equating Chicago with "chaos and violence" is reductive at best.

Indeed, reflecting on some of the changes she made, Ewing tweeted, "I never liked the idea of her being defined as a Chicagoan primarily by these extreme acts of gun violence she'd experienced" (Ewing 2019b). Thus, one of her aims was to add complexity to the representation of Chicago so that it would be meaningful for Riri on multiple levels and so that it would be recognizable to the "really good people trying to make an awesome life" there (Vargas 2019). The city, and how it informs who Riri is as a person, manifests most clearly in Vecchio and Libranda's art. For example, in issue #1, on pages dedicated to a late night in the lab, we see an open bag of "hot chips" on Riri's desk and a refrigerator full of bottles of orange soda. The iconography on the packaging of both is abstract enough to avoid acting as brand placements, but they are also visually evocative of two Chicago-original products, Vitner's Hot Corn Chips and Crush Orange Soda.

Issue #2 opens with a flashback sequence in which we see young Riri attending "King College Prep High School," also known as Dr. Martin Luther King Jr. College Preparatory High School, a real four-year magnet high school on the south side of Chicago. At the end of the same issue Riri soars over Daley Plaza, at the city's center, giving us a bird's-eye view of its famous Pablo Picasso sculpture; she then swoops over to Millennium Park, where she hovers over Anish Kapoor's Cloud Gate sculpture, more popularly known as "The Bean" (Ewing et al. 2020). Recognizable landmarks of the city are similarly used throughout the book, both on issue covers and as backdrops to Riri's adventures.

On the one hand, Ewing and Vecchio's use of Chicago imagery adheres to the "inseparable" tie between superhero comics and cities, which positions the city "as an important plot element, even an atmospheric, and symbolic protagonist" (Ahrens and Meteling 2010, 5). According to Jason Bainbridge, this is particularly true of Marvel Comics, which rely on a type of realism that sutures "the Marvel Universe to the real world, providing a material context for" its superheroes (2010, 172). On the other hand, *Ironheart*'s incorporation of Chicago(ness) amends some of the intersectional weaknesses of prior representations of Black female superheroes generally, and the weaknesses in iterations of Riri in particular. By showing readers Riri's habits that come from being a resident of Chicago (e.g., she has a fierce thirst for orange soda), or by providing details about her early education, Ewing, Vecchio, and the rest of the creative team make Riri a truly complex, multidimensional character who is therefore more representative of real Black girls and women. Moreover, by choosing diverse Chicago cityscapes as backdrops and highlighting the elements of Chicago life that appeal most to Chicagoans themselves, *Ironheart* centers the native perspective and makes Chicago "legible to a comic-reading community who may be otherwise unfamiliar with the city" beyond reductionist or racist stereotypes (Bainbridge 2010, 176).

This move to make previously ignored perspectives legible, like the other kinds of reparations described in this section, does not indicate an abandonment of generic conventions but rather a transformation of them. Said another way, the shifts in *Ironheart* should not be conceived of as external to, or separate from, the superhero genre. Instead, they convey a remixing of it, thus giving readers "a range of ideas, cultural points of interests, compelling themes, and multiple meanings that were not previously present" that become part of the legacy of superheroism (Nama 2011, 92).

REMIXING LEGACIES

In his book *Super Black: American Pop Culture and Black Superheroes,* Adilifu Nama compares the creation of legacy heroes to hip-hop DJs who "take a preexisting sonic artifact" like a recognizable baseline or melody and build on it to create something new. "These kinds of 'sampled' reinterpretations provide the listening audience the ability to aurally experience the rebirth of a familiar tune in a refreshingly distinct manner" (2011, 90–92).

From the first page of issue #1 of *Ironheart,* we see remixing at work; however, it is not only established superhero conventions that the creative team is building on—Black literature, music, and history are also sampled throughout the book. The comic opens with a two-page spread that is divided horizontally: a tier of five panels extends along the bottom and a splash of Riri soaring across the spread with inset panels on either side of her dominates the top. Captions convey Riri's thoughts as she ascends into the sky and then rockets across landscapes (fig. 4.3). With self-reflexivity characteristic of some Dark Age comics, Ewing's

Figure 4.3. Riri soars through the sky musing about her ability to fly. *Ironheart* #1 (2020).

captions in this opening spread can be read as a critique of historical shortcomings of the superhero genre. For example, the first caption reads, "I was never meant to fly." Nama asserts that the ability to fly is incredibly rare among superheroes, so given the markedly small number of Black female superheroes and their relative marginalization in the genre, Riri's existence defies convention (2011, 73).[13] By calling attention to Riri's defiance, the captions simultaneously summon and overcome the racialized and gendered history of the genre.

The captions may also convey a critique of Riri's origin story. In the panel second from the left in the bottom tier of the page, Riri sarcastically recognizes that "every super hero has their golly-gee, mild-mannered, humble origin story," but the particularly traumatic events of her own mean that she "shouldn't be here" (Ewing et al. 2020). Again, in drawing attention to the grisly details of Riri's background, Ewing appears to call into question the violent circumstances Riri was made to face, which seemed to define her superhero persona in such a narrow way. Opening the book with a splash page would certainly feel familiar to comics readers, but by combining it with a metacommentary on the genre, Ewing, Libranda, and Vecchio also revise what is conventionally accepted about the layout.[14]

What makes this initial spread even more "refreshingly distinct" is the literature Ewing samples in the captions; namely, the poetry of Maya Angelou.[15] As Riri flies high above the Earth and takes pleasure in her ascension, she recites two lines of Angelou's poem "Still I Rise": "Into a daybreak that's wondrously clear . . . I rise." These lines are striking because they echo Riri's movement on the page, but the choice of this particular poem is also powerful from an intersectional feminist perspective. Angelou's poem is written from a Black woman's point of view, and in each stanza, the narrator first recognizes the harmful lies, stereotypes, and acts of violence that have afflicted Black women's lives and then subsequently rejects the power of those wrongs to stop her from rising into a hopeful, joyful, desirous, expansive existence (1978). Using imagery and language that strongly resonate with Riri's own trajectory, the narrator of the poem recalls how her "sassiness" has been criticized; she asserts that she will not be cowed by the pain and trauma of her past and that she will leave behind the hate and fear that have surrounded her; and she will rise up to become the living embodiment of her ancestors' dreams.

Ewing's use of the poem therefore boldly opens the book with a recognition of the harm done in Riri's past but also rejects the power of her past to limit her future. In sampling Angelou's work, Ewing is also affirming Black women's knowledge, experiences, and work as central to the kind of character Riri will be. The captions are a declaration that Riri's rebirth as a superhero will manifest in the image of Black women—not in the image of the character types that have historically dominated the genre. Thus, the opening spread of *Ironheart* not only remixes Riri's own past but also mainstream superhero comics, to introduce a book that is "politically fresh and more contemporary than the original" (Nama 2011, 114).

Sampling and remixing are also used later in issue #1 to help establish the nature of Riri and Xavier's friendship and to give us further insights into the complexity of Riri's character. After falling asleep at her desk, Riri receives a video call from her neighborhood friend Xavier. Although the conversation starts out a bit rocky, Riri and Xavier eventually ease into what appears to be an hours-long chat about their interests. In this instance of sampling, the creative team draws on Black music. In fact, in one panel we see music literally being sampled. Xavier sits at his computer, which displays music-mixing software, and prepares to play Riri a track he has arranged. As the two listen, Xavier's unique lyrics are interspersed with lyrics from the song "Feeling Good," recorded by singer Nina Simone.[16] Riri recognizes the lyrics and praises her friend saying, "And the way you used that Nina Simone sample? So dope."

Matt Milla's coloring does a lot to convey the joy the two teens share as they listen to Xavier's track. The background of the panel appears light and airy, like pastel clouds, and behind Riri and Xavier floats a soft, spectral band of color that's textured like the grooves on a vinyl album. Blue-and-white lyrics are foregrounded in the middle of the panel. The lighting is warm and soft, and pastel yellow and fuchsia lens flares[17] float over Xavier and Riri respectively, giving the panel a shimmering, transcendent appearance. The panel evokes a form of joy that Audre Lorde characterizes as involving "love in all its aspects," as well as "creative power and harmony." She writes that this feeling manifests in "the power which comes from sharing deeply any pursuit with another person . . . whether physical, emotional, psychic, or intellectual," or in the way a body "stretches to music and opens in response, hearkening to its deepest rhythms" (1984, 55–56). Ewing, Libranda, Vecchio, and Milla enact another remix of Riri's personal legacy by focusing on shared Black joy, and they create a "refreshing" representation of Black life that eschews "mainstream media's attempts to fix Black people and Black life into a position of death and despair." Instead, they capture "Black people as fully human, capable of experiencing and expressing a full, dynamic range of emotion" (Lu and Steele 2019, 829).

Ewing's sampling of Black music also provides an opportunity to remix the figure of the Black nerd. Two pages prior to this sampling panel, Xavier and Riri begin discussing hip-hop and dispute what an appropriate top-five list should look like. Each aligns with a different generation of artist—Riri is a Tribe Called Quest fan, while Xavier lists Jay-Z. During this exchange, something catches Xavier's eye, forcing Riri to claim that the golden visor on her desk is for cosplaying the beloved *Star Trek* character Geordi La Forge. Riri speaks defensively, expecting to be criticized for her nerdiness, but instead Xavier excitedly launches into a discussion about his own love for *Star Trek*. As the conversation meanders, subsequent panels feature a debate over the deliciousness of sweet potatoes and strategies for beating video games.

Johnathan Flowers notes the paucity of Black nerds in popular culture, particularly "Black girl nerds." Endemic to representations of Black nerds (or "Blerds") that do exist—most of whom are male—there is a "perceived tension between 'black identity' and 'nerd identity,'" resulting in relatively narrow options to be a Blerd that are made even narrower by hegemonic norms of masculinity (2018). Riri and Xavier's conversation in issue #1 arguably constitutes the rebirth of the Black nerd in at least two important ways: first, Xavier excitedly discusses topics relevant to Black culture and to nerd culture in equally familiar ways, and we are given no textual or visual indicators that these discussions are meant to bolster or diminish his identity as a young Black man. Second, Riri's centrality as a Black girl nerd—evident not only via her conversation with Xavier but also in earlier close-up panels of her desk on which we see DVDs of Carl Sagan's TV show *Cosmos,* a Sherlock Holmes novel, an action figure of the Hulk,[18] and what appears to be an Iron Man comic—adds much-needed visibility to an underrepresented group.[19] Like Xavier, Riri's Black girl nerdiness manifests in ways that avoid playing into the controlling stereotypes of Black femininity discussed previously. That Riri and Xavier's conversation includes both what they have in common as well as their differences of opinion further adds to the refreshing way Black nerds are portrayed: it disrupts monolithic definitions of Blackness and nerdiness. Ultimately, Ewing's dialogue, and Libranda and Vecchio's art, remixes narrow or underdeveloped models of Black nerd representation and instead shows two characters who can "embrace their blackness while simultaneously engaging in their various interests, thereby distancing themselves from the controlling images" of hegemonic race and gender norms (Flowers 2018, 188).

As mentioned previously, while the legacy of Tony Stark in particular, and mainstream superheroes more broadly, is decentered in *Ironheart,* it does not mean that they aren't part of the material the creative team sampled. The cover of issue #4, for instance, created by Amy Reeder, shows Riri falling through the air while her armor seems to peel away from her piece by piece.[20] Within the issue Riri comes face-to-face with an incredibly dangerous and mystical adversary who pushes her beyond her physical and psychological limits (Ewing et al. 2020). In both appearance and content, this issue echoes issue #3 of *Invincible Iron Man,* in which Tony struggles with his own magical nemesis. The cover features him hurtling through the air headfirst while his armor flies off (Bendis et al. 2017). For both Riri and Tony, these battles also signal the forthcoming appearance of Dr. Strange, who aids both heroes in learning more about the mystical arts. Tony himself also appears in issue #8 of *Ironheart* during a video call with Riri. While it's clear by the excited expression on Riri's face and her eagerness to show Tony digital plans of her suit that she still looks up to Stark, the dialogue also indicates that he is no longer her active or primary mentor. Both Tony and Riri admit to having been busy, and by the end of the spread, Tony rushes off to another meeting.

Instead, Ewing makes clear in issue #1 and again in #12 that Riri has modeled herself as a hero by following the example of her stepfather, Gary, and not in the image of Tony Stark. In a remix of the famous Spider-Man proverb, "With great power comes great responsibility," we learn in issue #1 that Riri's primary motivation to become Ironheart was something her stepdad used to tell her: "Those who move with courage make the path for those who live with fear." In the first issue, Riri explains that the expression Gary taught her was one he learned from his mother. In issue #12, there is a flashback scene of young Riri watching a documentary about Harriet Tubman with Gary, who, we are led to believe, repeats the mantra as they watch, thus connecting it to Tubman as well (Ewing et al. 2020). Here again, by sampling established superhero traditions as well as Black history, Ewing remixes not only Riri's backstory but also the genre more widely. Riri's heroism is not rooted in a hyperindividualistic androcentric tradition; instead, it is inspired by family and by a desire for collective liberation, and it is modeled on the example of Black women (i.e., Gary's mother and Tubman).

Ewing similarly draws on both Black history and the history of the superhero genre in her remix of Riri's biological father's backstory. Issue #11 opens with a flashback sequence showing young Riri discovering the fate of her biological father, Demetrius; like so many other loved ones in Riri's life, Demetrius was originally written as another victim of gun violence. As the issue progresses, however, it is revealed that Demetrius is alive and is now the villain Dune. By the next issue, Riri has fallen into the Wellspring of Power—a vast underground source of magic—where she has a series of epiphanies and flashbacks, one of which shows Demetrius leaving his pregnant wife under the pretense of running errands. Instead, he goes to enroll himself in what turns out to be human experiments run by S.H.I.E.L.D. (a worldwide law-enforcement organization specializing in "strange occurrences"). Riri's epiphany reveals that Demetrius believed he was simply donating plasma to help support his growing family but instead was forcibly injected with a serum that eventually gave him superpowers and, apparently, erased his memory of who he was, paving the way for his rebirth as Dune.

This scene is highly evocative of Robert Morales and Kyle Baker's comic, *Truth: Red, White & Black* (2004), about a group of Black soldiers in World War II who become experimental test subjects for the US government's mission to recreate the super-soldier serum that was responsible for Steve Rogers's transformation into Captain America. Nama writes that in *Truth*, "Appallingly, the black men are forced to take an unstable version of the serum, which has unknown short-term and long-term side effects" (2011, 114). Similarly, in *Ironheart*, a conversation between S.H.I.E.L.D. agents reveals that subjects' reactions to the injection vary and many die as a result. As Consuela Francis notes, this narrative is not one of pure fiction: Morales and Baker based their story on "the Tuskegee syphilis experiments, in which, over the course of forty years, the US Public Health Service conducted an experiment on 399 black men in the late stages of syphilis, without their knowledge, in an effort to study the effects of nontreatment" (2015, 137).

Ewing's narrative use of involuntary experiments on predominantly working-class men of color, conducted by the seeming "good guys," functions in multiple ways. Namely, her sampling of Black history strongly aligns *Ironheart* with a comics history that demonstrates how comics may enact intersectional critiques of US institutions whose "goodness" is often taken for granted in our white supremacist society. Because Ewing is not just imitating historical examples of medical abuse but remixing them, Demetrius is no longer an expendable Black body, as were the men forced into the Tuskegee experiment. Although he has become a villain, he is nevertheless alive, underscoring his inherent worth as a human being.

Lastly, if, as Peter Coogan suggests, "superhero stories concern the responsible use of extraordinary power in the service of justice," comics like *Truth* and *Ironheart* not only enable intersectional critiques of US history and culture but also of the superhero genre itself (2013, 3). If a superhero-related organization like S.H.I.E.L.D. is in fact unjustly wielding biomedical power against historically oppressed people, what questions about justice, good, and evil become necessary? How do the ethics of the superhero genre fail when confronted with the realities of overlapping systems of oppression? It is precisely these types of questions that allow *Ironheart* to remix the genre in one more way, and in so doing, push superheroic conventions towards a reckoning with the "banality of evil."

Taking to Twitter to discuss her work on *Ironheart,* writer Eve Ewing teased that she had snuck her "ongoing rants about the banality of evil" into the book (2019a). The phrase "banality of evil" refers to the philosophy of Hannah Arendt, and specifically to her work during the Eichmann trials.

Otto Adolf Eichmann was a German Nazi SS lieutenant colonel and one of the major architects of the Holocaust. In 1960 Eichmann was captured in Argentina, put on trial in Israel, found guilty of war crimes, and was hanged in 1962. Arendt, who was living in the United States at this point, was sent by the *New Yorker* to report on the trial. Her resultant work was eventually compiled into a book titled *Eichmann in Jerusalem: A Report on the Banality of Evil* (1963).[21] Contrary to the overwhelming sentiment of those attending and following the trial, Arendt did not think it was sufficient to chalk Eichmann's crimes up to remarkable monstrosity. In fact, Arendt noted how underwhelming Eichmann was as a man—he seemed mediocre in every conceivable way, so to simply paint him as the hateful perpetrator of outrageous evil struck Arendt as unhelpful if the goal was to understand how these atrocities could be carried out on such a large scale. It is not to suggest that she did not think him guilty—she absolutely did. But the man himself was very ordinary. As such, "Arendt calls into question one of our oldest and most entrenched moral and legal convictions: namely, that people who do evil deeds must have evil motives and intentions. They are vicious, sadistic, wicked, demonic, pathological" (Bernstein 2012, 301). Arendt's conclusions were not that Eichmann was demonic or that he was a mindless "cog"; nor did he lack the ethical capacity to understand. Instead, he was a man who quieted his own moral reasoning to acquiesce to the demands of "respectable society," in this case, his Nazi superiors. The total compliance of his fellow Nazi officers, his esteem for Nazi leadership as being the "best people," and the fact that the law allowed for the deportation, torture, and murder of Jews all led Eichmann to conclude that "right action" was equivalent to performing his duty, and his duty was to abide by the laws of the land.

As Richard Bernstein writes, the primary lesson of Arendt's writing on the banality of evil is that "one does not have to be a monster, a sadist, or a vicious person to commit horrendous, evil deeds. Normal people in their everyday lives, 'decent citizens,' even respectable political leaders, who are convinced of the righteousness of their cause, can commit monstrous deeds" (2012, 303). For a character like Riri—who is intelligent, ambitious, has extraordinary access to technology and hence power—learning to recognize and choose what is morally right is a fraught and sometimes painful process. Moreover, her past trauma makes Riri wonder if something in her is irreversibly broken, predisposing her to evil. When one of her foes tries to appeal to Riri based on what he presumes to be a shared worldview, it is only through the love and support of her friends that Riri learns that evil is not inherent but rather something that one chooses to do.

Specifically, in issue #8 Nadia van Dyne, a.k.a. the Wasp, shares with Riri and Xavier her own lesson about Arendtian ethics. Raised in Russia, in the Red Room (a brainwashing and training program designed to turn young women into elite assassins), Nadia was groomed to believe that what was right was to do her duty, and her duty was to become a skilled assassin. At some point, Nadia realized that doing her duty meant inflicting grievous bodily harm on others and that she needed to reconsider what she thought was right. She says to Riri, "Evil isn't something you *are* or *are not*. Evil is something that any human can do or not do, given the circumstances. That's why we have to *choose*. To do the right thing" (Ewing et al. 2020). Nadia is very clearly a good person and performs as a superhero, but she also undeniably has harmed people in the past precisely because she was (initially) unthinkingly compliant with an inhumane, corrupt authority. Ewing's sampling of Arendt's work, and inclusion of Nadia's story in *Ironheart*, remixes taken-for-granted definitions of the superhero genre that suggest that "moral good and moral bad are always the actions of easily identifiable moral agents with unambiguous intentions and actions" (Pizarro and Baumesiter 2013, 20).

The more nuanced reformulation of superhero ethics Ewing produces is important in at least two ways: first, it makes characterizations of Riri as "a problem" untenable. As scholars like carrington (2016), Singer (2002), and Blair Davis (2015) observe, Black superheroes with secret identities often experience what W. E. B. Du Bois defined as "double consciousness." The result of institutionalized racism, double consciousness arises when Black subjects have to confront how they are perceived as "a problem" by white supremacist society. For Black superheroes who may be valued when they are in their disguises fighting for justice, double consciousness arises from also knowing how they are perceived and devalued as civilians. Interestingly, Riri does not have an alter ego; that she is Ironheart is well known. Thus, her double consciousness arises as a result of being a Black girl in a white supremacist society, as outlined by Du Bois.

Ewing describes how this dilemma worked itself into the book following early fan reactions: "When this character first came out, a weird critique of her character was that she was an unlikeable sociopath. I think that was rooted in a lot of bizarre misogynoir and straight-up trolling. But in a sense, I was like, 'okay, word. That's her fear about herself, then.' In a sense, it's like Riri has been able to hear all the hateful things people say about her on the internet, and because she's a teen and because she has real trauma, she's internalized them. Now it's time to face them," she tweeted. One of Ewing's aims, then, was to help Riri "confront and settle her biggest fear—that she is secretly somehow bad or has bad things inside her" (2019c). Thus, Riri's ability to determine what is right and to choose to pursue justice upends any misogynoir-fueled narratives about the essence of her character as being "a problem."

Second, Ewing's remixed Arendtian ethics in *Ironheart* are powerful because they speak to contemporary US politics. For example, in issue #5 Riri uncovers a petty crime ring being run by a corrupt politician who is exploiting poor children of color to drum up fear in the community and to steal data to help him win an upcoming election. As Riri faces off with Thomas Birch, he launches into an explanation of his motivations, saying that people crave panic, that they need fear to bring them together against a common enemy, and that the children he has forced to commit crimes for him have "criminal instincts," that they are "a bunch of filthy thugs" (Ewing et al. 2020).

While Ewing makes readers aware that the children in question are from low-income, working-class families and have been coerced with both monetary rewards and physical violence, she shows Birch trading on institutional racism and classism to keep the manufactured nature of the crisis invisible to the greater public. He espouses "big plans" and connections with "very powerful people." In his appearance—he is a white man with blonde hair and blue eyes who wears a red tie—and, more notably, his rhetoric and vocal patterns, Birch evokes the 45th president of the United States, who similarly used racist diatribes to demonize minority populations (BBC 2016), fabricate security threats (Cohen and Brown 2020), and justify his own unlawful activities (Mak 2020). Throughout his presidency (2016–2020), the 45th president stoked the flames of xenophobia, nationalism, racism, and sexism (Terrill 2017). His rhetoric and actions led to international human rights violations (United Nations 2019), to a rise in fascism (Braune 2020), and to an unchecked pandemic (Tollefson 2020).

In such circumstances, one is not required to personally commit hate crimes to do harm; rather, by merely accepting political authority (whether explicitly or tacitly), one becomes complicit in the harms of those who do. As Arendt argued, authoritarianism and totalitarianism rise under certain conditions and differ from other forms of government (1951). In other words, they are far from universal social and political states. Therefore, it seems that a superhero with what Coogan identifies as a "universal" mission may be alienating in times like these (2013, 3). If, as Francis suggests, the promise of superheroes lies in their ability to reflect "the kind of heroism we would like to imagine we are capable of," and their stories enable us to fantasize about "the ability of an ordinary citizen to become an extraordinary hero, all in a world that looks remarkably like our own," then it seems that Riri is exactly the type of hero the United States needs (2015, 138–141). Thus, Ewing's sampling of Arendtian ethics to ground Riri's mission as a superhero is more inclusive insofar as it combats misogynoir and demonstrates ideals of heroism that speak to the complexity of the political problems faced by contemporary readers.

The last legacy remix that merits discussion is that of superhero violence. While popular opinion and scholarly discourse have generally moved on from the moral panic created by studies like that of Fredric Wertham (1954), which suggested that superhero comics would incite delinquency in children, contemporary critiques still point towards the genre's seeming glorification of violence. Indeed, as scholars like Carolyn Cocca (2021), Blair Davis (2018), Chris Gavaler (2016; 2018), and Kevin J. Wanner (2016) have observed, it is rare for superhero comics to be published without depicting at least one fight; violence is often authoritarian or of a vigilante nature but it is also frequently presented as justified; and violence is often framed as the primary way to solve problems. Cocca asserts: "Most of these media have historically starred white, cisgender, heterosexual men, and through repetition have collapsed these four categories into a singular demographic profile and imbued it with the attributes of 'masculine,' 'American,' 'exceptional,' and 'violent'" (2021, 26). As a result, violence in superhero comics may, and frequently does, reinforce harmful norms of race, gender, and nationality.

Given that Riri is motivated by a desire to avoid doing harm—as a way to prove that she is not inherently bad—what does it mean that as a Black teen girl she continues to use physical fighting techniques and advanced armor? Martha McCaughey notes that "even as current feminist philosophy suggests that power operates at a level of the body, much of feminism—which always stood for a heightened consciousness of patriarchal modes of acting and thinking—rejects the possibility that anything good could come from violence" (1997, 2). How, then, might the depictions of physical violence in this comic challenge our ability to read it as a paradigm of intersectional feminist thought? McCaughey argues that a reevaluation of defensive violence and aggression has liberatory potential for women and is a necessary step for feminist theory. She asserts that "aggression is a primary marker for sexual difference. . . . The construction and regulation of a naturalized heterosexual femininity hinges on the taboo of aggression, and often what challenges femininity is labeled 'aggressive'" (1997, 2–3).

For white women, any perceived aggression results in the assumption that they are not sufficiently feminine; for Black women, whose identities are impacted by misogynoirist assumptions about innate aggression, this has meant an almost complete denial of their femininity. Indeed, as Cocca points out, violence performed by women in comics has generally only been palatable when characters are "white, conventionally attractive, and almost always portrayed as heterosexual—not women of color, not working-class, not impoverished, not disabled, not queer, not transgender" (2021, 27). However, McCaughey argues that in outright rejecting the use of any form of violence, feminist theorists may inadvertently leave intact sexist assumptions about women's bodies as passive objects to be acted upon, and about the inherent connection between masculinity and violence. Rejecting a reconception of aggression may also leave racist, sexist assumptions about the innateness of Black women's aggression untroubled. Rethinking defensive fighting and aggression, McCaughey argues, can change "what it means to be a woman" and "[throw] open for critique the gender ideologies to which we have all become more or less habituated" (1997, 3).

Following McCaughey, then, I suggest that while the use of physical force and fighting technology in *Ironheart* may seem to adhere to the status quo of violence in superhero comics, Ewing, Vecchio, Libranda, and Milla successfully remix many generic conventions in ways that disrupt hegemonic norms of gender and race both in superhero comics and in social discourse.

Early in issue # 1 Ewing addresses concerns about violence head-on. As Riri converses with visitors to her MIT lab, her dialogue establishes that her use of force is not unthinking. One of the visitors begins by bringing up the loss of Riri's father and best friend to gun violence and notes, "And yet Ironheart, much like Iron Man, is a weapon. Do you—?" Riri interjects, "Ironheart is *not* a weapon. Ironheart is an engineer who uses many tools. Including force, sometimes. But I try to avoid that" (Ewing et al. 2020).[22] Ewing draws an important distinction between weapons (objects used to hurt or kill people) and tools (objects used to accomplish tasks) and shows that Riri never employs her technology with the intent to harm or kill. Of course, this distinction has the potential to be shaky, but for a hero committed to Arendtian ethics, her active contemplation and intent work to stabilize it somewhat.[23]

This interaction emphasizes Riri's acumen for complex problem-solving. By calling herself an engineer, Riri implies that Ironheart operates first and foremost by being inventive, analytic, and practical. As such, the use of force is not her default, but Riri clarifies that when unavoidable, she will use it to accomplish her tasks.

The fight scene that unfolds a few pages later demonstrates this remixed approach to the use of force. Clash, a former foe of Spider-Man, has taken several world leaders hostage; prior to confronting him, Riri carefully analyzes her surroundings, researches her adversary and his victims, quickly reengineers a piece of her suit, and weighs various rescue strategies. When she arrives to face Clash, she continues to use her suit to analyze her options while simultaneously distracting the villain. Once the situation escalates and Clash fires at Riri, she spends several panels using evasive maneuvers before the need to disarm him becomes necessary, at which point she lets loose a mean right hook. Riri blasts the villain with her hand cannon only once in order to lay him flat and restrain him.

This scene is indicative of the fighting throughout *Ironheart*. The force Riri uses is overwhelmingly defensive. Her use of aggressive fighting techniques begins only after other tactics like humor, dialogue, distraction, and deflection have failed and the need to protect herself or others becomes paramount. She uses her armor—which (admittedly) is pretty much any time she wears it—overwhelmingly to defend, disarm, or to slow the advance of her nemeses. Even when fighting mindless yet aggressive zombies in issue #7, Riri, Nadia, and Xavier agree to "nonlethal" force only after they have been attacked (Ewing et al. 2020).

These depictions of young women fighting aggressively to defend themselves and to protect others, and defensively using technology, act as a powerful counter to what McCaughey identifies as "dominant representations in North American" media, which "display and eroticize women's inability to defend themselves." As part of an alternative set of images, *Ironheart* may "offer new fantasies of what women can be which rest on women's abilities to set boundaries, defend themselves, and enter into combat" (1997, 5). Further, because Riri is never irrational in her use of force; because wit, rather than anger, often accompanies her fighting; and because physical aggression is just one of the many tools Riri employs to save the day, *Ironheart* challenges racist readings of "kick-ass" Black women and girls in media "as hyperaggressive, wild, untamable, and vicious" (Tung 2004, 111).

Finally, the frank way this comic deals with the cost of violence productively remixes the tendency for the superhero genre to present violence as purely for entertainment (Cocca 2021, 32). Throughout the book, numerous panels show the injuries Riri sustains and the pain and discomfort that come from physical altercations. In issue #5, for instance, Riri spends three panels wincing in pain and clutching an ice pack to her forehead following an almost-deadly encounter with one of her adversaries in the previous issue. Her friend Xavier admonishes her for facing such a threat alone and for intending to pursue it further. Riri doubles down and insists that because she's a superhero, she has to solve the problem. Xavier shouts, "Well, you know what? Sometimes *super heroes* make *mistakes*. And get *hurt*. Super heroes can't fix everything. Super heroes need *help* sometimes" (Ewing et al. 2020). Ewing's dialogue functions as an implied critique of the superhero genre, particularly of its previously mentioned tendency to center on hyperindividualistic heroes and to treat violence as the primary way to solve problems. Xavier's reprimand paired with Riri's physical injuries demonstrates the danger in such assumptions. *Ironheart* also takes seriously the psychological cost of violence. There are three close-up panels of Riri throughout the book—in issues #2, #8, and #11—that visually draw the reader into her psychological state as she experiences or recalls physical violence. Two of the three panels, in issues #2 and #11, illustrate the result of her being triggered by her circumstances and show Riri dissociating, a reaction commonly brought on by trauma. In all three panels, Vecchio illustrates all or part of Riri's face, giving the reader a clear indication of her pain and fear. The remainder of the panels show traumatic scenes from Riri's past, like the shooting deaths of her father and Natalie, or recent altercations that weigh heavy on Riri's mind (Ewing et al. 2020). They underscore the psychological hurt a character like Riri would accrue and lend much-needed gravity to representations of violence in superhero comics. Vecchio's panels position the reader as a witness, rather than a voyeur, to Riri's pain, thus potentially evoking a more empathetic, ethical response to graphic representations of violence (Polak 2017) and to visualizations of Black suffering (Rankine 2016). Refreshingly, Ewing does not leave Riri traumatized. Issue #5 concludes with a sequence showing her and her mother attending a support group for survivors of gun violence. Within an intersectional feminist framework, this type of imagery is particularly important in our white supremacist, heteropatriarchal, ableist culture wherein significant stigma still exists around Black women seeking care for mental illness (Ward, Clark, and Heidrich 2009). Relatedly, by demonstrating Riri's vulnerability in conjunction with her courage, by surrounding her with love and support, and by showing the steps she takes to heal, *Ironheart* constructively counters the stereotype of the "strong Black woman" who supposedly deprioritizes her own feelings and who is entirely unbroken by the consequences of systemic violence (Harris-Perry 2011, 183–220).

Although their book still involves "fighting bad guys," Ewing, Vecchio, Libranda, and Milla's remix of the legacy of violence in superhero comics is significant in its avoidance of and active critiques of problematic constructions of the superhero as white, male, nationalist, and impervious. The reinterpretation of violence in *Ironheart* also enables a manifestation of Riri specifically, and representations of Black women generally, that avoids common intersectional weaknesses.

Despite the changes outlined above, and the numerous ways Ewing and the rest of the creative team remixed, and arguably improved upon, Riri's identity as a superhero, *Ironheart,* like many other Blue Age titles, was canceled after only twelve issues (Resha 2020, 79). This decision by Marvel has led certain scholars to argue that books like *Ironheart* merely represent an "illusion of change" (Roman and Lizardi 2018). Even less cynical analyses of the genre, in their attempt to focus on the root of its problems, curiously accentuate how exceptional more diverse superhero books are, thus (perhaps inadvertently) reducing further how impactful they can be (e.g., Guynes and Lund 2020, 8–9). As numerically marginal as *Ironheart* was, I have attempted to show its complexity and promise from an intersectional feminist perspective. To affirm the progress made by the book, despite its early cancellation and its minority status in the superhero genre, I will conclude the chapter by following the work of bell hooks (1996), Stuart Hall (2019), and andré carrington in recognizing the productivity, creativity, and radicality that thrive in the margins; and by realigning *Ironheart* with the "Black expressive tradition" of Afrofuturism (carrington 2016, 24).

FROM THE MARGINS INTO THE (AFRO)FUTURE

Scholars such as Nama (2011), Whaley (2015), and carrington (2016) all argue for the need to move beyond analyses that focus solely on the rarity of Black sequential subjects or that remain "stuck" in discourse about the racism and sexism of a title or genre. As carrington notes, "None of the aforementioned strategies encourage us to learn anything new, except perhaps who our enemies are; instead, they reinforce precepts that we already believe" (2016, 18). I don't deny that characters like Riri and books like *Ironheart* are indeed in a minority among mainstream superhero titles. Similarly, adopting such an assertion still acknowledges the risks attendant to analyses of texts produced by capitalist corporations like Marvel. Resha clarifies that "'diversity' in comics and their transmedia derivatives is at least as much about commodification as it is about representation, if not more" (2020, 78).

Nevertheless, methods such as reframing the discussion to recognize the margins as a site for creativity or drawing connections between genre-specific texts to encompass a larger cultural movement do not ignore these paradoxes. According to carrington, "The objective of a reparative knowledge project is not necessarily to forestall unpleasant surprises but to maintain the ability to keep itself intact in the face of the likelihood that some threats may indeed manifest" (2016, 20). Therefore, echoing Nama, Whaley, carrington, and others, this section shifts the conversation towards a cursory look at readings of *Ironheart* as an Afrofuturist text in order to move it beyond its minority status in the superhero genre.

Indeed, such an analysis focuses on *Ironheart*'s place within "a resistance movement that employs the imagination in inverting conventional thinking, destabilising previous analysis of blackness and creating an African space in the future" (Chikafa-Chipiro 2019, 2). Further, by reframing *Ironheart* as a "constituent" of Afrofuturism, "rather than viewing [it] as [an] isolated [minority] within a predominantly White community" of superhero comics, this final section "performs a reparation vis-à-vis the alienating effects of the putative Whiteness" of the genre (carrington 2016, 24).

Afrofuturism is an umbrella term for an aesthetic or cultural movement, for a field of study, for a kind of metaphysics, and more (Anderson and Jones 2016; Chikafa-Chipiro 2019; Eshun 1998; C. Jones 2018; Nelson 2002; Womack 2013). Although the roots of Afrofuturism can be traced back over a hundred years, its current manifestation began in the 1990s when cultural critic Mark Dery coined the term in an interview with Black authors like Samuel Delaney, Greg Tate, and Tricia Rose (Anderson and Jones 2016, viii). Summarizing Dery, Alondra Nelson suggests that "Afrofuturism can be broadly defined as 'African American voices' with 'other stories to tell about culture, technology and things to come'" (2002, 9). Indeed, Riri's relationship to advanced technology forms the foundation of *Ironheart* as an Afrofuturist text. According to Cassandra Jones, "Outside the realms of scholarship specifically exploring the relationship of race and technology, technology is often described as objective and ahistoric, a tendency that elides the racism from the level of the institution down to the very code informing the machines" (2018, 203). However, within mainstream pop culture and literary texts, "blackness is [often] constructed as the antithesis of technology" or as entirely absent from "discourses of technology and digital spaces." Jones goes on to say that the "rare occasions when race was explicitly mentioned in relation to technology were marked by a discourse of lack, such as the digital divide, highlighting the racialized division between the technological 'haves' and 'have-nots'" (2018, 204–205).

Ironheart defies these trends in numerous ways: first, it was Black fans on Twitter who overwhelmingly drew attention to Ewing as a viable replacement for Bendis and a Black fan who generated the Change.org petition. These examples point towards what Anna Everett has described as "significant black techno-mastery and new media activism" (2009, 149). Second, the book depicts all of the main characters (the majority of whom are Black) as having regular access to, and mastery of, technology, thus disrupting the stereotype of Black people as technological "have nots." And third, *Ironheart* affirms Riri's engineering acumen throughout.

In fact, I would argue that Riri can be characterized not just as a Black girl nerd but also as an Afrogeek.[24] An Afrofuturist metaphor developed by Everett, Afrogeeks do not "just access or alter off-limits programming or information. This group of technology early-adopters hack reality by inserting themselves into elite centers of technological development"—like MIT, for instance (Jones 2018, 213). Similarly, if Riri can be read as an Afrogeek, Xavier also resembles an Afrofuturist subject: the Rhythm Scientist. Jones points towards the work of Paul D. Miller, who

> invokes the vision of a griot, an African tribal storyteller who carries the history of his or her people, to think through how DJs—musicians who create through the disassembly and reassembly of prepackaged sounds—are digital storytellers. Just as griots do, the DJ connects us to the past through their archives, the portable libraries of vinyl crates or digital cuts; however, they endlessly remix these archival resources to create new meaning, new possibilities, and new future narratives. (2018, 210)

Xavier's sampling of Nina Simone, an artist associated with the civil rights era, demonstrates a concern with the history of Black Americans while his own lyrics illuminate his unique vision of the world—combined, they constitute a new narrative.

Like contemporary Afrofuturism (what Anderson and Jones identify as Afrofuturism 2.0 [2016]), *Ironheart* does not promote unfettered technophilia; rather, the book openly explores the epistemological and ethical tensions that arise with the use of advanced technology. One example of such tension centers on Riri's childhood friend Daija. Despite years of distance, Daija reenters Riri's life but soon reveals herself to be tied up with one of Riri's foes. To discover the nature of Daija's relationship with the villain, Riri proposes to run surveillance on Daija without her knowledge. The technology Riri develops to carry out this plan is a tiny audio recorder with a built-in GPS tracker that fits on a shoe, something she plants on Daija's kicks surreptitiously while Daija is injured in the hospital.

Aside from being an undeniable invasion of privacy, one could argue that Riri's actions constitute what Michel Foucault terms biopower (Foucault 1994); that is, Riri treats Daija's body as a resource for gaining knowledge in the hopes of seizing power from her enemy. The exploitative nature of Riri's actions is further underlined at the end of issue #5 wherein Riri sells the patent for the shoe tracker that she tested without consent and earns enough to put towards her own independent lab. The remaining cost of the lab, Riri reveals, came from wealthy investors who wanted to thank her for securing stolen data (Ewing et al. 2020).

In this latter instance, it was a villain who used surveillance to harvest information without consent and against the will of the people who were surveilled, but in the end Riri is still able to leverage this data for her own gains. For any academic reader, Riri's desire to acquire her own lab independent of MIT's corporate interests is surely understandable, but one has to wonder at the ethics of obtaining this goal by means of invasion, surveillance, and exploitation.

Ewing voices these concerns in issue #5 through Xavier, after Riri admits to him what she has done; he begins by expressing shock and quickly clarifies that her actions are "intrusive." His facial expressions become increasingly disapproving as the conversation progresses: for example, his eyebrows are furrowed in several panels, and he places his hands on his hips while telling Riri, "I don't like anything about this." In the following issue, in her search for Miles Morales, Riri similarly surreptitiously traces Miles's cellphone usage, an act NATALIE calls "data stalking," implying that what Riri has done may be read as threatening.

Further, as discussed previously, Riri's epiphany in issue #12 about S.H.I.E.L.D.'s involuntary human testing also draws on Black American history to offer a cautionary tale regarding unexamined assumptions about the innate "goodness" of technology. As Nelson writes, "The text and images [called Afrofuturist] reflect African diasporic experience and at the same time attend to the transformations that are the by-product of new media and information technology. They excavate and create original narratives of identity, technology, and the future and offer critiques of the promises of prevailing theories of technoculture" (2002, 9). Through creatively centering technology and including constructive critiques of normative assumptions surrounding its use, *Ironheart* performs as an Afrofuturist text.

Perhaps the second-most recognizable aspect of *Ironheart* that situates it within Afrofuturism is the choice of Wakanda for a major setting. A large portion of issues #6–12 takes place in Wakanda, the fictionalized African nation that has "developed technologies more advanced than those of any other nation" (Jones 2018, 202). According to Nama, "Wakanda is a high-tech African Shangri-La where African tradition and advanced scientific technology are fused together to create a wonderland of futuristic weapons and flying machines" (2011, 43). As in other Afrofuturist texts, the focus on Wakanda in *Ironheart* displaces "Eurocentric constructions of history that seek to center whiteness as the sole creators and arbiters of civilization" (Jones 2018, 211).

From the moment in issue #9 when she flies over Wakanda's capital city, Birnin Zana, Riri is moved by the combination of futuristic technology and architecture with a plurality of African fashions, people, and cultural traditions. Upon entering Shuri's lab, Riri encounters technology even she finds astonishing. Riri's trip to Wakanda is also the occasion upon which she teams up with other women of African descent—namely Shuri, Silhouette, and Okoye. Because Afrofuturist texts reject Eurocentric futurist ideals of the eradication of difference, what we discover about this group of women is their heterogeneity alongside their shared heritage.

Of futurist erasures, Sami Schalk writes that "while multiple forms of difference are erased in much speculative-fictional visions of the future, disability is perhaps the most unquestioned erasure" (2018, 87). By focusing on Riri, a Black teen coping with mental health issues, and by including Silhouette, who walks with the aid of crutches, as integral parts of the Wakanda team, *Ironheart* "actively resists the concept of a technology created, disability-free future and its assumed value" (Schalk 2018, 87).

Wakanda is, of course, also the location of the Wellspring of Power in which Riri experiences the aforementioned epiphanies and flashbacks. More specifically, though, once she falls into the Wellspring in issue #12, we see a full splash page of what looks like a galaxy of stars with inset panels of increasing sizes as the page progresses from the top down; the bottom panel provides a close-up of Riri's face. A full-body illustration of Riri, seated, also appears at the bottom of the page. What we discover as we read from top to bottom is that Riri has entered an alternate state of consciousness where dialogue is possible between her current self and her heightened consciousness (fig. 4.4). As the dialogue unfolds, Riri is shown visions of the past, she witnesses the truth about her biological father, she is reminded of recent events, and she is shown a possible future of herself where she lives happily and without fear. This sequence is indicative of Afrofuturist literature in two ways: first, as Kristen Lillvis argues: "In Afrofuturist cultural productions, historical experiences of disorientation converge with contemporary strategies for survival and futurist projections of vitality. As such, the black subject settles in multiple time periods simultaneously" (2017, 3). In other words, this sequence is Afrofuturist insofar as it shows "black identity as temporally flexible, based in the history of what has occurred as well as the potential of what is to come" (2017, 3). Second, these scenes may be read as an example of what Anderson and Jones define as

Figure 4.4. After falling in the Wellspring, Riri gains access to her own heightened consciousness. *Ironheart* #12 (2020).

Astro-Blackness, "an Afrofuturistic concept in which a person's black state of consciousness, released from the confining and crippling slave or colonial mentality, becomes aware of the multitude and varied possibilities and probabilities within the universe" (2016, vii). The dialogue Riri has with her heightened consciousness puts her fears of being inherently bad—fears that represent a version of double consciousness—permanently to rest, releasing her from the confines of misogynoir and allowing her to see the promise of her possible future.

Although this analysis of *Ironheart* as an Afrofuturist text is brief, I have attempted to demonstrate how the book's "intersection of imagination, technology, the future and liberation" resonates strongly with a broader field of creative and scholarly production centered on the past, present, and future of Black subjects (Chikafa-Chipiro 2019, 2). This reframing is intended to redress dismissive analyses of female-led and Black superhero comics as indicative of only an "illusion of change." Ironically, a recent article in the *New York Times* declared that "Afrofuturism is booming in comics" and that a "bumper crop" of books was sweeping the industry (Ito 2021). Thus, it hardly seems a stretch to assert that heroes like Riri, and books like *Ironheart,* are moving out of the margins and pushing comics into the (Afro)future.

Further, through calling attention to the intersectional weaknesses of previous iterations of Riri's narrative and of certain generic legacies more broadly, I argue that Ewing, Vecchio, Libranda, and Milla offer a reparative remix that creatively samples Black music, culture, and history to center Black people's experiences and ways of knowing. More specifically, by drawing from, and valuing, her own and other Black women's lives and thought, Ewing demonstrates that the creation of a Black girl superhero is not a supplementary or external creative process. As Wanzo argues, "By staying within the traditional framework, instead of suggesting that [it is] counter to the representative," this type of text suggests that its "characters are the most representative, replacing one set of ideal bodies with other kinds of bodies" (2015, 330).

Similarly, by sampling Arendtian ethics, Ewing remixes the superhero mission using ideas and images that derail fan misogynoir, disrupt assumptions about the universality of whiteness, and truly make the figure of the superhero more inclusive and just. Moreover, as I mentioned above, because authoritarianism and totalitarianism are not universal political states, looking to a superhero with a universal mission may be a fruitless, or even contradictory, endeavor. By anchoring Riri's mission as a superhero in Arendtian ethics, Ewing makes it possible for a character whose life is impacted by overlapping systems of oppression to be heroic by working towards a collective liberation that would also mean personal freedom, and by speaking to the precarity and complexity of a political atmosphere threatened by authoritarianism.

Again, to echo Wanzo, "As opposed to allowing someone with a body like Superman's to speak for 'truth, justice, and the American way,'"—that is, a white, straight, nondisabled, unflinchingly patriotic male character whose life is not subject to intersecting oppressions related to race, gender, sexuality, embodiment, and state-sanctioned violence—characters like Riri, "that are traditionally marginalized[,] speak the truth, decry injustice, and challenge the American way" (2015, 329). This qualitative change seems to me to be at least as important as increasing the numbers of Black girls and women on and behind the comics page. And, as I hope to have shown, the change is hardly illusory.

In December 2020 the president of Marvel Studios, Kevin Feige, announced that *Ironheart* would be adapted as a TV series for the streaming entertainment platform Disney+ (Dinh 2020). For feminist scholars and readers of *Ironheart,* this transmedia expansion is encouraging but should not be received uncritically. While we cannot know how this adaptation will turn out, or how current cultural tensions around race and gender will inform the creation of the series, continued intersectional analysis of representations of Black girlhood will surely remind us of "the dangers, possibilities, and pleasures in consuming ideas about Black women" (Whaley 2015, 26–27). However she appears on screen, Riri's manifestation in *Ironheart* has underlined the transformative potential of comics to show nuanced and complex depictions of Black girls and women. Perhaps even more importantly, *Ironheart* mobilizes genre conventions using techniques that affirm and celebrate Black lives, proving that intersectional justice is not mutually exclusive to superheroism. In keeping with Riri's mission, we must hope that, as a feminist superhero, she is not the last Black teen girl to "move with courage" through the pages of Marvel comics; rather, we anticipate that she has merely "[made] the path for those who" will follow.

CONCLUSION | ARCHIVING TRACES OF FEMINIST SUPERHEROES

In 2021 comics writer Jason Aaron generated a major Marvel Universe event in his run of *The Avengers*. Following Jean Grey's refusal to be a host, the Phoenix Force comes back to Earth looking for a new hero to wield its cosmic power. The Phoenix pairs Avengers old and new in one-on-one battles until it can find a suitable replacement for Jean. In issue #42 Maya Lopez, a.k.a. Echo, is forced to fight the antihero Namor, and much to everyone's dismay, it appears that she not only loses the battle but also her life (Aaron et al. 2021). However, by issue #44, after the fights have brought every Avenger to the brink of death, Echo rises from the ocean, aflame with the power of the Phoenix (Aaron et al. 2021).

Author Rebecca Roanhorse and artist Luca Maresca pick up where Aaron leaves off in the five-issue miniseries *Phoenix Song: Echo* to try to answer the questions of why the Phoenix chose Maya and whether she will be able to avoid losing herself to the cosmic power. Despite its brevity, Roanhorse and Maresca's comic reimagines what a Dark Phoenix story can be and in so doing broadens the potential for the Phoenix to be read as an intersectional feminist character.

One of the most obvious ways Roanhorse and Maresca mitigate the problems of previous Dark Phoenix stories is to center Indigeneity. Echo is a Cheyenne woman with Choctaw heritage. She is accompanied in her journey by River, an Indigenous man raised on "the Rez," a place Echo describes as being "for those of us who lost our languages, lost our culture and family connections, lost ourselves in the wake of genocide" (Roanhorse et al. 2021). And much to Echo's initial dismay, she and River are eventually aided by X-Men member Forge, also a Cheyenne man.

These characters make people indigenous to the United States integral to the Marvel Universe, and their histories serve as a critique of the cultural, political, and physical violence of American settler-colonialism. Together, the three characters traverse Echo's ancestral line through space and time as Echo tries to learn what it means to be the Phoenix, all while a powerful enemy called The Adversary pursues the group. The Adversary reinforces *Phoenix Song* as an Indigenous story not only because he previously appeared in Forge's history but also because he is characterized as a Trickster, a type of character that features in the stories of many North American Indigenous tribes.

This particular narrative arc enables Roanhorse and Maresca to focus their comic almost entirely on Indigenous characters—a much misrepresented and underrepresented group (Aldama 2020). Relatedly, both Echo and Forge have disabilities: Echo was born deaf and Forge lost a hand and a leg in combat. The comic demonstrates a social model of disability insofar as Echo only experiences problems in relation to her deafness when, for example, it's too dark for her to read lips (Roanhorse et al. 2021).[1] In other words, it is not an inherent failing of Echo's that creates difficulty but rather the exclusivity of certain environments. These representational choices diversify ideals of superhero embodiment and redress ableist genre norms that align disability with weakness, deficiency, and evil (Alaniz 2014).

The creative team's choice to center Indigeneity does not stop with the cast of characters. *Phoenix Song* also reinterprets the questions posed by "the Dark Phoenix problem" through metaphysical, epistemological, and ethical frameworks divorced from the colonial-settler binary logic endemic to Jean Grey comics. For example, unlike Jean, Echo is not chosen because she is a "loner" who can be easily controlled; instead, it is because she is strong and because she comes "from a long line of *warrior women*" who, through various scenes, are shown defending and leading their respective communities (Roanhorse et al. 2021). This means that the source of Echo's power is distinctly rooted in her female ancestry.

These depictions also disrupt what Shari Huhndorf describes as "the gendered paradoxes of colonial memory," in which "chiefs and warriors" are "gendered male in popular memory," while the "complicated historical roles" of Indigenous women are silenced, trivialized, or erased (2010, 181–182). The Phoenix Force (discussed either as an "it" or a "she") is not rendered as purely destructive but rather in more fluid terms as being capable of both destruction and creation, rage and beauty. The problem, Echo is told by a powerful female ancestor, is not the Phoenix Force itself but rather Echo's misguided attempts to "control" it and deny her connection to it (Roanhorse et al. 2021).

The book makes a distinction between Echo trying to "know" the Phoenix Force so that she can control it or fix it in place and her accepting it as part of herself. This distinction resonates with the differences Vine Deloria Jr. identifies between Western and Indigenous metaphysics. In Western thought, Deloria suggests, "knowledge seems to be divorced from experience," whereas the "Indian confronts the reality of the experience, and while he or she may not make immediate sense of it, it is not rejected as an invalid experience. In the Indian world, experience is not limited by mental considerations and assumptions regarding the universe" (1979, 1–5).

Thus, while Professor Xavier of the X-Men sought to understand the Phoenix Force so that he could control it by placing psychic barriers around it in Jean's mind to shield her from experiencing its power, Echo's ancestor Ohoyo Luak insists that Echo cannot possibly understand her own reality, let alone all possible realities, if she does not accept her lived experience *as* the Phoenix. Ohoyo Luak insinuates that trying to separate the Phoenix Force from one's lived experience will only manifest in rage—as it certainly did in *The Dark Phoenix Saga* when Jean consumed a planet. However, embracing it "can reveal the *wonders of the universe*" (Roanhorse et al. 2021). The creative team of *Phoenix Song* lets Echo *experience* the Phoenix Force, even when she is angry, confused, or unsure of herself. There are costs (she kills a jewel thief who threatens her life, for instance), but it is only through the process of becoming the Phoenix and making mistakes that Echo is eventually able to embody her power and exceed what has been previously imagined possible for female superheroes.

Roanhorse, Maresca, and the rest of the creative team also exceed the limitations placed on previous iterations of the Phoenix by eschewing a heteronormative romance as Echo's primary motivation and by letting her live as a fully powered woman. Like Jean Grey in *The Dark Phoenix Saga* or *Phoenix Resurrection*, Echo finds herself trapped in an illusion towards the end of *Phoenix Song*. She is determined to stand up to The Adversary, and on the advice of her ancestor, she takes him to the White Hot Room, an alternate reality that acts as "the center of The Phoenix's power" (Roanhorse et al. 2021). Once there, The Adversary gains the upper hand and lulls Echo into a fantasy-filled sleep so that he can siphon off her power. Although the fantasy she sees of a romance with River and a job as a professional artist fulfills her desires for "a great loft in New York, a kind boyfriend who is nuts about [her], a successful art career," Echo feels unsettled: she repeatedly states that she feels like something is missing, that there's more to her life. River is finally able to wake Echo from these illusions by shouting, "Remember your ancestral line. Remember *who you are*!" As she begins to come to, Echo thinks to herself: "Inheriting the Phoenix made me doubt myself. I am no longer the person I was before, but I am *more* than just a vessel for the Phoenix. Forge, The Adversary, even River . . . They all came to me for the Phoenix. But I am still *Maya Lopez*. I am still *Echo*. And that means I am still my *ancestors' wildest dreams*."

A few pages later, as Echo pursues The Adversary into "The Beginning of Time," she calls herself "*creator* and *destroyer*." A couple scenes later she recalls that "the Phoenix ancestor said that there's so much more to this power, and there's so much more to me. I know she's right" (Roanhorse et al. 2022). Although we are led to believe that Echo is interested in a romance with River, she recognizes that the fantasies she had were not right because they denied her her power and her ancestral heritage. Whereas Jean at the end of *Phoenix Resurrection* says that all she wanted from the Phoenix Force was to see her husband, Scott Summers, one more time, Echo desires more for herself (Rosenberg et al. 2018). It is not a heteronormative romantic connection that defines who Echo is but rather her connection to her female ancestors.

Similarly, Echo's dialogue about being the Phoenix *and* Echo, creator *and* destroyer—the same as before yet also different—parallels much of Jean's dialogue at the end of *The Dark Phoenix Saga*. Jean says of herself: "I am what was, what is, what will be—" and then later, "two beings—Jean Grey and Phoenix . . . separate . . . unique . . . bound together" (Claremont et al. 2006, 145, 181). However, Jean struggled with the complexity of being powerful and connected to both creation and destruction, the past and the present, her own life and the vastness of the universe. Her creative team concluded that to resolve these contradictions, she must be killed.

Within a white supremacist, patriarchal binary logic, liminality poses a threat; Jean's (repeated) annihilation or depowering is evidence of an obsession with upholding borders, no matter the cost. Echo's conclusion demonstrates a different logic. According to Inés Hernández-Avila, Native American imaginaries of the future are not unilateral or linear. She writes, "In imagining a future, we also imagine our past as we contemplate and enact our present. The imagination realized is praxis, and it is an imagination profoundly informed, as so many Native writers have said, by memory, by spirit, and by the land. The word and Native woman made one in self-(and community) realization and action/reflection" (2005, 2).

The fluidity demonstrated in *Phoenix Song* around the past, present, and future; between personal and collective memory; and around Echo's identity is not characterized as threatening or as indicative of instability. Instead, this multilayered imaginary provides the very conditions for Echo's ability to fully realize herself (as the culmination of her people's histories and cultures). To conceive of herself as the embodiment of cosmic power in terms of both creation and destruction is also untroubling from an Indigenous perspective. As Deloria argues, Indigenous "peoples do not cringe in superstition before nature and they are not fearful of natural processes. They are capable of creating situations in which they can use the forces of nature to their benefit" (2003, 154). Even if the Phoenix has the capacity to enact creation and destruction on a cosmic level, these are still natural processes that are normal phases in the cycles of existence. An imbalance or ill use of any natural process can of course be detrimental, but nothing suggests that such abuses are inevitable. In short, Echo's future as the Phoenix is not predetermined.

I include this brief discussion of *Phoenix Song: Echo* in this conclusion for two primary reasons. One, despite my own fraught history as a fan of the Phoenix and my declaration in the introduction that Jean Grey does not (currently) belong in this book, Roanhorse and Maresca's text offers confirmation that there is nothing inexorably antifeminist about superhero comics. Even a character type like the Phoenix, which has been historically limited as a mechanism to depict female empowerment, can be imagined differently. If Jean Grey brought me into superhero comics, Maya Lopez/Echo inspires me to stay. Two, *Phoenix Song* meets the criteria used to choose the other comics analyzed in this book and reinforces many of the qualities that I have argued make a superhero comic feminist. Like *Spider-Woman*, *America*, *The Unstoppable Wasp*, and *Ironheart*, *Phoenix Song: Echo* is an eponymous comic focused primarily on one female character; it is a discrete text that can be discussed in its entirety; and (probably owing to its relative newness) it has not received much scholarly attention thus far. *Phoenix Song* is also a Marvel comic and one that similarly demonstrates the publisher's continued efforts to diversify its team of creators and cast of characters—in this case by hiring Roanhorse, a woman with Black and Indigenous heritage, to write Echo, an Indigenous Deaf female character.

As is the case with the comics discussed in the previous chapters, *Phoenix Song* is a Blue Age comic in terms of its publication date (2021–2022), its availability via online platforms like Marvel Unlimited, its short run (five issues), and its aforementioned capacity to diversify Marvel's offerings by using a legacy character. As I mention above, there are aspects of Echo's story that mirror Jean's such that *Phoenix Song* remains recognizable as a "Dark Phoenix story." Nevertheless, in reimagining that story from the perspective of a disabled Native American woman whose cultural, political, social, and communal orientations are not rooted in white supremacist, imperialist, capitalist patriarchy, the creative team of *Phoenix Song* is able to ameliorate many of the problems attendant to earlier iterations (e.g., the link between female sexuality and psychosis, the violence of dichotomous logic, etc.). *Phoenix Song* also exhibits Blue Age qualities in its ability to make marginalized fans feel seen. In the back matter of issue #5, Roanhorse concludes her wrap-up statement by writing, "Thanks to all the fans who have reached out to tell me how much they loved the story, and especially to all the Indigenous and deaf [sic] fans who see themselves in Echo. Your ancestors are no doubt cheering you on!" (Roanhorse et al. 2022).

Phoenix Song also resembles *Spider-Woman, America, The Unstoppable Wasp,* and *Ironheart* in its explicit critique of overlapping systems of oppression and its purposeful re-creation of Indigenous women's roles as communal leaders. As mentioned previously, Roanhorse's dialogue about "the Rez" points towards the violence inherent in American settler-colonialism as it stripped Native people of their cultural, linguistic, and social traditions in addition to removing them from the land and even from their families (Dunbar-Ortiz 2014). Centering Echo's female ancestors also redresses the relative invisibility of Indigenous women in popular memory.

Although these engagements with contemporary issues are brief, they nonetheless signal some of the pressing concerns of Native American women such as self-determination and tribal sovereignty, recovering traditions and histories from the effects of colonization, and exploring "Native women's consciousness, power, and vision" (Hernández-Avila 2005, 1). Lastly, Maya Lopez/Echo—like Jessica Drew, America Chavez, Nadia van Dyne, and Riri Williams—has expanded beyond her comics appearances and is already diversifying other forms of media. Played by Deaf Menominee and Mohican actress Alaqua Cox, Echo appeared on the small screen in the streaming MCU series *Hawkeye* (Igla 2021). A titular spin-off series, *Echo,* also aired on Disney+ in January 2024. Although I have not yet seen the series, there is reason to believe that it will include similar themes and story arcs as *Phoenix Song.* Marvel Studios producer Stephen Broussard revealed that the series would be set in Oklahoma, for instance, the same location where Echo and River find some of Echo's ancestors in *Phoenix Song* (Oddo 2023). Roanhorse also thanks "the *Echo* TV show's writers' room" for working with her and acknowledges that they "inspired some of the peoples and locales Echo visited, including the Choctaw Lighthorsemen and Cahokia" (Roanhorse et al. 2022).

Thus, even though *Phoenix Song: Echo* occupies a relatively marginal place among Marvel's publications as a five-issue miniseries, its impact cannot be dismissed on that basis alone. Like the other comics analyzed in the previous chapters, *Phoenix Song* has the potential to push the genre in more feminist directions across narrative media.

The brevity of *Phoenix Song* also helps focus attention on additional feminist attributes that come to light when the comics discussed thus far are put into conversation. I suggest that if these characteristics are as apparent in a miniseries as they are in longer books, then they also play a vital role in the construction of feminist superhero comics. That Echo learns the most about her own potential from her ancestor Ohoyo Luak points to the importance of female mentors and mothers in feminist narratives. Although her own mother is absent from Echo's character history (as is characteristic of most female superheroes), *Phoenix Song* still pauses in issue #2 to show how much a relationship with her mother would mean to Echo. After River transports himself and Echo to the night Echo's parents met, he warns Echo that she should not interfere with this reality, but by chance Echo meets and talks to her mother anyway. A close-up panel of Echo's face shows immense pride, admiration, and fulfilment after just a brief moment of getting to know the kind of person her mother was (Roanhorse et al. 2021). The fact that Echo's power is rooted in her female lineage (Ohoyo Luak guides her progression) demonstrates that even in the absence of a mother, female characters need and deserve to learn from other women's knowledge and experiences.

This focus on mothers and mother figures plays out in each of the comics discussed previously. *Spider-Woman,* of course, cultivates this focus most directly by making Jess a mother herself. *Ironheart* also insists on the centrality of mothers by keeping Riri's mom in the picture and by developing Riri's motivations for heroism in relation to her need to keep her mother safe. *America* and *The Unstoppable Wasp* explore the desire a female superhero would have for her lost mother(s) in similar ways to *Phoenix Song*. Rather than acquiescing to the status quo of absent mothers, however, both comics also provide their main characters with the love and support of female mentors, female ancestors, or, as in America's case, both. The presence of mothers and female mentors in these comics cannot be collapsed into support for patriarchal norms that equate womanhood with maternity; instead, the varied depictions of these characters across titles emphasize the value of women's relationships and amend the genre's unexamined glorification of patriarchal modes of transmitting knowledge.

On the last pages of issue #44 of *The Avengers*, as Echo flies off after being newly empowered by the Phoenix Force, Jean Grey telepathically speaks to her, saying, "Maya . . . if you can hear me . . . don't try to do this alone" (Aaron et al. 2021). Although Echo has traditionally been characterized as something of a loner, *Phoenix Song* takes Jean's advice to heart and surrounds Echo with collaborators. The book's truncated format doesn't allow the relationships between Echo, River, and Forge to be very developed, but they nevertheless demonstrate the power of collaboration. Like all the women and girls analyzed in this book, Echo's journey eschews the hyperindividualism of traditional superhero narratives in favor of teamwork. Not only is Echo's realization *as* the Phoenix made possible by the collective actions of her ancestors, but River and Forge also use their unique powers to fight beside Echo to defeat The Adversary.

As Native American characters, Echo's, River's, and Forge's commitment to their people's survival and growth takes on a specific meaning; however, it also illustrates the tendency for feminist superhero comics to include collective fights for justice. In *Spider-Woman*, *America*, *The Unstoppable Wasp*, and *Ironheart*, the characters who are integral to the titular character's success also become a found family. For example, collaboration and her found family enable Jessica to be a mother *and* a superhero, and they give America the space to experience tenderness as she exudes toughness. Nadia gains a sense of belonging that would otherwise be impossible given her isolation, and Riri finds community and belonging despite a history of loss. By queering patriarchal conventions of the nuclear family, feminist superhero comics allow their heroes to retain more of their humanity by being able to experience vulnerability, cooperation, connection, and a shared sense of purpose regardless of their sexualities, familial histories, or heroic burdens.

The repeated depictions of teamwork and non-normative family structures also function as reminders that intersectional justice must be collective. As Cocca argues, "A punch to one white man's jaw from a glowing female fist doesn't dismantle multiple and overlapping systems of inequalities" (2021, 88). The seeming preference for collaboration and teamwork in feminist superhero comics and the inclusion of found families help to reinforce the fact that there is more at stake than just one character's victory. Systemic injustice cannot be fought by one person, no matter how exceptional, and until all women are free, none of us are.

Echo's recognition of the complexity of her identity as Maya Lopez, as Echo, as her ancestors' wildest dreams, as the Phoenix, and *more* is also indicative of a shared trait among the feminist superhero characters examined in this book. Regardless of existing scholarly literature that has suggested that dealing with duality is integral to mainstream superhero comics, feminist superheroes seem to exceed binary categories of identity and actively work against inflexible social norms. While it may have been the case that male superheroes like Batman, Superman, or Spider-Man strained under the weight of having to navigate both a public persona and a superhero alias, all the feminist characters in this book push beyond these simple dichotomies. Jessica Drew's pregnancy disturbs binary distinctions between self and other. As a working mom who experiences both "anger and tenderness," she defies patriarchal ideals of the "good mother," and as a woman with dynamic desires, Jess refuses to acquiesce to what is expected of her as a "top tier" superhero.

America's powers profoundly defy binaries and borders as she punches through space and time with greater fluidity and precision as her book unfolds. Her dialogue fluctuates between Spanish and English and requires readers to seamlessly navigate both. And her ability to act as a bridge between worlds, between species, and across social divides all work to celebrate her status as a borderlands subject.

Both *The Unstoppable Wasp* and *Ironheart* focus on the changeability and ambiguity of girlhood, a profoundly dynamic and unfixable state of being. Nadia contests taken-for-granted androcentric norms and reimagines the image of superhero teams in anti-essentialist ways. Riri's narrative explores the complexity of heroism in an age when doing what's right may also mean working against norms and defying authority. In short, Riri navigates superheroism through scenarios that go "beyond good and evil." This shared tendency to fight against binary logic and to exceed restrictive social norms speaks to the intersectional nature of women's lives. No woman or girl ever experiences herself through gender alone but always as a person whose life is also shaped by race, sexuality, embodiment, class, disability, nationality, geography, and so on. That these texts avoid homogenizing identity categories speaks to the responsibility their creators feel to reconstruct reality so that they may do justice to the plurality, complexity, and multivocality of women's experiences.

The polyvalence of these feminist narratives also reinforces the power of the margins. As a space that is already marked as outside, in excess or violation of "the norm," the margins of superhero comics arguably enable creators to imagine characters that speak more authentically to the diversity and dynamism of women's and girls' realities.

Phoenix Song takes on one of the most troubling, yet enduring Marvel superhero identities—that of the Phoenix—and does so using storylines that radically depart from tradition. This is a characteristic common among the comics featured in this book. The success with which each title reimagines genre conventions and previously established superhero identities reinforces the plasticity and adaptability of these stories and proves that more comics about other kinds of women and girls are not only possible but necessary.

As I suggest in the conclusion of chapter 1, gender-swap narratives in comics like *Spider-Woman* have paved the way for characters who not only allegorically speak to trans women's lives but who also explicitly represent trans women's experiences and stories. *America* shows us the power of borderlands narratives and hints at the diversity of Latinx identities. While America's purposeful adoption of latinidad affirms the variety of languages, cultures, traditions, ethnicities, and identities that inform the concept, it also reminds us that no single character can stand in for an entire demographic.

Although *The Unstoppable Wasp* focuses on Nadia's mission to build a truly diverse superhero team, the book is still ultimately about her journey as a white girl. That said, it also concludes by showing Indian American teen Priya learning to use her new powers, training to defend herself and others, daring to imagine her future as a superhero, and thus inviting readers to do the same. In surrounding Riri with other Black teens and then helping her find a sense of belonging in the fictional African nation of Wakanda, the creative team of *Ironheart* repaired the tokenism and isolation that marked Riri's character history. By demonstrating what it means to Riri to be connected to her Black community and to feel a sense of "home" in an Afrofuturist space, *Ironheart* also paves the way for more stories that enable traditionally marginalized characters to "speak the truth, decry injustice, and challenge the American way" (Wanzo 2015, 329).

It's important to note that none of these comics attempts to construct a storyworld that speaks to all women's lives, nor do they feature a superhero who can represent the experiences of all women and girls. The books mentioned above can be read as intersectional feminist texts because they depict the unique way a particular type of girl or woman's life is shaped by overlapping systems of oppression, and in their specificity, they also leave room for other distinct stories to come into being.

My aim in reiterating my research criteria and outlining these common themes is not to reconstruct the kind of taxonomy characteristic of the early history of the subfield of superhero studies. Taxonomies are not bad in and of themselves. They help us to clarify our studies and dig deep into our interests. The common vocabulary taxonomies give us can also enable us to exchange ideas more efficiently, and they make particular objects of knowledge recognizable as knowledge. As such, while I am not trying to construct a new taxonomy of superheroes, I am grateful for the work done by scholars like Coogan, Gavaler, and others that helped to establish superhero comics as a recognizable genre and thus lent credibility to superhero studies scholars who might otherwise have been ignored or dismissed because of their love for over-the-top, costume-wearing characters.

This is valuable work, but as a feminist scholar, I am not sure this is a viable aim for my project. Intersectional feminism is necessarily a contingent praxis. The varied forms of women's political, cultural, ideological, spiritual, and legal efforts to attain unmitigated access to the fullness of their lives pay testament to the dynamism of feminist orientations to the world. There simply cannot be a one-size-fits-all. And, as idealistic as it may be to say, I sincerely hope that someday the need for intersectional feminist praxis ceases to exist. Ideally, this is not an enduring project. In this sense, a codified taxonomy seems futile. Instead, I suggest that the criteria for, and the shared attributes of, the feminist superhero comics identified in this book provide the beginnings of an archive. Building from Sara Ahmed, a feminist superhero archive is not a thing I exclusively claim or control but something I hope to share with all scholars of the genre willfully following "nots." It will inevitably change as the comics do, and it will require that we care about and for what we've compiled.

As Ahmed writes, "Research involves being open to being transformed by what we encounter." And yes, perhaps using the designation of archive is strange, because, as Ahmed notes, "there is no building in which the documents are housed." Rather, a feminist superhero archive is a collection of "documents [whether comics or other media] that are passed down in which [feminism] comes up, as a trait, as a character trait" (2014, 13). It also includes concepts such as equity, solidarity, collective justice, and liberatory imaginaries. A feminist superhero archive like the one I am trying to compile includes affect and spaces of encounter: How do these superhero texts affect readers? Where do readers intersect their heroes?

And, of course, as I hope to have made clear, this assembly has begun because I have strayed from the genre's most normative paths. Marvel Studios producer Broussard says of the *Echo* series that "it's very different. . . . It's a very different tonal sort of thing," that is not easily compared to anything else in the MCU (Oddo 2023). I cannot yet say if the show parallels *Phoenix Song*, but Broussard's comments make me hopeful; perhaps *Echo* will find her way into our archive.

Like the shared themes I have identified above, this burgeoning archive of feminist superheroes "might create an even stronger impression" of the feminist superhero. That said, this project is *not* motivated by any desire to "fix" what it means to be a feminist superhero; I have no desire to define what "she *is*." As Ahmed reminds us, "We are following a depositing rather than finding what is deposited" (2014, 17). *Searching for Feminist Superheroes* represents my efforts to follow the "nots," the traces, the depositings. I have endeavored to walk the path established by other feminist scholars who have shown not only the shortcomings of the superhero genre but also the vast possibilities for the genre to reconstruct the complex realities of women's lives. Further, I have followed traces left by creative teams who willfully include and omit building blocks of reality to produce characters and storyworlds that speak to women's and girls' experiences of overlapping systems of oppression. Yet they also dare to imagine storyworlds free from such degradation. For all the talk of "superhero fatigue" (a discourse that has been unfolding for years), superheroes are and will remain an integral part of our culture. There is no reason we should cede such an impactful form of fantasy to the limitations determined by hegemonic social norms. We can have feminist superheroes.

Ahmed argues that feminist archives are "premised on hope: the hope that those who wander away from the paths they are supposed to follow leave their footprints behind" (2014, 21). I have followed the depositings of particular feminist superheroes as they proliferate across media, leaving my footprints behind in this book. My hope is that other scholars and fans will wander from the mainstream into the margins to search out the "nots" and meet me in the archive of feminist superheroes.

ACKNOWLEDGMENTS

One of the (unofficial) conventions of superhero scholarship is for authors to share their own origin stories as comics fans. Like many, I inherited my first superhero comics from my older brother. However, weaving a narrative from that point forward would be slightly disingenuous on my part. Sure, I loved the old *Spider-Man* floppies and their corresponding 45 RPM records, but I don't remember them inspiring me to seek out more or different comics. My Spider-Man treasures went into my toy chest alongside Star Wars toys, Barbies, and My Little Ponies and were simply one part of the expansive imaginary landscape I built through play.

To be perfectly honest, my love for superheroes grew more through seeing them on film than it did from reading their comics. I was devastated when Christopher Reeve's Superman renounced his powers. My cousins and I practiced saying, "I'm Batman," in our best Michael Keaton voices until we were hoarse. And Famke Janssen's turn as Jean Grey in *X-Men* (Singer 2000) was so captivating that I too became a redhead from the mid-2000s onwards. Jean was intelligent, beautiful, compassionate, and, to my eyes, more powerful than she seemed. As I watched her character become more godlike over the subsequent films, my interest in her grew, and my desire to understand her as both powerful and *empowering* intensified. I was invigorated by seeing a female character who was unstoppable, full of rage, and yet somehow still loved. Looking for more of that, for more Jean, is what brought me back to comics and what set me on the path towards this book.

For better or worse, by the time I came to comics studies, I had not only revived my status as a comics reader, but I was also a new PhD. This meant that the superhero comics I read, including those centered on Jean, were treated with the same feminist lenses I had learned to apply to my doctoral research. This often left me feeling frustrated and deflated rather than captivated and empowered. Like the materials I analyzed for my thesis, however, I was determined to find more creative ways to read superhero comics such that feminist readers like me could still find something inspiring in their pages. I am immensely grateful to Ken Koltun-Fromm and Assaf Gamzou for giving me the opportunity to apply this strategy and to publish my first piece on feminism and superhero comics. It was also at Ken and Assaf's symposium, Sacred Texts and Comics, that I met Aaron David Lewis, Elizabeth Rae Coody, and Jeff Richey, all of whom became treasured comics studies buddies and collaborators, and to whom I am thankful for their support and friendship.

I also owe Aaron David Lewis a debt of gratitude for introducing me to the Comics Studies Society. Joining CSS opened innumerable doors, gave me a community, and encouraged me to continue to develop my comics scholarship. I am especially grateful to Carol Tilley, who did so much to support my early work; Candida Rifkind, whose commitment and passion taught me what kind of leader I want to be; Biz Nijdam, whose immense kindness is matched by her outstanding capability; and Nhora Serrano and Susan Kirtley, who have become some of my favorite collaborators. I am immensely grateful to Carolyn Cocca, whose work is foundational to any feminist study of superhero comics and whose guidance and feedback on my first peer-reviewed journal article made it a piece I am truly proud of. My journey as a feminist scholar of superhero comics would also not have been possible without Anna Peppard. The bibliography of this book reads a little like Anna's CV, which is a testament not only to my admiration but also to her creativity, sharp analysis, and love of the medium. I am thankful for Kate McClancy, another "OG" comics studies buddy, whose work with the Comics Arts Conference gave me numerous opportunities to lay the groundwork for this book.

Enormous thanks go to my "Monstrous Women" crew, so many of whom I am lucky enough to call friends. I am particularly grateful to Ayanni Hanna Cooper and Charlotte Johanne Fabricius, who were kind enough to read drafts of chapters in this book. Huge thanks to J. Richard Stevens, Dan Yezbick, Christy Knopf, and Justin Wigard, who have all supported my work, shared their own witty and brilliant scholarship, and extended their friendship into a galaxy far, far away. Speaking of rebel alliances, I cannot say thank you enough to my best partners in crime, John Edward Martin and Spencer Keralis. Every scheme we've cooked up together has been life giving, I simply could not have done the last half decade without you. I love you both.

There is also no way for me to express enough gratitude to Adam Benkato. I am one of many, many PhDs for whom a stable academic job is unlikely. No matter how precarious my employment situation has been, Adam has never stopped encouraging me to push forward, reminding me of my worth, or refusing to let me quit. This book exists because Adam believed it should and because he did whatever it took to ensure I had the time and resources to write it. You saved the day, RB. Lub ub ub. I am also so thankful for the unwavering love and support of my family (Gentners, Langsdales, Karsenos, and Benkatos alike), my best ones, witches, and Baysties, my murder puppy, and all the sparkly people I am fortunate enough to count as friends. Your love means the world to me.

Finally, I want to extend heartfelt thanks to the series editors of the World Comics and Graphic Nonfiction Series at the University of Texas Press: Christopher González, Deborah Elizabeth Whaley, and especially Frederick Luis Aldama, whose encouragement gave me the confidence to submit my book proposal. I am also so grateful to my editor Jim Burr for all his constructive feedback and positive reinforcement, as well as to my copyeditor Leslie Tingle for her humor and precision. And thank you to my peer reviewers: your insights, questions, and guidance made this book better.

NOTES

INTRODUCTION. "A WILLFUL METHOD"

1. Any type within quotations set in italics or boldface reflects the source typography.
2. For a historical synthesis of feminisms across eras and geographies, see Freedman (2003). For a comprehensive introduction to the diversity of feminist thought, see Tong and Botts (2018).
3. Although related to the present study, an analysis of feminist men and boys in superhero comics would present its own challenges and promises and thus deserves to be treated separately.
4. Of the four female characters discussed in this book, America Chavez, as she appears in Gabby Rivera and Joe Quinones's solo run, is the subject of the most scholarly studies. That said, at the time of writing, these publications are still far outnumbered by those on the other characters listed above.
5. Unfortunately, the Warner Bros. takeover of streaming channel HBO Max, where the *Batgirl* film was set to debut, resulted in the film's cancellation (Coggan 2023).
6. At one point in *The Dark Phoenix Saga*, Jean is brainwashed and has visions of being on a slave plantation in the South. Storm, an African goddess, appears to Jean in this vision as an enslaved woman bound in shackles. All of this, we are led to believe, is a part of Jean's deepest, darkest desires (Claremont et al. 2006).
7. See "A Short History of 'Retcon,'" accessed November 28, 2023, https://www.merriam-webster.com/wordplay/retcon-history-and-meaning.
8. Including texts such as José Alaniz's *Death, Disability, and the Superhero* (2014), Deborah Elizabeth Whaley's *Black Women in Sequence* (2015), Ramzi Fawaz's *The New Mutants* (2016), Adilifu Nama's *Super Black* (2011), Jeffrey A. Brown's *Black Superheroes, Milestone Comics, and Their Fans* (2001) and *Panthers, Hulks, and Ironhearts* (2021), Frederick Luis Aldama's *Latinx*

Superheroes in Mainstream Comics (2017), Lee Easton and Richard Harrison's *Secret Identity Reader* (2010), and the anthology *Superheroes and Identities* (Gibson, Huxley, and Ormrod 2014).

9. More specifically, Lillian S. Robinson's *Wonder Women* (2004), Jeffrey A. Brown's *Dangerous Curves* (2013a) and *Beyond Bombshells* (2015), Carolyn Cocca's *Superwomen* (2016) and *Wonder Woman and Captain Marvel* (2021), the edited volume *Supersex* (Peppard 2020), Jennifer Stuller's *Ink-Stained Amazons and Cinematic Warriors* (2010), the edited volume *Gender and the Superhero Narrative* (Goodrum, Prescott, and Smith 2018), and Frederick Luis Aldama's anthology *The Routledge Companion to Gender and Sexuality in Comic Book Studies* (2021).

CHAPTER 1. WHOA MOMMA!

1. While still widely used in academic literature, the label "French feminists" is not without problems. Its use tends to homogenize a diverse field of scholars and ignores the fact that many of these women have openly contested the term "feminist." It also belies the fact that the scholars in question are not exclusively French (e.g., Irigaray is Belgian-born, Cixous is of Algerian origin, and Kristeva is Bulgarian). For further discussion, see Cavallaro (2003, ix–xvii).
2. Even if to be socialized through language in a patriarchal system means being inured to phallogocentrism, Cixous does not believe that there is no escape. On the contrary, she, like other French feminists, argues for different ways of thinking, speaking, and writing that expose the illusory nature of the inevitability of the "Law of the Father" and explore femininity for its own sake. See, for example, Cixous (1976).
3. Ross Murray's work on Marvel's X-Men character Mystique further reinforces the trope of monstrous mothers in superhero comics (2011).
4. To explore just how impossible this and other female superhero poses are, female journalists attempted to recreate the poses for a photo shoot. Every pose, including Manara's, required multiple props, bodily discomfort, and heavy photo editing. None of the resultant photos perfectly recreated the comic book images, thus underscoring the fantastical nature of the poses (Fustich 2015).
5. These assumptions do not just occur in-text. Upon hearing the news of a pregnant Spider-Woman, pop-culture website *CBR* invited Hopeless for an interview about the forthcoming title. Among the first set of questions posed was, "Is the father of her child in the picture?" (Richards 2015).
6. Because feminist theory is no more homogenous a field than comics studies or cultural studies, and because feminism as a praxis varies through time and according to the concerns of its practitioners, my discussion here

cannot adequately capture the varying positions feminists have taken regarding women's reproductive capacities, health, rights, etc. For a sample of the sometimes-divergent views on motherhood that feminist thinkers have held, see Moyra Davey's edited volume, *Mother Reader* (2001).

7. Jessica's relationship with Roger arguably constitutes a point of paradox. As I assert above, denying Jess the opportunity to pursue a sexual and romantic relationship would perpetuate harmful cultural expectations for mothers to be "pure" and asexual. However, as two white characters in a heterosexual relationship, Jess and Roger adhere to the status quo for romantic pairings in superhero comics. Moreover, as Kristen Hoerl and Casey Ryan Kelly argue, recent media focused on single women as mothers tends to conclude with heteronormative romances that work to reinforce assumptions about the connection between heterosexuality and parenthood, even if in nontraditional ways (2010). Thus, it is true that while *Spider-Woman* disrupts sexist expectations for mothers to be asexual, it also reinforces white heterosexual relationships as the norm.
8. See also "Motherhood according to Giovanni Bellini" for further discussion of the maternal subject (Kristeva 1980b, 237–270).
9. Whether Kristeva de-essentializes gender in relation to maternity or traffics in essentialist stereotypes is debatable. For a synthesis of several theorists whose readings differ from Edelstein's, see Cavallaro (2003, 172–173).
10. McCloud identifies a "bleed" as an instance "when a panel runs off the edge of the page" (1994, 103).
11. According to Anne Enke, the prefix "cis" means "on the same side or staying with the same orientation," so in terms of gender, a cis person is someone who stays with or is "perceived to stay with the gender and/or sex one was assigned at birth" (2012, 20). I was assigned female at birth, and I identify as a woman, therefore, I am a cis woman. "Trans" means "on or to the other side," and as an identity "may include a gender identity that differs from sex assigned at birth; a gender expression that differs from that conventionally expected of people according to their bodily sex; and/or a desire for alteration of the body's sex/gender characteristics" (Enke 2012, 19).
12. Jamie Capuzza and Leland Spencer argue that "television often has supported the cisgender status quo. Across television genres, a standardized television narrative typically employed a 'wrong body discourse' and privileged the traditional notion of 'transgender as transition,' thus aligning gender with sex and supporting the gender binary. In short, television has normalized and reified as monolithic one particular experience of transgender identity and expression" (2016, 216).
13. Rob Lendrum argues that storylines featuring gay superheroes often celebrate fatherhood as a way to heteronormalize them (2004). Jesse's paternity may similarly complicate a trans or queer reading of his circumstances.

14. Unfortunately, there are those who identify themselves as feminists but who also deliberately exclude trans people, particularly trans women, from their theory and practice. The identifier for a person who takes this position, TERF, is an acronym for trans-exclusionary radical feminist. Although the term was coined in cisgender circles, it is now used widely to designate those who weaponize their interpretation of feminism to discriminate and even enact violence against trans people. Cristan Williams writes that "while *TERF*, as a lexical unit, can carry unflattering overtones in the same way that *bigot*, *misogynist*, or *racist* might, it nonetheless constructs a much-needed way to disentangle the sometimes subjugative, violent, and even murderous anti-trans behavior and rhetoric of TERF activism from radical feminism itself, even as TERFs work tirelessly to represent their activism as 'radical feminism' on popular, social, and academic media platforms" (2021). From my perspective, trans-exclusionary versions of feminism and intersectional feminism are mutually exclusive; as such, the former is irrelevant beyond this note to recognize the harm such a position causes.
15. In her synthesis of Ellis's work, Garbes is clearly making reference to people who choose to transition via hormonal therapies, surgery, or both; however, it is important to note that these are not choices universally made among trans people.
16. The version of Jessica in *Spider-Verse* is presented as cis and is voiced by cisgender actress Issa Rae. Thus, while this new iteration of Jess may not expand pregnancy in ways that disrupt cisnormative expectations, the film will still add a much-needed and similarly marginalized perspective to superhero media and representations of motherhood.

CHAPTER 2. *AMERICA* AND THE NEW MESTIZA

1. Quinones is the primary penciler and provides most of the covers for the series. That said, a large team of other pencilers, inkers, and colorists have also worked on the title at various points, making Rivera the only constant among the creators. (See the "Primary Sources" section of the references for more precise attributions.) As such, this chapter will refer to Rivera and Quinones when discussing issues on which Quinones is indeed the primary artist. In discussions of issues with larger creative teams (e.g., issue #7, which features the work of eight artists), or in discussing the book generally, credit will be given to "the creative team."
2. The term "Latinx" was developed by activists and scholars in order to avoid the inherent androcentrism of using the masculine "Latinos" to refer to a group of people and to be more inclusive of gender identities beyond man and woman. At the time of writing, the term "Latine" (pronounced

Lah-TEEN-ay) is also being used with greater frequency by those who wish to retain the inclusivity of "Latinx" but who find the *-e* more indicative of other Spanish word endings. Because of its prevalence in the relevant literature, this chapter will use the term "Latinx" when referring to a group of people with various gender identities or to nonbinary individuals, and "Latina" or "Latino" when referring to individuals who identify as a woman or a man. The use of "Latinos" to refer to a group is used by some authors who are quoted here.

3. Aldama is careful to note that while some Latinx people are born with fairer skin and European facial features, their overrepresentation in comics has functioned to all but erase "phenotypically dark and/or non-Caucasian featured Latinx" characters (2017, 122).
4. As popular as she is, Beyoncé's self-identification as a feminist is also controversial. For a discussion of the debates around Beyoncé's feminism, see Hobson 2016.
5. Stuller is specifically addressing women and girls in the genre, but scholars like Christopher Paul Wagenheim note how poorly mothers are treated throughout superhero comics, regardless of the gender of the child (2014).
6. Agent Peggy Carter first appeared in *Captain America* comics as part of the French Resistance in World War II. She is skilled in espionage and hand-to-hand combat.
7. One can assume this group is nonbinary (i.e., they do not identify with binary categories of gender like girl or boy or woman or man) because as America carries one character (Imani) to safety, she avoids using gendered pronouns, saying she needs to "get this kid to their family" (Rivera et al., issue #1). In issue #2 another character, Zulai, is described in a caption box as "Imani's right-hand amigx." Here, the Spanish word for friend, *amiga/o,* is treated like the word "Latinx," where the gendered ending is replaced with *-x* to be more inclusive. The Chavez Guerrillas may be read as femme because as nonbinary teens they adopt traditionally feminine styles of comportment, such as cosmetics and hairstyles.
8. This fact becomes apparent about Imani and Zu in *America* issue #3; readers learn this about David in issue #1; X'andria's ambitions are explored in issue #8.
9. Chicana is the Spanish word for a Mexican American woman; "*tejana*" more specifically refers to a Texan woman of Mexican descent.
10. According to Juana María Rodríguez, "*Latinidad* serves to define a particular geopolitical experience, but it also contains within it the complexities and contradictions of immigration, (post)(neo)colonialism, race, color, legal status, class, nation, language, and the politics of location" (2003, 9–10). The utility and constructiveness of the concept is debated among Latinx scholars, as are the terms "mestiza" and "mestizaje"; for a synthesis of these debates, see Rodríguez (2003, 5–36). Similar concerns arise for

comics scholars analyzing *America*. Grace Martin, for example, argues that the creative team's construction of America as a mestiza and the presentation of latinidad in her storyworld are achieved via a "haphazard saturation of hodge-podge Latinx cultural elements" that "often [reproduce] common stereotypes about Latinx subjects to the point of nearly caricaturizing them" (2020, 35–36). Conversely, Ande Davis argues that the "surface erasure of nationality" is "a broader call toward a transcultural feminism," and "a call toward Anzaldúan solidarity" (2021, 74). For other sources that recognize the risks of latinidad and mestizaje yet find their application in *America* constructive, see Castillo Planas (2021) and Jiménez (2018).

11. For more on the importance of masks and costuming in *lucha libre* and how Mexican wrestling plays a central role in Hernandez's comics, see Gil-Gómez (2016, 109–129).

CHAPTER 3. *THE UNSTOPPABLE WASP*

1. *The Unstoppable Wasp* issues #1–4 are collected in *Vol. 1: Unstoppable!* (Whitley et al. 2017); issues #5–8 appear in *Vol. 2: Agents of G.I.R.L.* (Whitley et al. 2018).
2. Issues #1–5 appear in *The Unstoppable Wasp Unlimited Vol. 1: Fix Everything* (Whitley and Gurihiru 2019); and issues #6–10 appear in *Vol. 2: G.I.R.L. vs. A.I.M.* (Whitley, Gurihiru, and Firmansyah 2019).
3. Nadia was originally created by writer Mark Waid and artist Alan Davis for Marvel's 2016 *Free Comic Book Day Civil War II* "event" (Waid et al. 2016).
4. As a white man, Whitley adheres to the status quo for creators at Marvel. Nevertheless, his commitment to writing female-led, feminist comics (like *Princeless, Raven: Pirate Princess,* and *School for Extraterrestrial Girls*) is worth noting.
5. While Whitley is reimagining who Janet is and can be, it is arguably the case that the history of her character as a superhero is steeped in androcentric assumptions. As Peppard notes, "Many of Marvel's female superheroes of the 1960s, including the Invisible Girl, the Wasp, and Marvel Girl, become and remain superheroes primarily to stay close to their male love interests" (2017, 111).
6. For example, Robert Weiner, Robert Peaslee, and Duncan Prettyman use this phrasing to describe the overwhelming characterization of villains in the Golden Age (2020, xxviii).
7. My suggestion that Janet's actions are akin to feminist abolitionist praxis is tentative. While prison abolition has been a longstanding movement in the United States and is participated in by myriad people with varying inspirations, contemporary abolitionist movements have overwhelmingly been led and defined by Black people and people of color. According to Elizabeth

Whalley and Colleen Hackett, white women's involvement in the criminal legal system has, in some instances, made the carceral state stronger (2017). Further, while economically disadvantaged white women do make up a substantial portion of imprisoned women, Black women and women of color are the majority. Thus, the scene in question runs the risk of appropriating the foundational work of Black women like Angela Davis (2003) and Michelle Alexander (2010); of obscuring the anti-abolitionist relationship between some white liberal feminists and the carceral state; and of erasing the women who are most harmed by the prison-industrial complex.

8. In issue #7 of the relaunch, for instance (*Unlimited Vol. 2: G.I.R.L. vs. A.I.M.*), she giddily accepts a "team-up" brawl as a birthday gift (Whitley et al. 2019).
9. Portions of this introductory paragraph have been adapted from material that first appeared in *Signs: Journal of Women in Culture and Society* (see Langsdale 2020).
10. For further discussion of this identification, see chapter 4 in this book.
11. One of the villains Nadia faces in *The Unstoppable Wasp* is in fact disabled. A cyborg called Mother, whose flesh appears decrepit and whose mobility is impaired, certainly seems to adhere to the status quo of disabled "villains coded as monstrous Others" (Fabricius 2020, 87). While I cannot sufficiently address the design and narrative function of Mother here, there is marked potential for future research on the intersections of disability, monstrosity, and motherhood in relation to this character and to the feminist politics of the book.
12. Even if Taina's desire is being represented as heterosexual, it is important to note how her sexuality queers or disrupts ableist assumptions about disabled women being "sexless and barren due to [their] disabled [bodies]" (Fabricius 2020, 92).
13. Romantic interest and sexual desire are not the same thing and do not necessarily simultaneously manifest in every relationship; however, in the case of Shay and Ying, both are relevant.
14. Thanks to Ayanni CH Cooper for identifying these as "love bubbles."
15. In issue #7 of the relaunch, for example (*Unlimited Vol. 2: G.I.R.L. vs. A.I.M.*), Nadia, Priya, and Ying all end up jumping up and down, holding hands, and screaming in celebration of the revelation that Ying and Shay have just kissed (Whitley et al. 2019).
16. Thanks to Spencer Keralis for helping me to clarify this point.
17. According to Miller, sex-normativity centers on "the idea that sexual desire is foundational to human identity" (2017, 356).
18. Whitley was also the writer for a short run of comics called *Marvel Action: Chillers*, in which Nadia also appears and wherein she makes another explicit statement about her interests. In issue #3, as Nadia finds herself confronted with the villain Venom, she calls G.I.R.L. headquarters for help and hears Taina on the other end of the line. Taina teases Nadia, saying she thought

Nadia had a date with Spider-Man, to which she responds "It's not a date, Taina! I don't like *like* him! It was for science!" Taina continues to give Nadia a hard time, which eventually prompts Nadia to shout, "Taina, I know you think you're funny . . . but the two things I'm least interested in are romantic relationships *and being eaten!*" (Whitley et al. 2020).

19. Note that while this separation does appear, the two women in question are still nondisabled, upper-middle-class, well educated, white, thin, conventionally attractive, and heterosexual. Thus, while removing motherhood from the equation may result in a slightly less hegemonic discursive construction of "woman," the feminine identities Janet and Bobbi embody are not entirely free from hegemonic norms.
20. María Lugones and Elizabeth Spelman point towards the "history of clumsy missionaries, and the white suffragists of the 19th century (who couldn't imagine why Black women 'couldn't see' how crucial getting the vote for 'women' was)" in demonstrating how even supposedly good intentions (e.g., enacting women's suffrage) can cause harm when they are formulated by a single group who assumes that their own version of things is universal (1983, 579). Because Black women were not free citizens, winning the vote was not their priority. White women, however, saw emancipation (of all enslaved Black people) as a secondary issue that threatened to enfranchise Black men before themselves. Thus, they rejected Black women's participation and leadership in the early women's movement, claiming that what was in the best interest of "women" was to gain the vote before any other group of men, even if Black men's enfranchisement would also mean the emancipation of Black women (Angela Davis 1981).

CHAPTER 4. SAMPLING *IRONHEART*

1. There is some debate about this. Technically Riri had a brief cameo in issue #7 of *Invincible Iron Man*, but her first full appearance was not until issue #9.
2. In print, the book was first available as twelve monthly issues published in 2018. Issues #1–6 then became available as the trade paperback *Ironheart Vol. 1: Those with Courage* (2019) and then issues #7–12 were published in *Ironheart Vol. 2: Ten Rings* (2020). A trade paperback containing all twelve issues has also been published: *Ironheart: Meant to Fly* (2020). Finally, as with all Blue Age comics, *Ironheart* can be read digitally via online platforms.
3. Jeffrey A. Brown writes, "Where male characters usually strike heroic action poses, superheroines are far more likely to be illustrated as pin-ups or centerfolds" (Brown 2013a, 134). There were two versions of Campbell's cover: the one described above in which Riri wears street clothes, and one where Riri

stands in the same pose but wearing her Iron Man armor. While the cover featuring her in armor is arguably more action-oriented—she appears to be preparing to blast her hand cannon—she is still fairly inert, standing with planted feet and popped hips.

4. The implication that young Black women are inherently "sassy" is a point to which I will return.
5. According to Moya Bailey and Whitney Peoples, "*misogynoir* describes the co-constitutive, anti-Black, and misogynistic racism directed at Black women, particularly in visual and digital culture. The term is a combination of *misogyny*, 'the hatred of women,' and *noir*, which means 'black' but also carries film and media connotations. It is the particular amalgamation of anti-Black racism and misogyny in popular media and culture that targets Black trans and cis women" (2007, 2–3).
6. Luciano Vecchio is credited as the artist for issues #1–5 and #7–12, while Kevin Libranda is credited as the artist on issues #1 and #6. Where I discuss the art of the book as a whole, I use both their names; in discussions of specific issues I identify which artist is primarily credited.
7. Randy Duncan and Matthew J. Smith define "synecdoche" as a "prevalent reductive device in comics" that uses "a part to represent the whole or vice versa. For example, in the majority of panels, only a portion of a characters' body is drawn to represent the reality of the entire body" (2009, 133).
8. Feminist scholars Dill and Kohlman (2014) assert that intersectional approaches that simply include differences or incorporate diverse identities are weak, whereas approaches that acknowledge and critique how systems of inequality relate to one another to subjugate marginalized groups are strong.
9. In her feedback on the first draft of this chapter, Ayanni CH Cooper noted that there is potential for further research on Tony's naming of Riri. Because of the roles of naming or nicknaming in African American history and culture, more could be said about the racial politics of Tony naming Riri rather than Riri choosing a name for herself.
10. Robin DiAngelo writes that within white supremacist societies, "whites can represent humanity, while people of color, who are never just people but always most particularly black people, Asian people, etc., can only represent their own racialized experiences" (2011, 59).
11. Bendis has articulated his desires to contribute to more diverse representation in superhero comics in numerous interviews. He also frequently credits his two Black daughters for inspiring the creation of heroes like Miles Morales. Such interviews help to make Bendis's intentions clear, but the impact of his narrative choices varies, and it is the *impact* in which I am primarily interested here. For an example of Bendis's own explanation of his desires and inspirations, see Parker (2020).

12. Thanks to Ayanni CH Cooper for pointing out that Riri's *girlhood* matters here. This shift not only affirms Black women but also Black girls. For more on Black girlhood, see Brown (2009) and Jordan-Zachery and Harris (2019).
13. For further discussion of the significance of Riri's ability to fly, see Stringfield (2022).
14. Duncan and Smith write that "many splash pages, and most double-page spreads, simply operate as pinups of the hero leaping into action" (2009, 139).
15. Maya Angelou (1928–2014) was an American poet, writer, and civil rights activist. Incredibly prolific throughout her fifty-year career, she published autobiographies, collections of essays, books of poetry, plays, and worked in TV and film. Angelou's work garnered multiple awards, and she is widely considered to be one of the most important Black women writers in US history.
16. Nina Simone (1933–2003) was an American singer, songwriter, musician, arranger, and civil rights activist. Although her career was tumultuous, she was admired for her powerful performance style, and her protest songs and activist anthems made her one of the most influential artists of her time.
17. Ayanni CH Cooper has suggested that these lens flares are also reminiscent of "love bubbles" from shojo manga, a relevant observation given the shared joy being portrayed in the panel in question.
18. The figure of the Hulk is visually reminiscent of a Funko Pop! collectible figurine; they are particularly popular at "nerd culture" events such as comic conventions.
19. Riri's technical genius could also be included here; however, that is a point to which I will return later in the chapter.
20. This cover was also chosen as the cover for the trade paperback that collects all twelve issues of the comic, *Ironheart: Meant to Fly* (2020).
21. Arendt's coverage of the trial was highly controversial, and subsequent scholarship has continued to debate her work, including the various inaccuracies in her initial reporting of the trial proceedings. It is not the point of this chapter to contribute to these debates or to assess the veracity of Arendt's work more generally. Instead, I am specifically interested in how Ewing used her observations about the "banality of evil" as a phenomenon to explore Riri's ethical identity as a superhero.
22. This short dialogue raises a point of tension for a feminist analysis of *Ironheart*. Although Ewing and the rest of the creative team try to distance Riri from Iron Man via this distinction between weapons and tools and a redesigned suit, the question remains whether Riri's use of technologically advanced armor can be truly separated from Tony's tech and, by extension, militarism. Because Tony's Iron Man suit was built with the knowledge he gained as a weapons manufacturer for the military-industrial complex, and because Riri begins her journey by building her own version of Tony's suit,

it is difficult to completely extract *Ironheart* from other forms of militainment. As Carolyn Cocca writes, militainment involves "technofetishism" as part of "a liberal fantasy of the military" that translates state violence into a form of "pleasurable consumption" (2021, 30). Although I suggest below that *Ironheart* is largely successful in avoiding uncritical "technophilia," the history of Riri's suit as an offspring from Tony's complicates a feminist reading and points towards the need for further research.

23. It's not to say that Riri *never* causes harm—her use of force, particularly defensively, does occasionally inflict injury—but because that is never her intent, Ewing's distinction arguably remains intact. The distinction between destruction caused by weaponry or by tool use also complicates the matter, because even when Riri does not intend to be destructive, she sometimes is (e.g., blasting through walls, front doors, etc.). In these instances, Riri's frequent attempts to repair the damage (e.g., issue #6 shows Riri replacing a blasted front door) suggest that the use of superheroic force is never treated with total impunity in *Ironheart*.
24. Ravynn Stringfield builds on similar scholarship of Black technomastery to argue that Riri's story serves as an example of "technomagic girlhood" (2023).

CONCLUSION. ARCHIVING TRACES OF FEMINIST SUPERHEROES

1. That is not to say that the representation of Echo's deafness is entirely without problems. Although *Phoenix Song* does include a few panels in which she uses sign language, Echo is overwhelmingly shown lip-reading, which "assimilates her into the dominant hearing culture that permeates both American comics and beyond." As Jules Chin Greene writes, "While superhero stories necessitate readers to suspend their disbelief, the misrepresentation of Echo's deafness provides both an inaccurate depiction of how many hard of hearing and d/Deaf people navigate the world, as well as a shallow understanding of what 'diversity' looks like in real life" (2022).

REFERENCES

PRIMARY SOURCES

Legend: (w) writer, (p) penciler, (i) inker, (c) colorist, (l) letterer.

America

Issue #1. 2017. Gabby Rivera (w), Joe Quinones (p, i), José Villarrubia (c), and Travis Lanham (l). Marvel Comics.

Issue #2. 2017. Gabby Rivera (w), Joe Quinones (p), Ming Doyle (p, i), Joe Rivera (i), José Villarrubia (c), Travis Lanham (l). Marvel Comics.

Issue #3. 2017. Gabby Rivera (w), Joe Quinones (p), Stacey Lee (p, i), Joe Rivera (i), José Villarrubia (c), Jordan Gibson (c), and Travis Lanham (l). Marvel Comics.

Issue #4. 2017. Gabby Rivera (w), Joe Quinones (p, i), Ming Doyle (p, i), Joe Rivera (i), José Villarrubia (c), Jordan Gibson (c), and Travis Lanham (l). Marvel Comics.

Issue #5. 2017. Gabby Rivera (w), Ramon Villalobos (p, i), Tamra Bonvillain (c), and Travis Lanham (l). Marvel Comics.

Issue #6. 2017. Gabby Rivera (w), Ramon Villalobos (p, i), Tamra Bonvillain (c), and Travis Lanham (l). Marvel Comics.

Issue #7. 2017. Gabby Rivera (w), Jen Bartel (p, i, c), Annie Wu (p, i), Aud Koch (p, i), Joe Quinones (p, i), Ming Doyle (p, i), Jordan Gibson (c), Rachelle Rosenberg (c), and Travis Lanham (l). Marvel Comics.

Issue #8. 2017. Gabby Rivera (w), Joe Quinones (p), Joe Rivera (i), Jordan Gibson (c), and Travis Lanham (l). Marvel Comics.

Issue #10. 2017. Gabby Rivera (w), Flaviano (p, i), Jen Bartel (p, i), Chris O'Halloran (c), Jordan Gibson (c), and Travis Lanham (l). Marvel Comics.

Issue #11. 2018. Gabby Rivera (w), Stacey Lee (p, i), Flaviano (p, i), Jordan Gibson (c), Chris O'Halloran (c), and Travis Lanham (l). Marvel Comics.

Issue #12. 2018. Gabby Rivera (w), Stacey Lee (p, i), Flaviano (p, i), Jordan Gibson (c), Chris O'Halloran (c), Annie Wu (p, i), and Travis Lanham (l). Marvel Comics.

The Avengers

Issue #42. 2021. Jason Aaron (w), Luca Maresca (p, i), David Curiel (c), and Cory Petit (l). Marvel Comics.

Issue #44. 2021. Jason Aaron (w), Javier Garrón (p, i), David Curiel (c), and Cory Petit (l). Marvel Comics.

Champions

Issue #2. 2018. Jim Zub (w), Emilio Laiso (p, i), Andy Troy (c), and Clayton Cowles (l). Marvel Comics.

Issue #22. 2018. Jim Zub (w), Kevin Libranda (p, i), Marcio Menyz (c), and Clayton Cowles (l). Marvel Comics.

Chesty Sanchez

Issue #1. 1995. Steve Ross (w). Antarctic Press.

Cihualyaomiquiz, The Jaguar

1996. Laura Molina (w). Insurgent Comix.

Invincible Iron Man

Issue #3. 2017. Brian Michael Bendis (w), Stefano Caselli (p, i), Marte Gracia (c), and Clayton Cowles (l). Marvel Comics.

Issue #6. 2017. Brian Michael Bendis (w), Stefano Caselli (p, i), Marte Gracia (c), and Clayton Cowles (l). Marvel Comics.

Issue #9. 2016. Brian Michael Bendis (w), Mike Deodato (p, i), Frank Martin (c), and Clayton Cowles (l). Marvel Comics.

Ironheart Vol. 1: Those with Courage

Issues #1–6. 2019. Eve Ewing (w), Kevin Libranda (p, i), Luciano Vecchio (p, i), Geoffo (p), Matt Milla (c), and Clayton Cowles (l). Marvel Comics.

Ironheart Vol. 2: Ten Rings

Issues #7–12. 2020. Eve Ewing (w), Luciano Vecchio (p, i), Geoffo (p), Matt Milla (c), and Clayton Cowles (l). Marvel Comics.

Ironheart: Meant to Fly (Complete series)

Issues #1–12. 2020. Eve Ewing (w), Luciano Vecchio (p, i), Kevin Libranda (p, i), Geoffo (p), Matt Milla (c), and Clayton Cowles (l). Marvel Comics.

Jean Grey

Issue #1. 2017. Dennis Hopeless (w), Victor Ibanez (p, i), Jay David Ramos (c), and Travis Lanham (l). Marvel Comics.

Marvel Action: Chillers

Issue #3. 2020. Jeremy Whitley (w), Gretel Lusky (p, i), Bowen McCurdy (p, i), Nahuel Ruiz (c), and Valeria Lopez (l). Marvel Comics.

Phoenix Song: Echo

Issue #1. 2021. Rebecca Roanhorse (w), Luca Maresca (p, i), Carlos Lopez (c), and Ariana Maher (l). Marvel Comics.

Issue #2. 2021. Rebecca Roanhorse (w), Luca Maresca (p, i), Kyle Charles (p, i), Carlos Lopez (c), Bryan Valenza (c), and Ariana Maher (l). Marvel Comics.

Issue #3. 2021. Rebecca Roanhorse (w), Luca Maresca (p, i), Kyle Charles (p, i), Bryan Valenza (c), Carlos Lopez (c), and Ariana Maher (l). Marvel Comics.

Issue #4. 2022. Rebecca Roanhorse (w), Luca Maresca (p, i), Kyle Charles (p, i), Bryan Valenza (c), Carlos Lopez (c), and Ariana Maher (l). Marvel Comics.

Issue #5. 2022. Rebecca Roanhorse (w), Luca Maresca (p, i), Kyle Charles (p, i), Carlos Lopez (c), and Ariana Maher (l). Marvel Comics.

Phoenix Resurrection: The Return of Jean Grey

Issue #1. 2017. Matthew Rosenberg (w), Leinil Francis Yu (p), Gerry Alanguilan (i), Rachelle Rosenberg (c), and Travis Lanham (l). Marvel Comics.

Issue #3. 2018. Matthew Rosenberg (w), Rachelle Rosenberg (c), Joe Bennett (p), Lorenzo Ruggiero (i), and Travis Lanham (l). Marvel Comics.

Issue #5. 2018. Matthew Rosenberg (w), Leinil Francis Yu (p), Gerry Alanguilan (i), Rachelle Rosenberg (c), Joe Bennett (p), Belardino Brabo (i), and Travis Lanham (l). Marvel Comics.

Spider-Woman

Issue #1. 2015. Dennis Hopeless (w), Javier Rodriguez (p, c), Alvaro Lopez (i), and Travis Lanham (l). Marvel Comics.

Issue #2. 2015. Dennis Hopeless (w), Javier Rodriguez (p, c), Alvaro Lopez (i), and Travis Lanham (l). Marvel Comics.

Issue #3. 2016. Dennis Hopeless (w), Javier Rodriguez (p), Alvaro Lopez (i), Rachelle Rosenberg (c), and Travis Lanham (l). Marvel Comics.

Issue #4. 2016. Dennis Hopeless (w), Javier Rodriguez (p), Alvaro Lopez (i), Rachelle Rosenberg (c), and Travis Lanham (l). Marvel Comics.

Issue #5. 2016. Dennis Hopeless (w), Javier Rodriguez (p), Alvaro Lopez (i), Rachelle Rosenberg (c), and Travis Lanham (l). Marvel Comics.

Issue #6. 2016. Dennis Hopeless (w), Joëlle Jones (p, i), Rachelle Rosenberg (c), and Travis Lanham (l). Marvel Comics.

Issue #7. 2016. Dennis Hopeless (w), Joëlle Jones (p), Lorenzo Ruggiero (i), Rachelle Rosenberg (c), and Travis Lanham (l). Marvel Comics.

Issue #12. 2016. Dennis Hopeless (w), Tigh Walker (p, i), Rachelle Rosenberg (c), and Travis Lanham (l). Marvel Comics.

Issue #17. 2017. Dennis Hopeless (w), Veronica Fish (p, i), Rachelle Rosenberg (c), and Travis Lanham (l). Marvel Comics.

Truth: Red, White & Black

2004. Robert Morales (w), and Kyle Baker (p). Marvel Comics.

Ultimate Spider-Man
Issue #98. 2006. Brian Michael Bendis (w), Mark Bagley (p), John Dell (i), Justin Ponsor (c), and Cory Petit (l). Marvel Comics.
Issue #105. 2007. Brian Michael Bendis (w), Mark Bagley (p), Andrew Hennessy (i), Justin Ponsor (c), and Cory Petit (l). Marvel Comics.
Ultimate Comics Spider-Man
Issue #25. 2013. Brian Michael Bendis (w), David Marquez (p, i), Justin Ponsor (c), and Cory Petit (l). Marvel Comics.
The Unstoppable Wasp Vol. 1: Unstoppable!
Issues #1–4. 2017. Jeremy Whitley (w), Elsa Charretier (p, i), Megan Wilson (c), and Joe Caramagna (l). Marvel Comics.
The Unstoppable Wasp Vol. 2: Agents of G.I.R.L.
Issues #5–8. 2018. Jeremy Whitley (w), Elsa Charretier (p, i), Megan Wilson (c), Joe Caramagna (l), Veronica Fish (p, i), Ro Stein (p, i), and Ted Brandt (p, i). Marvel Comics.
The Unstoppable Wasp Unlimited Vol. 1: Fix Everything
Issues #1–5. 2019. Jeremy Whitley (w), Gurihiru (p, i, c), and Joe Caramagna (l). Marvel Comics.
The Unstoppable Wasp Unlimited Vol. 2: G.I.R.L. vs. A.I.M.
Issues #6–10. 2019. Jeremy Whitley (w), Gurihiru (p, i, c), Alti Firmansyah (p, i), Espen Grundetjern (c), and Joe Caramagna (l). Marvel Comics.
Vengeance
Issue #1. 2011. Joe Casey (w), and Nick Dragotta (p). Marvel Comics.
X-Men: The Dark Phoenix Saga
2006. Chris Claremont (w), John Byrne (p), Terry Austin (i), Glynis Wein (c), Bob Sharen (c), and Tom Orzechowski (l). Marvel Comics.

GENERAL REFERENCES

Acevedo, Nicole. 2019. "Nearly 900 Women's Health Clinics Have Lost Federal Funding over Gag Rule." NBC News online, October 22. https://www.nbcnews.com/news/latino/nearly-900-women-s-health-clinics-have-lost-federal-funding-n1069591.

ACLU. 2023. "Mapping Attacks on LGBTQ Rights in US State Legislatures." ACLU online, March 14. https://www.aclu.org/legislative-attacks-on-lgbtq-rights.

Ahmed, Sara. 2014. *Willful Subjects*. Durham, NC: Duke University Press.

Ahrens, Jörn, and Arno Meteling. 2010. Introduction to *Comics and the City: Urban Space in Print, Picture and Sequence*, edited by Jörn Ahrens and Arno Meteling, 1–18. New York: Continuum International.

Alaniz, José. 2014. *Death, Disability, and the Superhero: The Silver Age and Beyond.* Jackson: University Press of Mississippi.

Aldama, Frederick Luis. 2009. *Your Brain on Latino Comics: From Gus Arriola to Los Bros Hernandez.* Austin: University of Texas Press.

Aldama, Frederick Luis. 2017. *Latinx Superheroes in Mainstream Comics.* Tucson: University of Arizona Press.

Aldama, Frederick Luis. 2020. "Graphic Indigeneity: Terra America and Terra Australasia." In *Graphic Indigeneity: Comics in the Americas and Australasia,* edited by Frederick Luis Aldama, xi–4. Jackson: University Press of Mississippi.

Aldama, Frederick Luis. 2021. *The Routledge Companion to Gender and Sexuality in Comic Book Studies.* New York: Routledge.

Alexander, Michelle. 2010. *The New Jim Crow: Mass Incarceration in the Age of Colorblindness.* New York: New Press.

Anderson, Reynaldo, and Charles Jones. 2016. "Introduction: The Rise of Astro-Blackness." In *Afrofuturism 2.0: The Rise of Astro-Blackness,* edited by Reynaldo Anderson and Charles Jones, vii–xviii. Lanham, MD: Lexington Books.

Angelou, Maya. 1978. *And Still I Rise.* New York: Random House.

Anzaldúa, Gloria. 1999. *Borderlands/La Frontera: The New Mestiza.* 2nd ed. San Francisco: Aunt Lute Books.

Anzaldúa, Gloria. 2002. "Preface: (Un)Natural Bridges, (Un)Safe Spaces." In *This Bridge We Call Home: Radical Visions for Transformation,* edited by Gloria Anzaldúa and Analouise Keating, 1–5. New York: Routledge.

Arendt, Hannah. 1951. *The Origins of Totalitarianism.* New York: Schocken Books.

Arendt, Hannah. 1963. *Eichmann in Jerusalem: A Report on the Banality of Evil.* New York: Viking Press.

Arrant, Chris. 2021. "WandaVision's Success Leads to a Run on Related Comics, Leaving Marvel Out of Stock for Months." *GamesRadar+,* "Newsarama" section, March. https://www.gamesradar.com/wandavisions-success-leads-to-a-run-on-related-comics-leaving-marvel-out-of-stock-for-months/?fbclid=IwAR3jdVtQX6-WUpZo6DYroJOUJwBmtrCVAC2YiGugcC4KeC1RplCG4h5RAZM.

Austin, Allan, and Patrick Hamilton. 2019. *All New, All Different? A History of Race and the American Superhero.* Austin: University of Texas Press.

Bailey, Moya, and Whitney Peoples. 2007. "Towards a Black Feminist Health Science Studies." *Catalyst: Feminism, Theory, Technoscience* 3 (2): 1–27.

Bainbridge, Jason. 2010. "'I Am New York': Spider-Man, New York City, and the Marvel Universe." In *Comics and the City: Urban Space in Print, Picture and Sequence,* edited by Jörn Ahrens and Arno Meteling, 163–179. New York: Continuum International.

BBC. 2016. "'Drug Dealers, Criminals, Rapists': What Trump Thinks of Mexicans." BBC News online, August 31. https://www.bbc.com/news/av/world-us-canada-37230916.

Bernstein, Richard. 2012. "Are Arendt's Reflections on Evil Still Relevant?" In *Politics in Dark Times: Encounters with Hannah Arendt*, edited by Seyla Benhabib, 293–304. Cambridge: Cambridge University Press.

Betancourt, David. 2017. "Marvel Hired Gabby Rivera, a Queer Latina Writer, for Its Queer Latina Superhero. That Matters." *Washington Post*, March 8. https://www.washingtonpost.com/news/comic-riffs/wp/2017/03/08/marvel-hired-gabby-rivera-a-queer-latina-writer-for-its-queer-latina-superhero-that-matters/.

Billard, Thomas J., and Brian L. MacAuley. 2017. "'It's a Bird! It's a Plane! It's a Transgender Superhero!': Transgender Characters in Marvel, DC, and Image Comics." In *Heroes, Heroines, and Everything in Between: Challenging Gender and Sexuality Stereotypes in Children's Entertainment Media*, edited by CarrieLynn D. Reinhard and Christopher J. Olson, 233–252. New York: Lexington Books.

Boden, Anna, and Ryan Fleck, dirs. 2019. *Captain Marvel*. Walt Disney Studios Motion Pictures.

Boeckner, McKenna James, Monica Flegel, and Judith Leggatt. 2020. "'Not My Captain America': Racebending, Reverse Discrimination, and White Panic in the Marvel Comics Fandom." In *Fandom, Now in Color: A Collection of Voices*, edited by Rukmini Pande, 181–195. Iowa City: University of Iowa Press.

Boym, Svetlana. 2001. *The Future of Nostalgia*. New York: Basic Books.

Braune, Joan. 2020. "The Outsider as Insider: Steve Bannon, Fourth Turnings, and the Neofascist Threat." In *Spectres of Fascism*, edited by Samir Gandesha, 207–222. London: Pluto Press.

Brigid-Prehn, Jean. 2022. "All-New Ultimates #4 PROVES that Jessica Drew Is the Best Trans Coded Genetic Clone of Peter Parker." *Shelfdust*, December 21. https://shelfdust.com/2022/12/21/all-new-ultimates-4-proves-that-jessica-drew-is-the-best-trans-coded-genetic-clone-of-peter-parker/.

Brown, Jeffrey A. 2001. *Black Superheroes, Milestone Comics, and Their Fans*. Jackson: University Press of Mississippi.

Brown, Jeffrey A. 2013a. *Dangerous Curves: Action Heroines, Gender, Fetishism, and Popular Culture*. Jackson: University Press of Mississippi.

Brown, Jeffrey A. 2013b. "Panthers and Vixens: Black Superheroines, Sexuality, and Stereotypes in Contemporary Comic Books." In *Black Comics: Politics of Race and Representation*, edited by Sheena Howard and Ronald Jackson II, 125–138. New York: Bloomsbury Academic.

Brown, Jeffrey A. 2015. *Beyond Bombshells: The New Action Heroine in Popular Culture*. Jackson: University Press of Mississippi.

Brown, Jeffrey A. 2021. *Panthers, Hulks, and Ironhearts: Marvel, Diversity, and the Twenty-First-Century Superhero*. New Brunswick, NJ: Rutgers University Press.

Brown, Nicole R. 2009. *Black Girlhood Celebration: Toward a Hip Hop Feminist Pedagogy*. New York: Peter Lang.

Bychowski, M. W. 2016. "Super Trans: Transgender in Comic Books." *Transliterature: Things Transform* (blog), March 21. http://www.thingstransform.com/2016/03/super-trans-transgender-in-comic-books.html?m=1.

Capuzza, Jamie C., and Leland G. Spencer. 2016. "Regressing, Progressing, or Transgressing on the Small Screen?" *Communication Quarterly* 65 (2): 214–230.

carrington, andré m. 2016. *Speculative Blackness: The Future of Race in Science Fiction*. Minneapolis: University of Minnesota Press.

Castillo Planas, Melissa. 2021. "Superheroine Latinidad: The Diasporic Identities of America Chavez and La Borinqueña." *Journal of Popular Culture* 54 (5): 1–19. https://doi.org/10.1111/jpcu.13055.

Cavallaro, Dani. 2003. *French Feminist Theory: An Introduction*. London: Continuum International.

Cavanaugh, Patrick. 2019. "'Captain Marvel': Brie Larson Addresses the Smiling 'Controversy.'" *Comicbook*, February 27. https://comicbook.com/marvel/2019/02/27/captain-marvel-brie-larson-smile-smiling-trolls/.

Century, Sara. 2019. "The Queer Fanbase of Jean Grey." *SyFy Wire*, April 19. https://www.syfy.com/syfy-wire/the-queer-fanbase-of-jean-grey.

Chang, Clio. 2016. "How Black Girls Are Locked Out of America's Schools." *New Republic*, March 14. https://newrepublic.com/article/131482/black-girls-locked-americas-schools.

Chikafa-Chipiro, Rosemary. 2019. "The Future of the Past: Imagi(Ni)Ng Black Womanhood, Africana Womanism, and Afrofuturism in Black Panther." *Image and Text* 33: 1–20.

Chin Greene, Jules. 2022. "Echo's MCU Show Needs to Fix Her Biggest Marvel Comics Problem." *Screen Rant*, May 23. https://screenrant.com/echo-marvel-deaf-disability-representation-marvel-comics/.

Chute, Hillary. 2010. *Graphic Women: Life Narrative and Contemporary Comics*. New York: Columbia University Press.

Chute, Hillary. 2017. *Why Comics? From Underground to Everywhere*. New York: Harper Collins.

Cipolla, Cyd, Kristina Gupta, David A. Rubin, and Angela Willey, eds. 2017. *Queer Feminist Science Studies*. Seattle: University of Washington Press. http://www.jstor.org.libproxy.berkeley.edu/stable/j.ctvcwn8vd.

Cixous, Hélène. 1976. "The Laugh of the Medusa." Translated by Keith Cohen and Paula Cohen. *Signs: Journal of Women in Culture and Society* 1 (4): 875–893.

Cixous, Hélène. 1997. "Sorties: Out and Out: Attacks/Ways Out/Forays." In *The Feminist Reader: Essays in Gender and the Politics of Literary Criticism*, edited by Catherine Belsey and Jane Moore, 2nd ed., 91–103. London: Macmillan.

Clark, Nicole. 2018. "Brie Larson Was Told to Smile, So She Put Smiles onto Marvel Dudes." *Vice*, September 21. www.vice.com/en_us/article/gynvnw/brie-larson-was-told-to-smile-so-she-put-smiles-onto-marvel-dudes.

Cocca, Carolyn. 2016. *Superwomen: Gender, Power, and Representation*. New York: Bloomsbury Academic.

Cocca, Carolyn. 2021. *Wonder Woman and Captain Marvel: Militarism and Feminism in Comics and Film*. New York: Routledge.

Coggan, Devan. 2023. "New DC Boss Says Canceling Batgirl Was the Right Move: 'That Film Was Not Releasable.'" *EW* online, January 31. https://ew.com/movies/new-dc-boss-stands-by-batgirl-cancellation/.

Cohen, Zachary, and Pamela Brown. 2020. "US Intelligence Officials Say There's No Evidence to Back Up Trump's Claims about Threats to Mail-in Voting." CNN online, August 26. https://www.cnn.com/2020/08/26/politics/election-security-officials-mail-in-voting-trump/index.html.

Collins, Patricia Hill. 1991. *Black Feminist Thought: Knowledge, Consciousness, and the Politics of Empowerment*. New York: Routledge.

Collins, Patricia Hill, and Sirma Bilge. 2016. *Intersectionality (Key Concepts)*. Cambridge, MA: Polity Press.

Coogan, Peter. 2013. "The Hero Defines the Genre, the Genre Defines the Hero." In *What Is a Superhero?*, edited by Robin Rosenberg and Peter Coogan, 3–10. Oxford: Oxford University Press.

Cowling, Sam, and Wesley D. Cray. 2022. *Philosophy of Comics: An Introduction*. London: Bloomsbury Academic.

Davey, Moyra, ed. 2001. *Mother Reader: Essential Writings on Motherhood*. New York: Seven Stories Press.

Davis, Ande. 2021. "Queer, Latina, and Punching Nazis: A New America Breaking Borders." In *Intersectional Feminist Readings of Comics: Interpreting Gender in Graphic Narratives*, edited by Sandra Cox, 62–80. New York: Routledge.

Davis, Angela Y. 1981. *Women, Race and Class*. New York: Random House.

Davis, Angela Y. 1990. *Women, Culture, and Politics*. New York: Vintage Books.

Davis, Angela Y. 2003. *Are Prisons Obsolete?* New York: Seven Stories Press.

Davis, Blair. 2015. "Bare Chests, Silver Tiaras, and Removable Afros: The Visual Design of Black Comic Book Superheroes." In *The Blacker the Ink: Constructions of Black Identity in Comics and Sequential Art*, edited by Frances Gateward and John Jennings, 193–212. New Brunswick, NJ: Rutgers University Press.

Davis, Blair. 2018. *Comic Book Movies*. New Brunswick, NJ: Rutgers University Press.

De Dauw, Esther. 2021. *Hot Pants and Spandex Suits: Gender Representation in American Superhero Comic Books*. New Brunswick, NJ: Rutgers University Press.

Deloria, Vine, Jr. 1979. *The Metaphysics of Modern Existence*. Golden, CO: Fulcrum Publishing.

Deloria, Vine, Jr. 2003. *God Is Red: A Native View of Religion*. 30th anniversary ed. Golden, CO: Fulcrum Publishing.

DiAngelo, Robin. 2011. "White Fragility." *International Journal of Critical Pedagogy* 3 (3): 54–70.

Díaz-Barriga, Miguel, and Margaret Dorsey. 2020. *Fencing In Democracy: Necrocitizenship and the US-Mexico Border Wall*. Durham, NC: Duke University Press.

Dill, Bonnie Thornton, and Marla Kohlman. 2014. "Intersectionality: A Transformative Paradigm in Feminist Theory and Social Justice." In *The Handbook of Feminist Research: Theory and Praxis*, edited by Sharlene Nagy Hesse-Biber, 2nd ed., 154–174. Thousand Oaks, CA: Sage Publications.

Dinh, Christine. 2020. "Just Announced: Riri Williams Heading to Disney+ with New 'Ironheart' Series." Marvel online, "TV Shows" section, December 11. https://www.marvel.com/articles/tv-shows/riri-williams-ironheart-disney-plus-series.

Dittmer, Jason. 2013. *Captain America and the Nationalist Superhero: Metaphors, Narratives, and Geopolitics*. Philadelphia: Temple University Press.

Dockterman, Eliana. 2016. "Exclusive: Marvel's New Iron Man Is a Black Woman." *Time*, July 6. https://time.com/4394478/iron-man-riri-williams-tony-stark/.

Dos Santos, Joaquim, Kemp Powers, and Justin K. Thompson, dirs. 2023. *Spider-Man: Across the Spider-Verse*. Sony Pictures.

Dunbar-Ortiz, Roxanne. 2014. *An Indigenous Peoples' History of the United States*. Boston: Beacon Press.

Duncan, Randy, and Matthew J. Smith. 2009. *The Power of Comics: History, Form, and Culture*. New York: Bloomsbury Academic.

Duster, Michelle. 2019. "From the Suffrage Movement to the Women's March: Black Women's Fight for Inclusion." *Black History Bulletin* 82 (2): 10–11.

Easton, Lee, and Richard Harrison. 2010. *Secret Identity Reader: Essays on Sex, Death and the Superhero*. Hamilton, Ontario: Wolsak and Wynn Publishers.

Edelstein, Marilyn. 1993. "Toward a Feminist Postmodern Polèthique." In *Ethics, Politics, and Difference in Julia Kristeva's Writings*, edited by Kelly Oliver, 196–214. London: Routledge.

Ellis, Simon Adriane, Danuta M. Wojnar, and Maria Pettinato. 2015. "Conception, Pregnancy, and Birth Experiences of Male and Gender Variant Gestational Parents: It's How We Could Have a Family." *Journal of Midwifery and Women's Health* 60 (1): 62–69.

Emmott, Emily H., Sarah Myers, and Abigail E. Page. 2021. "Who Cares for Women with Children? Crossing the Bridge between Disciplines." *Philosophical Transactions of the Royal Society B: Biological Sciences* 376. https://doi.org/10.1098/rstb.2020.0019.

Enke, Anne, ed. 2012. *Transfeminist Perspectives In and Beyond Transgender and Gender Studies*. Philadelphia: Temple University Press.

Enlow, Courtney. 2021. "The Comics That Sold Out Thanks to WandaVision Are Going Back to Press." *Gizmodo*, March 14. https://www.gizmodo.com.au/2021/03/the-comics-that-sold-out-thanks-to-wandavision-are-going-back-to-press/.

Eshun, Kodwo. 1998. *More Brilliant than the Sun: Adventures in Sonic Fiction.* London: Quartet Books.

Espinoza, Mauricio. 2016. "The Alien Is Here to Stay: Otherness, Anti-Assimilation, and Empowerment in Latino/a Superhero Comics." In *Graphic Borders: Latino Comic Books Past, Present, and Future,* edited by Frederick Luis Aldama and Christopher González, 181–202. Austin: University of Texas Press.

Everett, Anna. 2009. *Digital Diaspora: The Race for Cyberspace.* Albany: SUNY Press.

Ewing, Eve L. 2018. *Ghosts in the Schoolyard : Racism and School Closings on Chicago's South Side.* Chicago: University of Chicago Press.

Ewing, Eve (@eveewing). 2019a. "In which I sneak my ongoing rants about the banality of evil into a comic book in my continued attempts to indoctrinate the youth with my SJW agenda." Twitter, July 28, 2019. (Tweet no longer available.)

Ewing, Eve (@eveewing). 2019b. "The other thing I wanted to do was bring back her biological dad. I never liked the idea of her being defined as a Chicagoan primarily by these extreme acts of gun violence . . ." Twitter, December 5, 2019. (Tweet no longer available.)

Ewing, Eve. 2019c. "When this character first came out, a weird critique of her character was that she was an unlikeable sociopath. I think that was rooted in a lot of bizarre misogynoir and straight-up trolling." Twitter, December 5, 2019. (Tweet no longer available.)

Fabricius, Charlotte Johanne. 2020. "New and Improved? Disability and Monstrosity in Gail Simone's *Batgirl.*" In *Monstrous Women in Comics,* edited by Samantha Langsdale and Elizabeth Rae Coody, 84–98. Jackson: University Press of Mississippi.

Faludi, Susan. 1991. *Backlash: The Undeclared War against American Women.* New York: Three Rivers Press.

Favreau, Jon, dir. 2008. *Iron Man.* Marvel Studios.

Fawaz, Ramzi. 2016. *The New Mutants: Superheroes and the Radical Imagination of American Comics.* New York: NYU Press.

Fleisher, Mark S. 2019. "Historical Roots of Chicago's Contemporary Violence: An Interpretation of Chicago's Early Sociologists' Texts on Black Assimilation." *Journal of Black Studies* 50 (8): 767–786. https://doi.org/10.1177/0021934719883358.

Flood, Alison. 2016. "Marvel Pulls Iron Man Cover after Accusations of 'Sexualising' Teen Girl." *Guardian,* October 21. https://www.theguardian.com/books/2016/oct/21/marvel-iron-man-cover-sexualised-j-scott-campbell-riri-williams.

Flowers, Johnathan Charles. 2018. "How Is It Okay to Be a Black Nerd?" In *Age of the Geek: Depictions of Nerds and Geeks in Popular Media,* edited by Kathryn E. Lane, 169–191. Cham, Switzerland: Springer International.

Foucault, Michel. 1994. *Power. Essential Works of Foucault,* vol. 3. Edited by James D. Faubion. London: Penguin Books.

Francis, Consuela. 2015. "American Truths: Blackness and the American Superhero." In *The Blacker the Ink: Constructions of Black Identity in Comics and Sequential Art*, edited by Frances Gateward and John Jennings, 137–152. New Brunswick, NJ: Rutgers University Press.

Francisco, Eric. 2019. "'Captain Marvel' Review Bombing: It's Happening Again, This Time on IMDb." *Inverse*, March 8. www.inverse.com/article/53892-captain-marvel-brie-larson-is-being-review-bombed-again-on-imdb.

Freedman, Estelle. 2003. *No Turning Back: The History of Feminism and the Future of Women*. New York: Ballantine Books.

Friedman, Marilyn. 1989. "Feminism and Modern Friendship: Dislocating the Community." *Ethics* 99 (2): 275–290.

Fustich, Kate. 2015. "What Happens When Women Recreate Comic Book Poses." *Bustle*, December 11. https://www.bustle.com/articles/129398-real-women-recreate-comic-book-hero-poses-the-results-show-how-problematic-the-depiction-of.

Garbes, Angela. 2018. *Like a Mother: A Feminist Journey through the Science and Culture of Pregnancy*. New York: Harper Collins.

García, Enrique. 2018. "The Latina Superheroine: Protecting the Reader from the Comic Book Industry's Racial, Gender, Ethnic, and Nationalist Biases." In *Comics Studies Here and Now*, edited by Frederick Luis Aldama, 163–179. New York: Routledge.

Gateward, Frances, and John Jennings, eds. 2015. *The Blacker the Ink: Constructions of Black Identity in Comics and Sequential Art*. New Brunswick, NJ: Rutgers University Press.

Gavaler, Chris. 2016. "The Rise and Fall of Fascist Superpowers." *Journal of Graphic Novels and Comics* 7 (1): 70–87.

Gavaler, Chris. 2018. *Superhero Comics*. London: Bloomsbury Academic.

Gibson, Mel. 2020. "Queer Girlhoods in Contemporary Comics: Disrupting Normative Notions." *Girlhood Studies* 13 (1): 1–16.

Gibson, Mel, David Huxley, and Joan Ormrod, eds. 2014. *Superheroes and Identities*. London: Routledge.

Gil-Gómez, Ellen M. 2016. "Wrestling with Comic Genres and Genders: *Luchadores* as Signifiers in *Sonambulo* and *Locas*." In *Graphic Borders: Latino Comic Books Past, Present, and Future*, edited by Frederick Luis Aldama and Christopher González, 109–129. Austin: University of Texas Press.

Gillespie, Rosemary. 2003. "Childfree and Feminine: Understanding the Gender Identity of Voluntarily Childless Women." *Gender and Society* 17 (1): 122–136.

Gilman, Charlotte Perkins. 1911. *The Man-Made World: Or, Our Androcentric Culture*. New York: Charlton Co.

Glenn, Cerise, and Landra Cunningham. 2009. "The Power of Black Magic: The Magical Negro and White Salvation in Film." *Journal of Black Studies* 40 (2): 135–152.

Goodrum, Michael. 2014. "'Oh c'Mon, Those Stories Can't Count in Continuity!' Squirrel Girl and the Problem of Female Power." *Studies in Comics* 5 (1): 97–115.

Goodrum, Michael, Tara Prescott, and Philip Smith, eds. 2018. *Gender and the Superhero Narrative.* Jackson: University Press of Mississippi.

Goodwin, Amber K., and Tj Grayson. 2020. "Investing in the Frontlines: Why Trusting and Supporting Communities of Color Will Help Address Gun Violence." *Journal of Law, Medicine & Ethics* 48 (December): 164–171. https://doi.org/10.1177/1073110520979418.

Gould, Helen. 2019. "Subtle Forms of Racism to Avoid in SFF." *Black Fem Geekery* (blog), April 20. https://blackfemgeekery.wordpress.com/2019/04/20/subtle-forms-of-racism-to-avoid-in-sff/.

Griffin, Susan. 2001. "Feminism and Motherhood." In *Mother Reader: Essential Writings on Motherhood,* edited by Moyra Davey, 33–46. New York: Seven Stories Press.

Grzanka, Patrick. 2014. "Introduction: Intersectional Objectivity." In *Intersectionality: A Foundations and Frontiers Reader,* edited by Patrick Grzanka, xi–xxvii. New York: Routledge.

Gumbs, Alexis Pauline, China Martens, and Mai'a Williams, eds. 2016. *Revolutionary Mothering: Love on the Front Lines.* Oakland, CA: PM Press.

Guthertz, Asher. 2018. "No Borders for America Chavez: An Interview with Gabby Rivera." *Book Riot,* February 21. https://bookriot.com/america-chavez-gabby-rivera/.

Guynes, Sean, and Martin Lund. 2020. "Not to Interpret, But to Abolish: Whiteness Studies and American Superhero Comics." In *Unstable Masks: Whiteness and American Superhero Comics,* edited by Sean Guynes and Martin Lund, 1–18. Columbus: Ohio State University Press.

Hall, Stuart. 2019. "What Is This 'Black' in Black Popular Culture?" In *Essential Essays: Identity and Diaspora,* edited by David Morley, 2:83–94. Durham, NC: Duke University Press.

Haraway, Donna. 1992. "Promising Monsters: A Regenerative Politics for Inappropriate/d Others." In *Cultural Studies,* edited by Lawrence Grossberg, Cary Nelson, and Paula A. Treichler, 295–331. New York: Routledge.

Harris-Perry, Melissa. 2011. *Sister Citizen: Shame, Stereotypes, and Black Women in America.* New Haven, CT: Yale University Press.

Hassel, Holly. 2008. "The 'Babe Scientist' Phenomenon: The Illusion of Inclusion in 1990s American Action Films." In *Chick Flicks: Contemporary Women at the Movies,* edited by Suzanne Ferriss and Mallory Young, 190–203. New York: Routledge.

Hawthorne, Sîan. 2005. "Rethinking Subjectivity in the Gender-Oriented Study of Religions: Kristeva and the 'Subject-in-Process.'" In *Gender, Religion and Diversity: Cross-Cultural Perspectives,* edited by Ursula King and Tina Beattie, 40–50. London: Continuum International.

Held, Jason, ed. 2017. *Wonder Woman and Philosophy: The Amazonian Mystique.* Hoboken, NJ: Wiley Blackwell.

Hernández-Avila, Inés, ed. 2005. *Reading Native American Women: Critical/Creative Representations.* New York: AltaMira Press.

heroeswhohappentobewomen (djthulktra-blog). 2014. "Ultimate Jessica Drew Is Queer and Here's Why." Tumblr. https://www.tumblr.com/heroeswhohappentobewomen/73461994564/ultimate-jessica-drew-is-queer-and-heres-why.

Hobson, Janell. 2016. "Feminists Debate Beyoncé." In *The Beyoncé Effect: Essays on Sexuality, Race, and Feminism,* edited by Adrienne Trier-Bienieck, 11–26. Jefferson, NC: McFarland.

Hoerl, Kristen, and Casey Ryan Kelly. 2010. "The Post-Nuclear Family and the Depoliticization of Unplanned Pregnancy in *Knocked Up, Juno,* and *Waitress.*" *Communication and Critical/Cultural Studies* 7 (4): 360–380.

hooks, bell. 1996. "Choosing the Margin as a Space of Radical Openness." In *Women, Knowledge, and Reality: Explorations in Feminist Philosophy,* edited by Ann Garry and Marilyn Pearsall, 2nd ed., 48–56. New York: Routledge.

hooks, bell, and Melissa Harris-Perry. 2013. "Black Female Voices: Who Is Listening–A Public Dialogue between bell hooks + Melissa Harris-Perry." *YouTube,* posted by the New School, November 11. https://www.youtube.com/watch?v5SOmgqXao1ng

Hopeless, Dennis (@hopelessDent). 2017. "For what it's worth, there is a character in our Spider-Woman run with whom I relate a great deal . . . Her name is Jessica Drew." Twitter, March 23, 2017. https://twitter.com/hopelessdent/status/847660323267985408.

Howard, Sheena, and Ronald Jackson II, eds. 2013. *Black Comics: Politics of Race and Representation.* New York: Bloomsbury Academic.

Huhndorf, Shari M. 2010. "Indigenous Feminism, Performance, and the Politics of Memory in the Plays of Monique Mojica." In *Indigenous Women and Feminism: Politics, Activism, Culture,* edited by Cheri Suzack, Shari M. Huhndorf, Jeanne Perreault, and Jean Barman, 181–198. Vancouver: University of British Columbia Press.

Igla, Jonathan, dir. 2021. *Hawkeye.* Disney+.

Ito, Robert. 2021. "Beyond 'Black Panther': Afrofuturism Is Booming in Comics." *New York Times,* February 7. https://www.nytimes.com/2021/02/07/books/afrofuturism-comics-graphic-novels.html.

Jiménez, Laura. 2018. "PoC, LGBTQ, and Gender: The Intersectionality of America Chavez." *Journal of Lesbian Studies* 22 (4): 435–445.

Johnston, Rich. 2018. "Marvel Has Sold Half a Million Infinity Gauntlet Trade Collections." *Bleeding Cool,* "News and Rumors" section, August 31. https://bleedingcool.com/comics/marvel-half-million-infinity-gauntlet/.

Johnston, Rich. 2023. "Warren Ellis and Bryan Hitch's Authority Sells Out Thanks to James Gunn." *Bleeding Cool,* February 3. https://bleedingcool.com/comics/warren-ellis-bryan-hitch-authority-sells-out-thanks-to-james-gunn/.

Jones, Cassandra. 2018. "The Data Thief, the Cyberflaneur, and Rhythm Science: Challenging Anti-Technological Blackness with Metaphors of Afrofuturism." *CLA Journal* 61 (4): 202–217.

Jones, Jonathan. 2022. "Marvel's First LGBTQ+ Spider-Hero Debuted Years Ago, But No One Remembers." *ScreenRant*, July 3. https://screenrant.com/marvel-first-lgbtq-spider-hero-spiderwoman/.

Jordan-Zachery, Julia S., and Duchess Harris. 2019. *Black Girl Magic beyond the Hashtag: Twenty-First-Century Acts of Self-Definition*. Tucson: University of Arizona Press.

Kamaloni, Sunshine. 2019. *Understanding Racism in a Post-Racial World: Visible Invisibilities*. Cham, Switzerland: Palgrave Macmillan.

Keller, Jean. 2008. "Dialogue among Friends: Toward a Discourse Ethic of Interpersonal Relationships." *Hypatia* 23 (4): 158–181.

Kinberg, Simon, dir. 2019. *Dark Phoenix*. 20th Century Fox/Marvel Entertainment.

Kirkman, Robert, and Simon Racioppa, dirs. 2021. *Invincible*. Amazon Prime Video.

Kripke, Eric, dir. 2019. *The Boys*. Amazon Prime Video.

Kristeva, Julia. 1980a. *Desire in Language: A Semiotic Approach to Literature and Art*. Translated by T. Gora, A. Jardine, and L. Roudiez. New York: Columbia University Press.

Kristeva, Julia. 1980b. "Motherhood according to Giovanni Bellini." In Kristeva, *Desire in Language*, 237–270.

Kristeva, Julia. 1986. "Stabat Mater." In *The Female Body in Western Culture: Contemporary Perspectives*, edited by Susan Rubin Suleiman, 99–118. Cambridge, MA: Harvard University Press.

Lang, Cady. 2018. "'Reviews Matter': Brie Larson Calls for More Diversity in Movie Reviews with Speech." *Time*, June 14. http://time.com/5312618/brie-larson-women-in-film/.

Langsdale, Samantha. 2018. "The Dark Phoenix as 'Promising Monster': An Interdisciplinary Approach to Teaching Marvel's *X-Men: The Dark Phoenix Saga*." In *Comics and Sacred Texts: Reimagining Religion and Graphic Narratives*, edited by Assaf Gamzou and Ken Koltun-Fromm, 153–171. Jackson: University Press of Mississippi.

Langsdale, Samantha. 2020. "Moon Girls and Mythical Beasts: Analyzing Race, Gender, and Monstrosity." *Signs: Journal of Women in Culture and Society* 45 (2): 394–420.

Lendrum, Rob. 2004. "Queering Super-Manhood: The Gay Superhero in Contemporary Mainstream Comic Books." *Journal for the Arts, Sciences, and Technology* 2 (2): 69–73.

Lillvis, Kristen. 2017. *Posthuman Blackness and the Black Female Imagination*. Athens: University of Georgia Press.

Lincoln, Anne, and Michael Patrick Allen. 2004. "Double Jeopardy in Hollywood: Age and Gender in the Careers of Film Actors, 1926–1999." *Sociological Forum* 19 (4): 611–631.

Lind, Dara. 2017. "Nazi Slogans and Violence at a Right-Wing March in Charlottesville on Friday Night." *Vox*, August 12. https://www.vox.com/2017/8/12/16138132/charlottesville-rally-brawl-nazi.

Lindelof, Damon, dir. 2019. *Watchmen*. HBO.

Linton, Matthew. 2019. "Blood and Fire: Monstrous Women in *Carrie* and 'The Dark Phoenix Saga.'" In *Gender and Contemporary Horror in Comics, Games and Transmedia*, edited by Robert Shail, Steven Gerrard, and Samantha Holland, 9–18. Bingley, UK: Emerald Publishing.

Lorde, Audre. 1984. *Sister Outsider*. Freedom, CA: Crossing Press.

Lu, Jessica H., and Catherine Knight Steele. 2019. "'Joy Is Resistance': Cross-Platform Resilience and (Re)Invention of Black Oral Culture Online." *Information, Communication and Society* 22 (6): 823–837.

Ludlow, Jeannie. 2020. "Kicking Ass in Flip-Flops: Inappropriate/d Generations and Monstrous Pregnancy in Comics Narratives." In *Monstrous Women in Comics*, edited by Samantha Langsdale and Elizabeth Rae Coody, 115–134. Jackson: University Press of Mississippi.

Lugones, María, and Elizabeth Spelman. 1983. "Have We Got a Theory for You! Feminist Theory, Cultural Imperialism and the Demand for 'The Woman's Voice.'" *Women's Studies International Forum* 6 (6): 573–581.

Luthar, Suniya S., and Lucia Ciciolla. 2015. "Who Mothers Mommy? Factors That Contribute to Mothers' Well-Being." *Developmental Psychology* 51: 1812–1823.

Mak, Tim. 2020. "Senate Report: Former Trump Aide Paul Manafort Shared Campaign Info with Russia." NPR online, August 18. https://www.npr.org/2020/08/18/903512647/senate-report-former-trump-aide-paul-manafort-shared-campaign-info-with-russia.

Martin, Grace. 2020. "I Don't Have Any Ancestors, OK? Let's Just Drop It: Miss America and (Pan)Latinx Representation in Marvel's *America*." In *Performativity, Cultural Construction, and the Graphic Narrative*, edited by Leigh Anne Howard and Susanna Hoeness-Krupsaw, 35–53. London: Routledge.

McCaughey, Martha. 1997. *Real Knockouts: The Physical Feminism of Women's Self-Defense*. New York: NYU Press.

McCloud, Scott. 1994. *Understanding Comics: The Invisible Art*. New York: Harper Perennial.

Mickwitz, Nina, Ian Horton, and Ian Hague, eds. 2020. Introduction to *Representing Acts of Violence in Comics*, 1–16. New York: Routledge.

Midgley, Mary. 1992. "Philosophical Plumbing." *Royal Institute of Philosophy Supplements* 33: 139–151.

Miller, Nicholas. 2017. "Asexuality and Its Discontents: Making the 'Invisible Orientation' Visible in Comics." *INKS: Journal of the Comics Studies Society* 1 (3): 354–376.

Mireles, Michelle Alejandra. 2022. "Paisa Aesthetics: Streetwear Fashion and Latinx Aesthetic Labor." MA thesis, University of California, Santa Barbara.

Morris, Tom, and Matt Morris, eds. 2005. *Superheroes and Philosophy: Truth, Justice, and the Socratic Way.* Peru, IL: Open Court Publishing.

Murray, Ross. 2011. "The Feminine Mystique: Feminism, Sexuality, Motherhood." *Journal of Graphic Novels and Comics* 2 (1): 55–66.

Nama, Adilifu. 2011. *Super Black: American Pop Culture and Black Superheroes.* Austin: University of Texas Press.

Nash, Elizabeth, and Isabel Guarnieri. 2023. "Six Months Post-Roe, 24 US States Have Banned Abortion or Are Likely to Do So: A Roundup." Guttmacher Institute, January 9. https://www.guttmacher.org/2023/01/six-months-post-roe-24-us-states-have-banned-abortion-or-are-likely-do-so-roundup.

Nelson, Alondra. 2002. "Introduction: FUTURE TEXTS." *Social Text* 20 (2 [71]): 1–15.

Oddo, Marco Vito. 2023. "'Echo' Producer Teases Series as a 'Very Different' Type of MCU Project." *Collider,* February 8. https://collider.com/echo-series-tone-producer-stephen-broussard-comments/.

Pantozzi, Jill. 2014. "Marvel, This Is When You Send an Artist Back to the Drawing Board." *The Mary Sue,* August 19. https://www.themarysue.com/marvel-spider-woman-variant-butt/.

Panuska, Sarah. 2020. "'Super-Gay' Gay Comix: Tracing the Underground Origins and Cultural Resonances of LGBTQ Superheroes." In *Supersex: Sexuality, Fantasy, and the Superhero,* edited by Anna Peppard, 129–150. Austin: University of Texas Press.

Parker, Johnny, II. 2020. "Put Some Light into the World: An Interview with Brian Michael Bendis and David Walker." In *With Great Power Comes Great Pedagogy,* edited by Susan Kirtley, Antero Garcia, and Peter Carlson, 68–82. Jackson: University Press of Mississippi.

Peppard, Anna. 2017. "'This Female Fights Back!': A Feminist History of Marvel Comics." In *Make Ours Marvel: Media Convergence and a Comics Universe,* edited by Matt Yockey, 105–137. Austin: University of Texas Press.

Peppard, Anna. 2018. "'I Just Want to Feel Something Different': Re-Writing Abuse and Drawing Strength in Brian Michael Bendis and Michael Gaydos's *Alias.*" *Feminist Media Histories* 4 (3): 157–178.

Peppard, Anna. 2019. "'We Ought to Be Friends': Investigating the Potential and Pitfalls of the Female Superhero Friendships, from the Second-Wave 1970s to the Postfeminist 2010s." Paper presented at the Second Annual Conference of the Comics Studies Society: Comics/Politics, Ryerson University, Toronto, Canada, July 27.

Peppard, Anna, ed. 2020. "Introduction: Presence and Absence in Theory and Practice: Locating Supersex." In *Supersex: Sexuality, Fantasy, and the Superhero,* edited by Anna Peppard, 1–30. Austin: University of Texas Press.

Phelps, Jordyn. 2019. "Trump Defends 2017 'Very Fine People' Comments, Calls Robert E. Lee 'a Great General.'" ABC News online, April 26. https://abcnews

.go.com/Politics/trump-defends-2017-fine-people-comments-calls-robert/story?id=62653478.

Phillips, Todd, dir. 2019. *Joker.* Warner Bros. Pictures.

Pizarro, David, and Roy Baumesiter. 2013. "Superhero Comics as Moral Pornography." In *Our Superheroes, Ourselves,* edited by Robin Rosenberg, 19–36. New York: Oxford University Press.

Polak, Kate. 2017. *Ethics in the Gutter: Empathy and Historical Fiction in Comics.* Columbus: Ohio State University Press.

Polo, Susana. 2017. "Marvel Exec Insists Wave of Cancellations Not Motivated by Books' Diversity." *Polygon,* December 22. https://www.polygon.com/comics/2017/12/22/16810138/marvel-exec-insists-wave-of-cancellations-not-motivated-by-books-diversity.

Raimi, Sam, dir. 2022. *Doctor Strange in the Multiverse of Madness.* Walt Disney Studios Motion Pictures.

ramonzer0. 2021. "R/TwoBestFriendsPlay." Reddit. https://www.reddit.com/r/TwoBestFriendsPlay/comments/rqc3t2/friendly_reminder_that_ultimate_spiderwoman_is_a/.

Rankine, Claudia. 2016. "The Condition of Black Life Is One of Mourning." In *The Fire This Time: A New Generation Speaks about Race,* edited by Jesmyn Ward, 145–156. New York: Scribner.

Resha, Adrienne. 2020. "The Blue Age of Comic Books." *INKS: Journal of the Comics Studies Society* 4 (1): 66–81.

Reynolds, Nick. 2023. "Republicans Declare War on Sex Education." *Newsweek,* January 30. https://www.newsweek.com/republicans-declare-war-sex-education-seek-restrictions-public-schools-1777650.

Rhodan, Maya. 2018. "Here Are the Facts about President Trump's Family Separation Policy." *Time,* June 18. https://time.com/5314769/family-separation-policy-donald-trump/.

Rich, Adrienne. 2001. "Anger and Tenderness." In *Mother Reader: Essential Writings on Motherhood,* edited by Moyra Davey, 81–98. New York: Seven Stories Press.

Richards, Dave. 2015. "Hopeless Talks 'Spider-Woman' and Balancing Crime Fighting with Motherhood." *CBR,* August 10. https://www.cbr.com/hopeless-talks-spider-woman-and-balancing-crime-fighting-with-motherhood/.

Robinson, Lillian. 2004. *Wonder Women: Feminisms and Superheroes.* New York: Routledge.

Rockett, Darcel. 2018. "Chicago's Eve Ewing Will Pen Marvel's 'Ironheart.'" *Chicago Tribune,* August 20. https://www.chicagotribune.com/entertainment/ct-ent-marvel-ironheart-eve-ewing-0821-story.html.

Rodríguez, Juana María. 2003. *Queer Latinidad: Identity Practices, Discursive Spaces.* New York: NYU Press.

Roman, Zak, and Ryan Lizardi. 2018. "'If She Be Worthy': The Illusion of Change in American Superhero Comics." *INKS: Journal of the Comics Studies Society* 2 (1): 18–37.

Rosza, Matthew. 2017. "Via Milkshake Selfie, Anti-Feminists Expose Themselves as the Real 'Fake Geeks.'" *Salon*, August 2. https://www.salon.com/2017/08/02/milkshake-club-heather-antos-marvel-comics-twitter/.

Rothman, Michael. 2017. "Marvel's 'Legacy' Will 'Break the Internet,' Says Axel Alonso." ABC News online, April 22. https://abcnews.go.com/Entertainment/marvels-legacy-break-internet-axel-alonso/story?id=46936769.

Russo, Anthony, and Joe Russo, dirs. 2018. *Avengers: Infinity War*. Walt Disney Studios Motion Pictures.

Sage, Terrence. 2018. "Marvel Comics Is Calling Black Minds to Breathe New Life into Its Heroes." *Vibe*, December 20. https://www.vibe.com/features/editorial/marvel-comics-black-writers-625082/.

Schalk, Sami. 2018. *BodyMinds Reimagined: (Dis)Ability, Race, and Gender in Black Women's Speculative Fiction*. Durham, NC: Duke University Press.

Schiller, Vanessa F., Diana S. Dorstyn, and Amanda M. Taylor. 2021. "The Protective Role of Social Support Sources and Types against Depression in Caregivers: A Meta-Analysis." *Journal of Autism and Developmental Disorders* 51 (4): 1304–1315.

Schlesinger, Alex. 2022. "Marvel Makes History with Their First Ever All-Trans Superhero Team." *ScreenRant*, June 26. https://screenrant.com/marvel-new-transgender-superhero-team-transistors-pride/.

Schweitzer, Ivy. 2016. "Making Equals: Classical Philia and Women's Friendship." *Feminist Studies* 42 (2): 337–364.

Scott, Darieck, and Ramzi Fawaz. 2018. "Introduction: Queer about Comics." *American Literature* 90 (2): 197–219.

Scott, Suzanne, and Ellen Kirkpatrick. 2015. "Trans Representations and Superhero Comics: A Conversation with Mey Rude, J. Skyler, and Rachel Stevens." *Cinema Journal* 55 (1): 160–169.

Shakman, Matt, dir. 2021. *WandaVision*. Disney+.

Shiach, Morag. 1999. *Feminism and Cultural Studies*. London: Routledge.

Silliman, Jael, and Anannya Bhattacharjee, eds. 2002. *Policing the National Body: Sex, Race, and Criminalization*. Cambridge, MA: South End Press.

Singer, Bryan, dir. 2000. *X-Men*. 20th Century Studios.

Singer, Marc. 2002. "'Black Skins' and White Masks: Comic Books and the Secret of Race." *African American Review* 36 (1): 107–119.

Spender, Dale. 1998. *Man Made Language*. 2nd ed. London: Pandora.

Stanley, Marni. 2017. "Unbalanced on the Brink: Adolescent Girls and the Discovery of the Self in *Skim* and *This One Summer* by Mariko Tamaki and Jillian Tamaki." In *Graphic Novels for Children and Young Adults: A Collection of Critical Essays*, edited by Michelle Anne Abate and Gwen Athene Tarbox, 191–204. Jackson: University Press of Mississippi.

Steinke, Jocelyn, Maria Knight Lapinski, Nikki Crocker, Aletta Zietsmann-Thomas, Yaschica Williams, Stephanie Higdon Evergreen, and Sarvani

Kuchibhotla. 2007. "Assessing Media Influences on Middle School-Aged Children's Perceptions of Women in Science Using the Draw-A-Scientist Test (DAST)." *Science Communication* 29 (1): 35–64.

Sternberg, Robert J. 2015. "Successful Intelligence: A Model for Testing Intelligence beyond IQ Tests." *European Journal of Education and Psychology*. 8 (2): 76–84. https://doi.org/10.1016/j.ejeps.2015.09.004.

Stringfield, Ravynn KaMia. 2022. "When Black Girls Fly: An Exploration of Black Girls' Multimedia Fantasy Narratives as Sites of Legacy, Lineage, and Creative Freedom." PhD diss., College of William & Mary, Williamsburg, VA.

Stringfield, Ravynn KaMia. 2023. "Flying toward a Twenty-First Century Aesthetics of Technomagic Girlhood." *Vault of Culture*, August 9. https://www.vaultofculture.com/vault/feature/stringfield/technomagicgirlhood?fbclid=IwAR0rHbB6dL5RXfjpZsU_tB1XhCwRhcaHhL0K_IGa08wHoVKmgFZemDM8F5o.

Stuller, Jennifer. 2010. *Ink-Stained Amazons and Cinematic Warriors: Superwomen in Modern Mythology*. London: IB Tauris.

Szaniawska, Aleksandra. 2019. "Gestural Refusals, Embodied Flights: Janelle Monáe's Vision of Black Queer Futurity." *Black Scholar* 49 (4): 35–50.

Tarver, Erin. 2011. "New Forms of Subjectivity: Theorizing the Relational Self with Foucault and Alcoff." *Hypatia* 26 (4): 804–825.

Tasker, Yvonne. 1993. *Spectacular Bodies: Gender, Genre and the Action Cinema*. London: Routledge.

Tasker, Yvonne, and Diane Negra. 2007. "Introduction: Feminist Politics and Postfeminist Culture." In *Interrogating Postfeminism: Gender and the Politics of Popular Culture*, edited by Yvonne Tasker and Diane Negra, 1–25. Durham, NC: Duke University Press.

Taylor, Tate, dir. 2011. *The Help*. DreamWorks Pictures.

Terrill, Robert E. 2017. "The Post-Racial and Post-Ethical Discourse of Donald J. Trump." *Rhetoric and Public Affairs* 20 (3): 493–510. https://doi.org/10.14321/rhetpublaffa.20.3.0493.

Tinsley, Omise'eke Natasha. 2018. *Beyoncé in Formation: Remixing Black Feminism*. Austin: University of Texas Press.

Tollefson, Jeff. 2020. "How Trump Damaged Science—and Why It Could Take Decades to Recover." *Nature* online, "News Feature" section, October 5. https://www.nature.com/articles/d41586-020-02800-9.

Tong, Rosemarie, and Tina Fernandes Botts. 2018. *Feminist Thought: A More Comprehensive Introduction*. 5th ed. New York: Westview Press.

Totenberg, Nina, and Sarah McCammon. 2022. "Supreme Court Overturns Roe v. Wade, Ending Right to Abortion Upheld for Decades." NPR online, "Roe v. Wade and the Future of Reproductive Rights in America" section, June 24. https://www.npr.org/2022/06/24/1102305878/supreme-court-abortion-roe-v-wade-decision-overturn.

Truitt, Brian. 2014. "Marvel Gives Spider-Woman a Modern Makeover." *USA Today*, December 18. https://www.usatoday.com/story/life/2014/12/18/spider-woman-new-costume-exclusive/20574271/.

Tullis, Brittany. 2018. "Mapping Transamerican Mestizaje in Love and Rockets." In *Comics Studies Here and Now*, edited by Frederick Luis Aldama, 252–266. New York: Routledge.

Tung, Charlene. 2004. "Gender, Race, and Sexuality in La Femme Nikita." In *Action Chicks: New Images of Tough Women in Popular Culture*, edited by Sherrie Inness, 95–121. Gordonsville, VA: Palgrave Macmillan.

Ulibarri, Kristy. 2022. *Visible Borders, Invisible Economies: Living Death in Latinx Narratives*. Austin: University of Texas Press.

United Nations. 2019. "UN Rights Chief 'Appalled' by US Border Detention Conditions, Says Holding Migrant Children May Violate International Law." *UN News*, "Migrants and Refugees" section, July 8. https://news.un.org/en/story/2019/07/1041991.

Vargas, Alani. 2019. "'What Keeps Us Coming Back Is the Human Struggle': Eve Ewing on Writing Marvel's *Ironheart*." *The AV Club*, April 24. https://aux.avclub.com/what-keeps-us-coming-back-is-the-human-struggle-eve-1834094447.

Vary, Adam. 2022. "'Batgirl': Ivory Aquino Cast as Trans Character Alysia Yeoh." *Variety*, January 24. https://variety.com/2022/film/news/batgirl-ivory-aquino-alysia-yeoh-trans-character-dc-1235162262/.

Wagenheim, Christopher Paul. 2014. "Representations of Motherhood in *X-Men*." In *Heroines of Comic Books and Literature: Portrayals in Popular Culture*, edited by Maja Bajac-Carter, Norma Jones, and Bob Batchelor. Lanham, MD: Rowman & Littlefield.

Waid, Mark, Alan Davis, Mark Farmer, Matt Hollingsworth, and Clayton Cowles. 2016. *Free Comic Book Day Civil War II: Buzzed*. Marvel.

Wanner, Kevin J. 2016. "In a World of Super-Violence, Can Pacifism Pack a Punch? Nonviolent Superheroes and Their Implications." *Journal of American Culture* 39 (2): 177–192.

Wanzo, Rebecca. 2015. "It's a Hero? Black Comics and Satirizing Subjection." In *The Blacker the Ink: Constructions of Black Identity in Comics and Sequential Art*, edited by Frances Gateward and John Jennings, 314–332. New Brunswick, NJ: Rutgers University Press.

Ward, Earlise C., Le Ondra Clark, and Susan Heidrich. 2009. "African American Women's Beliefs, Coping Behaviors, and Barriers to Seeking Mental Health Services." *Qualitative Health Research* 19 (11): 1589–1601.

Weiner, Robert, Robert Moses Peaslee, and Duncan Prettyman. 2020. "Introduction: It's All about the Villain!" In *The Supervillain Reader*, edited by Robert Moses Peaslee and Robert Weiner, xiv–xl. Jackson: University Press of Mississippi.

Wertham, Fredric. 1954. *Seduction of the Innocent*. New York: Rinehart.

Whaley, Deborah. 2015. *Black Women in Sequence: Re-Inking Comics, Graphic Novels, and Anime*. Seattle: University of Washington Press.

Whalley, Elizabeth, and Colleen Hackett. 2017. "Carceral Feminisms: The Abolitionist Project and Undoing Dominant Feminisms." *Contemporary Justice Review* 20 (4): 456–473. https://doi.org/10.1080/10282580.2017.1383762.

Whedon, Joss, dir. 2015. *Avengers: Age of Ultron*. Walt Disney Studios Motion Pictures.

Wheeler, Andrew. 2014. "Oh Thank God: Spider-Woman Rocks a Great New Look, Courtesy of Kris Anka." *Comics Alliance*, December 19. https://comicsalliance.com/spider-woman-new-look-kris-anka/.

Whitley, Jeremy (@jrome58). 2021a. "Being completely candid, this is a hard question for me: I do picture Nadia as a very physically affectionate person. Obvs she's a hugger, a snuggler . . ." Twitter, April 28, 2021. https://twitter.com/jrome58/status/1387409778176049154.

Whitley, Jeremy (@jrome58). 2021b. "I do also see her as aromantic or perhaps more specifically quoiromantic. She loves a lot of people platonically and affectionately in a way that might be mistaken by others as romantic, but doesn't have much interest in pursuing those relationships as romantic." Twitter, April 28, 2021. https://twitter.com/jrome58/status/1387411597082116100.

Whitley, Jeremy (@jrome58). 2021c. "Was thinking about Nadia being an ace character and how I think it's important because she's a character who's shown to be caring and passionate, not playing into the stereotype that aces are robotic and don't feel. Then I thought about how surprisingly horny Marvel robots are." Twitter, April 28, 2021. https://twitter.com/jrome58/status/1387398108728995843.

Williams, Cristan. 2021. "TERFs." *The SAGE Encyclopedia of Trans Studies*, vol. 2, edited by Abbie Goldberg and Genny Beemyn, 823–825. SAGE Publications, Inc.

Womack, Ytasha. 2013. *Afrofuturism: The World of Black Sci-Fi and Fantasy Culture*. Chicago: Chicago Review Press.

Woods, Heather Suzanne, and Leslie A. Hahner. 2019. *Make America Meme Again: The Rhetoric of the Alt-Right*. New York: Peter Lang.

INDEX